The Small and Mighty Real Estate Investor

The **SMALL** and **MIGHTY**
Real Estate Investor

Build Big *Financial Freedom*
with Fewer Rental Properties

CHAD CARSON

BiggerPockets®
PUBLISHING
Denver, Colorado

The Small and Mighty Real Estate Investor: Build Big Financial Freedom with Fewer Rental Properties
Chad Carson

Published by BiggerPockets Publishing LLC, Denver, CO
Copyright © 2023 by Chad Carson
All rights reserved.

Publisher's Cataloging-in-Publication Data
Names: Carson, Chad, author.
Title: Small and mighty real estate investor : how to reach financial freedom with fewer rental properties / Chad Carson.
Description: Includes bibliographical references. | Denver, CO: BiggerPockets Publishing LLC, 2023.
Identifiers: LCCN: 2023936549 | ISBN: 9781960178008 (paperback) | 9781960178015 (ebook)
Subjects: LCSH Real estate investment--United States. | Investments. | Finance, Personal. | BISAC BUSINESS & ECONOMICS / Real Estate / General | BUSINESS & ECONOMICS / Investments & Securities / Real Estate | BUSINESS & ECONOMICS / Personal Finance / Investing
Classification: LCC HD1382.5 .C364 2023 | DDC 332.63/240973--dc23

Printed in Canada
MBP 10 9 8 7 6 5 4 3 2 1

DEDICATION

To the small investors everywhere.
Your hopes and dreams were my motivation for writing this book.
You are mightier than you know!

TABLE OF CONTENTS

PART I
THE SMALL AND MIGHTY MANIFESTO

PART II
THE JOURNEY OF A SMALL AND MIGHTY REAL ESTATE INVESTOR

PART III
HOW TO BUY PROFITABLE INVESTMENT PROPERTIES

PART IV
FUNDING YOUR PROPERTIES

PART V
GUIDE TO RENTAL PROPERTY
OWNERSHIP

PART VI
HOW TO WIN THE REAL ESTATE GAME

FOREWORD

Most Americans struggle to save enough to retire. In contrast, Chad Carson began traveling the world with his family with the cash generated by his real estate investments in his thirties. His story is inspiring, illuminating a path that you can follow today to become financially independent.

There are a lot of books on investing in real estate. This one is different.

Chad's message is *not* how to get rich quick. It's *not* about flipping or other time-consuming, high-risk strategies. Simply getting rich or owning a lot of property is *not* his goal.

His purpose is to live well enjoying life to its fullest every day.

He can do this because he owns property that supports his family's lifestyle. Chad recognizes that time is the most valuable asset. In this book, he details a step-by-step plan to efficiently acquire and manage property that will make you financially independent. Once you learn how to it effectively, you can do it while working and while raising your family like Chad has done.

Chad is a rising star in the field of real estate education. He earned the title of "Coach" by helping thousands of other investors buy properties that produce the income they need to enjoy life. He is a hands-on investor and shares both the mistakes he made and the strategies that he learned that had made him successful. His approach is ethical, and practical.

This book will teach you the finer points of acquiring, financing, and managing property. In particular, Chad has proven that great management is the key to enjoying the long-term cash flow from property—he lives abroad and manages his property remotely because of his systems.

Without good management systems, landlords burn out before they make the large profits available to those who hold quality properties for a longer term.

An exciting part about investing is that you are always learning and improving your investing skills. As we all know, real estate and financial markets will continue to change, and your ability to adapt to that change is important. Real estate is the mighty power that has made me wealthy, as it has Chad and millions of other small investors.

You won't find a better teacher and "Coach" than Chad Carson.

John W. Schaub
Author, *Building Wealth One House at a Time*

INTRODUCTION

"Isn't it curious that the richer you are, the less time you can spare from tending your riches? By switching to a new game ... time becomes the only possession and everyone is equally rich in it ... Money, of course, is still needed to survive, but time is what you need to live."
— Ed Buryn, *Vagabonding in Europe and North Africa*

Private jets. Expensive cars. Luxury mansions on the beach. You've seen the photos and videos of these types of successful real estate investors. These empire builders followed the popular advice to "go big or go home." Now they've made it; they own thousands of properties and can buy and do anything they want. And if you believe their sales pitch, complete freedom is also yours if you follow in their footsteps.

Luxury goods and having a lot of money are fine. And a healthy ambition and drive to succeed are admirable. But the "go big" approach to business and real estate investing success isn't for everyone. A big real estate portfolio requires *big* risks; *big* investments of time; and *big,* complex organizations that require constant attention and tending.

We hear the stories of the "go big" entrepreneurs who successfully finish the race. They cash in on their wealth and ride off into the sunset. But we rarely hear the stories of those trapped in growth cycles that never end, chasing goalposts that always move. Or the anxiety and depression some entrepreneurs experience trying to reach the top. Or the "successful" people who have enough money to buy big stuff, but they've lost the things that really matter in the process.

The purpose of this book is to show a different path to building wealth through real estate. You don't have to go big to live a luxury life or accomplish amazing goals. Freedom isn't just found at the top of the biggest real estate empires or businesses. And you don't have to sacrifice what matters in the process of building wealth.

I wrote this book because a lot of us—and hopefully that includes you—want one thing more than anything else: freedom. You're tired of the grind of a 9-to-5 job that controls your life. You feel stuck and trapped in a rut. Life isn't bad, but you sense that it could be so much more if you could break out of your financial situation.

Freedom for people like you and me means having options. It means the flexibility to choose your schedule, your work, and the people you spend time with. It means the mobility to travel, explore, and rekindle long-forgotten hobbies. It means the energy and space to contribute to meaningful projects or causes. And most of all, it means becoming rich in the most precious and rare of resources in the modern age: time.

THE RISE OF THE SMALL AND MIGHTY REAL ESTATE INVESTOR

I wrote this book for people who believe that money is important but who also know that time is what you need to live. This book will teach you to build enough wealth to accomplish all your dreams. You'll find a detailed plan to find, acquire, finance, and own enough rental properties to pay for whatever you want in life.

But a plan that simply makes you more money isn't enough. The investing strategies and tactics you'll learn in this book are also designed to maximize your time and flexibility. This approach to real estate investing is something I call "small and mighty," and the people who embrace it are "small and mighty real estate investors."

The "small" in the book's title means different things to different people. There isn't a specific number of properties that gets you into the small and mighty club. Over the following chapters, you'll hear about investors who happily own two rental units, and you'll hear about others who own fifty units or more (like me). Different people have different goals, and different locations and strategies yield different financial results.

Instead of a set number of properties, small and mighty investors are unified by a practical philosophy and an approach to building wealth.

These investors share a few common principles, such as:
- The goal is to have enough, not the most.
- An abundance of time is more luxurious than private planes or yachts.
- Life comes first; business comes second.
- Slower and safer is better than faster and riskier.
- The craft and the quality of your real estate matter.
- People and relationships matter.
- Life doesn't begin at the top; it's to be enjoyed now *and* later.
- Debt and growth are tools, not religions.

If the small and mighty approach to real estate investing resonates with you, I hope you'll join us by reading this book! Throughout this book, I will teach you the practical strategies and tactics you need to accomplish your financial goals. And I'll share many real-life stories of people from a variety of backgrounds, locations, and starting points who've successfully built wealth using the same approach.

Even if you're someone who has been overwhelmed or stuck trying to learn real estate investing, my aim with this book is to present things simply so you can make progress. You don't need to learn fancy math or complex techniques to succeed as a small and mighty real estate investor. You just need a strong desire to learn and the persistence to stick with it.

And if you find yourself with unique challenges, such as lack of money, credit, or time, don't worry—I've written this book for you, too. Real estate investing is the most accessible path to building wealth for regular people like you and me. Even if you've had setbacks or struggles before now, I hope you'll find strategies in this book that will inspire and empower you to continue. The journey is worth it, and your life goals are worth it.

ABOUT YOUR GUIDE FOR THIS BOOK

The most important small and mighty investor is you! This book was written for your journey, and my goal is to help you accomplish your real estate and financial goals. But since I will be your trusty guide during this journey, you might want to learn a little more about me, Chad Carson.

I began investing in real estate in 2003 right after graduating college from Clemson University (Go Tigers!). I was drawn to real estate investing for the flexibility and freedom that it promised. I joined forces with a friend who became my business partner, and we're still having fun and working together twenty-one years later.

In the beginning, neither of us had much money, so we focused on paying the bills by flipping houses (buying, renovating, and reselling properties). Within a couple of years, we also started buying and holding on to rental properties, which has become our favorite strategy. We made a lot of mistakes, most of which I'll share in this book so that you can learn from them. And one of our biggest mistakes was growing too fast right before the Great Recession in 2008.

We were fortunate to survive that big mistake. I'll share the details of how we did it in Chapter 2. But we got into trouble by blindly following the "go big" real estate philosophy. We copied big real estate goals from "successful" investors, and we thought achieving those goals would lead to all our dreams. But as we grew fast and made progress, we experienced the negative side effects of the "go big" real estate model, like financial risk, stress, and lack of free time. We decided to pivot and do something different.

At about the same time, I was fortunate to read books like *Building Wealth One House at a Time* by John Schaub, *The 4-Hour Workweek* by Tim Ferriss, and *Your Money or Your Life* by Vicki Robin and Joe Dominguez. The books all shared an approach to business and investing that focused on simplicity and "enough," instead of the manic, never-ending pursuit of more. These authors motivated me to build a rental property business that incorporated the same principles. The blueprint for that business is the book you have in your hands.

Using a small and mighty approach to rental property investing has given me the freedom and life options I always dreamed of. As I write this, my wife and I are living in southern Spain for twelve months with our two kids (12 and 10 years old). The purpose of the trip is to spend more time together as a family, improve our Spanish language skills, and have fun exploring a different culture. We took a similar seventeen-month trip to Ecuador when the kids were 3 and 5 years old. Our rental income back home has paid for it all; and these days I typically spend only a couple of hours per week on real estate–related tasks.

This free time allows me to exercise, explore, and take Spanish classes while here in Spain. It's also allowed me to pursue passion projects, like writing this book and my first book, *Retire Early with Real Estate*. I also actively educate others on my Coach Carson media platform and as a contributor and speaker for BiggerPockets. And I'm also very involved in my local community in Clemson, South Carolina, with a nonprofit I co-founded. Our mission is to build an alternative transportation network for walking and biking in my hometown.

My hope is that the stories and lessons in this book will empower you to pursue your own dreams. Whatever your life goals, the small and mighty real estate business you'll learn in this book can help you get there. And I'm honored that you've allowed me to be your guide!

Let's get started.

Chad "Coach" Carson
January 16, 2023
Granada, Spain

PART I

THE SMALL AND MIGHTY MANIFESTO

CHAPTER 1
GO SMALL OR GO HOME

I was 26 years old, sitting in a hotel at a real estate conference when I heard a story that changed the direction of my career and my finances. Up to this point as a brand-new real estate investor, all my role models of successful investors had a similar path—grow fast, own hundreds of properties, and strive for more, more, and more. The characters in this story were different, and their example changed my opinion of what success as a real estate investor looks like. Here's the story.

THE SMALL AND MIGHTY PARABLE

One summer, three real estate investing friends and their spouses decide to travel together on a trip to Europe. As beginner investors, they had all become friends while chatting regularly on the BiggerPockets forums. Fifteen years later, they've each found success with real estate investing in their own ways.

Couple No. 1: Ten Local Single-Family Houses

The first couple, let's call them Liz and Tom, are in their fifties. They live, invest, and self-manage their properties in a small suburb of St. Louis,

Missouri. During the early years, they bought ten single-family houses, one by one, in good neighborhoods using mortgage financing. Then, over the past few years, they used extra rental cash flow and savings from their jobs to aggressively pay off their mortgages early.

Their houses now produce $10,000 per month, or $120,000 per year, of positive cash flow. Because of that, they've now both retired early from their careers. They also have a lot of free time because their houses only require a few hours of work per month to do some bookkeeping and other small tasks.

Couple No. 2: Fifty Long-Distance Apartment Units

The second couple, let's call them Tiffany and Darius, are in their early forties and have two kids. They live in Oakland, California, but they invest long-distance in North Carolina using a property manager. Fifteen years after starting, they now own several small multifamily apartments that total fifty units.

Originally, they bought properties in their own backyard by house hacking and renting their former residences in Oakland. But as prices increased and their wealth grew, they decided to cash out and trade the money in their California properties for better cash flow with these fifty units in North Carolina. Even with long-term mortgages, their properties still produce over $10,000 per month, or $120,000 per year, of cash flow.

Because Tiffany and Darius have a competent local property manager, they also only spend a few hours per month on their real estate. This has allowed them to spend more time with their kids and work part-time on projects they're passionate about.

Couple No. 3: 1,000-Unit Multi-State Apartment Empire

These two, Lauren and Mike, are in their late forties. They live in Nevada and own properties all over the country. Fifteen years after starting, they now partially own more than 1,000 apartment units, and they're continuing to grow. They began with smaller rentals in one location, but in the last few years, they've built a team and expanded their business.

Lauren and Mike use a technique called syndication to pool money from a larger group of investors to buy larger deals (hence the partial ownership of those 1,000 units). And as they've found out, syndications are a way to *supercharge* your wealth building and cash flow. As the general partner, they have become multimillionaires and their portion of the rental income equals $60,000 per month, or over $700,000 per year!

Lauren and Mike clearly produce the most cash flow out of all three couples, but everyone can easily afford to pay for this nice European vacation. After all, trips like this are why they wanted to make money in the first place!

Let's Extend the Trip!

The story gets a little more interesting as they approach the end of the trip. All three couples are having a fabulous time. It's so great, in fact, that Couple No. 1 (Liz and Tom) propose that they all stay a few weeks longer to explore more.

Liz and Tom have tenants who automatically deposit their rent online each month. When they do have maintenance issues, they simply text a message to their local contractors who can solve it. And with no debt or immediate plans to buy more properties, they have little pressure, and their schedule is amazingly flexible.

Couple No. 2, Tiffany and Darius, check their calendars. Because their kids are on summer break from school and because they don't have full-time jobs, their schedule is flexible. Their property manager is in control of day-to-day issues at their properties, and with no major financing or remodel projects looming, they happily agree to stay longer as well.

But Couple No. 3, Mike and Lauren, have challenges. They want to stay and can easily afford the expense of extending the trip, but there are projects that require their attention back home. For example:

- Due diligence on a new property purchase has raised some serious questions, and they need to meet people on the ground to figure it out.
- Remodeling contractors on another project are waiting for Lauren's guidance on design choices.
- Their corporate bookkeeper and administrator need help with some unresolved issues.
- And while it's not required, they really need to attend an upcoming conference where they can meet equity investors to raise capital for upcoming deals.

With so much on their plate, Lauren and Mike regretfully decline to extend their trip.

THE THREE CURRENCIES OF A GOOD LIFE

When I began my real estate career, it seemed obvious that more properties and more money are always better. I personally looked up to investors like Lauren and Mike, who bought the most deals and made the most money. And for the first few years, I modeled my real estate business after them.

But hearing this story was a lightbulb moment for me. It wasn't that Lauren and Mike had a *bad* business. In fact, it was financially very successful. But their financial success didn't translate into maximum personal freedom.

Why not?

All three couples had plenty of money to take the trip. But it turns out that money isn't the only currency you need to maximize your personal options. You also need other currencies like *time* and *mobility*. Lauren and Mike had the money, but they were missing a full bank account of the other currencies. And that translated into less freedom and fewer options in their life.

In *The 4-Hour Workweek,* author Tim Ferriss says that "People don't want to be millionaires—they want to experience what they believe only millions can buy... $1,000,000 in the bank isn't the fantasy. The fantasy is the lifestyle of complete freedom it supposedly allows."[1]

Ferriss also points out that earning $100,000 per year while working sixty hours per week stuck at one location is less wealthy than earning $50,000 per year working two hours per week from any location you want. Instead of simply maximizing money, Ferriss suggests measuring and maximizing *relative wealth*, which is a balance of all three currencies—time, money, and mobility.

That vision of balanced, relative wealth is what this book is all about. Getting more of one currency (for example, money) while sacrificing the other essential currencies (for example, time and mobility) is not true wealth for small and mighty real estate investors. Instead, the goal of this book is to help you find the sweet spot where you have *enough* of all three currencies. The goal isn't to impress people because you maximized your number of properties. The goal is to have enough wealth from properties so that you maximize your life options and have the time and mobility to enjoy and explore life.

---

1 Timothy Ferriss, *The 4-Hour Workweek* (New York: Crown Publishers, 2007), p. 8.

SMALL AND MIGHTY REAL ESTATE INVESTING

Rental business   Owner

GO BIG REAL ESTATE INVESTING

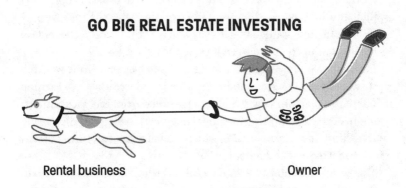

Rental business   Owner

THE SEVENTEEN-MONTH FAMILY TRIP OF A LIFETIME

I began really putting these ideas into practice as a real estate investor in my late twenties, and by the time I turned 37, I finally experienced the full power of having all three currencies. That year, I moved with my wife and our two daughters (3 and 5 years old at the time) to South America to live in Ecuador for seventeen months. We enrolled our daughters in local schools so they could learn to speak Spanish, and we all had one of the best experiences of our lives.

During this trip, I still had real estate investments back at home in Clemson, South Carolina. The steady monthly cash flow from these properties paid for our expenses to live there. Just as important as the money, however, these properties also required very little of my time, and I didn't have to be there in person.

For most of my properties, I had property managers locally who handled the day-to-day affairs like rent collection, maintenance, bill paying, and tenant placement. I also chose to "press pause" on my business for a time. I wasn't adding more properties, growing, or taking on new projects that would require my personal time or presence.

The result was that I spent about a couple of hours per week (remotely) on my real estate, and the rest of my time was focused on taking Spanish classes, writing my first book (*Retire Early with Real Estate),* and enjoying the experience of living in another country with my family.

You may or may not want to travel like my family did, but I bet if you had full bank accounts of money, time, and mobility, you could fulfill amazing dreams that you've always wanted to experience. Maybe you want to stay at home from work with your kids, volunteer for a worthwhile cause, learn a new skill, or start a more fulfilling career or business—even if it pays less. Whatever your dreams are, I wrote this book to give you the practical tools to make them happen.

And that's really what separates the small and mighty investor philosophy from other approaches to real estate investing. Small and mighty investors start with their ideal life and dreams, and they work backward to use money to serve those dreams. They make money to live, not live to make money.

For small and mighty real estate investors, the goal is always the same—the freedom to do whatever you want, whenever you want, for as long as you want, for the rest of your life. Achieving that freedom, however, requires you to shift your mindset away from the traditional approach to business and investing. You can begin that shift by embracing the seven rules of a small and mighty investor.

CHAPTER 2
THE SEVEN RULES OF A SMALL AND MIGHTY REAL ESTATE INVESTOR

You are the hero of this book. The lessons, strategies, and tactics you will read are designed to make you a more successful small and mighty real estate investor. But before we get into those nitty-gritty details, I want to talk about what makes a small and mighty real estate investor different.

If you watch action movies or read comic books, the greatest superheroes have a code or set of rules that set them apart. Batman and Superman don't kill villains or use weapons. Spiderman lives by the mantra "with great power comes great responsibility." And Wonder Woman is motivated to use her powers to protect humanity and make the world a better place.

In our case, a small and mighty real estate investor has seven rules that I'll explain in this chapter. No one will be perfect with these rules, including me, but you can use them to guide your journey and to give you more confidence. The rules begin with putting your life—not your business—first.

RULE NO. 1: LIFE FIRST, BUSINESS SECOND (AND HOW TO AVOID THE BEAST)

In the 1700s, a gifted and enthusiastic scientist decides to attempt his most ambitious experiment ever. During prior experiments, he had learned to make small, inanimate objects come alive. This time, he plans to bring forth an entirely new creature that will be human-like, beautiful, strong, and intelligent. When the creature is finally ready, he uses a massive jolt of electricity to bring it to life.

But instead of a beautiful creature, the scientist's creation is hideous and monstrous. As soon as it wakes up and looks at him, the scientist runs away in horror. In the long, painful story that follows, the creature pursues the scientist and wreaks havoc and destruction on everything in his life. The new creation turns out to be strong, intelligent, and powerful, but it has a life and a will of its own beyond the control of its creator.

This is, of course, the horror story of *Frankenstein*. And the moral of Mary Shelley's story is extremely relevant to anyone who builds a real estate investing business. When you begin, you probably plan for the business to grow quickly and become beautiful, useful, and within your control. But as many entrepreneurs find out, if a business grows too much or too fast, it takes on a life of its own!

You can also think of this phenomenon as "The Beast" of business.[2] As you add more expenses, employees, and debt to your growing business, it can become a beast that eats up all your money, time, and flexibility. Rather than serving *your* life, you are forced to serve *the beast* and give it your freedom and most precious personal resources for many years.

I got to know the business beast early in my real estate investing career. Between 2003 and 2007, my business partner and I grew our business very quickly. To buy and fix up more properties, we spent more money on marketing and hired more people to help us. Other than setting aside cash for reserves, most of our profits from flipping houses were reinvested into feeding the growing business. We also used high levels of debt to buy properties because we didn't have enough of our own cash.

This focused growth worked, in a way. By 2007, we were able to make thirty-three purchases in one year, and when the dust settled, we had more than fifty buy-and-hold rental units. On top of that, I got married that same year. It was one of the busiest and most exciting times of my life!

But growing fast also led to mistakes. While we made money on many properties, we lost money or had negative cash flow on others. During our frantic growth, we underestimated repairs, ignored some rental expenses, and picked bad locations. We also faced the harsh reality of an economy that was sinking into the worst recession in over seventy years. We were worried about our ability to continue paying for our substantial business overhead.

During late 2007, my business partner and I had a heart-to-heart. We questioned the overall strategy and direction of our real estate investing business. Things felt out of control.

We both did an exercise to help us get clear on why we were investing in real estate in the first place. We wrote down the activities that would make our lives fulfilling. On my piece of paper, I wrote down things like:

- Play basketball for two hours in the middle of the day
- Hike to nearby waterfalls when the weather is nice
- Travel to other countries for extended periods of time
- Read books and learn new skills that I'm interested in
- Teach, write, and share with others
- Have children and be present in their lives

---

2 Danielle LaPorte, as cited in Paul Jarvis, *Company of One* (New York: Mariner Books, 2020), p. 30.

My business partner had his own list of personal goals. We were both stunned to realize that money was not the primary factor keeping us from these goals. Most of our goals didn't cost anything, and even the ones that did cost money, such as travel, could be easily quantified and saved for.

Instead of money, lack of *time* and *mobility* kept us from our life goals. The business beast was eating all of those, and our current trajectory would only make it worse. Our business, not our lives, had become the priority. So, we decided to change that.

As a result of this conversation, our guiding business value became: **More freedom is better than more money.**

Money and growth were still important, but we balanced it with other priorities. Before, we had primarily used money to judge the success of each business decision, but now we also asked how the decision would affect our personal time and mobility. The goal became maximizing freedom, not maximizing money.

In practical terms, this changed our business decisions. For example, we narrowed the locations where we were looking for investment properties. Although the nearby city of Greenville, South Carolina, had many good opportunities, it was also a forty-five-minute drive away. We didn't want to spend half our lives in a car, so we stopped looking there and only focused within a ten-minute drive from our small town of Clemson. We had to adapt our business strategies to this new reality, but it worked fine in the end. And in the process, we increased our free time, mobility, and enjoyment of life.

This shift in priorities eventually led to an amazing transformation, as well as to the small and mighty real estate model that you'll learn about in this book. But those early decisions were only the beginning. More urgently, we had to financially survive the Great Recession that hit everyone hard for the next few years. This was no easy task. But one practical change that saved us was Rule No. 2: Be the real estate tortoise (not the hare).

RULE NO. 2: BE THE REAL ESTATE TORTOISE (NOT THE HARE)

"There is more to life than increasing its speed."
—Mahatma Gandhi (attributed)[3]

Paul Jarvis is an entrepreneur and author of the book *Company of One*. He defines a "company of one" as any business that questions growth.[4] In this book, Jarvis points out that a "study done by the Startup Genome Project, which analyzed more than 3,200 high-growth tech startups, found that 74 percent of those businesses failed, not because of competition or bad business plans, but because they scaled up too quickly."[5]

Fast-growing real estate investing businesses fail in the same way. I vividly remember a fellow investor who got started around the same time that I did. In a short time, he grew to hundreds of properties, an office, a big team, and many moving parts. He was smart and did a lot of things right, like mastering the process of using private and seller financing. But in the end, his real estate business failed during the recession of 2008–2009, along with many others.

The market downturn exposed some fatal mistakes he made during his frantic growth spurt. To get more volume, he compromised on the quality of his properties, the quality of his tenants, and the profit margins of his deals. I'll talk more about these subjects in detail later in the book. By becoming too big, too fast, he couldn't recover from those mistakes, and the whole business crumbled.

The alternative approach, a small and mighty real estate business, doesn't mean you never grow. It just means you grow *sustainably* by carefully considering how fast and when you grow. It means everything you do is more conservative, including how you buy, finance, and manage your properties. And while you still take risks, you keep the risks smaller so that failure doesn't knock you out of the game forever.

To give you a concrete example, I'm a big fan of cash reserves in real estate investing. (In Chapter 18, I'll explain how much cash I recommend

---

3 Susan Ratcliffe (editor), *Oxford Essential Quotations* (5th ed.) (Oxford: Oxford University Press, 2017).

4 Paul Jarvis, *Company of One* (New York: Mariner Books, 2020), p. 6.

5 Ibid., p. 27.

you set aside.) But saving cash takes time. It also takes away cash that you could use to grow faster. On the surface, cash reserves slow down your progress as an investor. But over the long haul, reserves ensure you finish the journey, which is what really matters.

Longtime investor John Schaub has an approach he describes as "building wealth one house [or property] at a time," which is also the title of his well-known book. By growing at a deliberate pace, especially early in your career, you give yourself time to improve and learn from your mistakes. With every purchase, you will learn and improve your ability to buy, finance, and manage properties. If my fellow investor had followed John's advice, he'd still be in business and would have an enormous amount of wealth and freedom today.

The small and mighty investor approach is like being the tortoise instead of the hare in Aesop's famous story. You may envy the faster, hare-like investors from time to time. It may appear on social media that they're winning the race. But like the tortoise, your deliberate forward progress will get you to the finish line in the end. It's not about how many properties you buy in the first few years. It's about how much freedom you have in the end.

As you plod deliberately up the financial mountain, one of the most important early milestones is simply buying four properties, the next rule of a small and mighty investor.

RULE NO. 3: JUST START WITH FOUR PROPERTIES

Big goals are exciting. But they can also be overwhelming and difficult to start. A great solution is to break your big goal into smaller, more manageable pieces. If the journey is 1,000 miles, break it into many smaller segments of one mile or less.

Michael Zuber, a fellow real estate investor and author of the book *One Rental at a Time*, always tells new real estate investors to start with a short-term goal of four or fewer properties. Not ten. Not twenty. Not one hundred. Just four.

I wholeheartedly agree with this advice. Buy why just four?

A goal of four properties is extremely achievable. By using the one property at a time approach and buying a new property every six to twelve months, you can buy four properties in two to four years. Hitting a major milestone in a few years is much easier to get excited about than something twenty years from now.

Starting with four properties also has a financing advantage. Getting approved for traditional investor mortgages is easier with the first four properties. After four loans, lenders make the process more difficult by requiring larger cash reserves and more income. Financing isn't impossible after four, but you may need to adapt your financing strategy.

Keeping your first goal small and achievable also helps you avoid the need to be perfect. It's very likely that your first deal will not be as good as your fourth deal. That's okay!

John Schaub points out that it's "not even important that your first house is a great deal. The first house I bought, I paid retail price for and made a 20 percent down payment."[6] But because Schaub was patient and bought in a good location, the house is now free of debt and worth many times what he paid for it.

For some of you, four properties may be all you need to buy to achieve your financial goals. For others, four properties may just be a solid foundation that will help you make the leap to bigger goals. But whatever your goals, aiming for the first four will keep you on the right path and help you to build momentum. And those first four properties will help you become a craftsman.

RULE NO. 4: BE A CRAFTSMAN

Shortly after I graduated from college, I decided to come back to my alma mater Clemson University to take a few voluntary classes for fun. Entrepreneurship and small business intrigued me, so I wanted to learn more. Although the classes were helpful, the life-changing event for me was meeting one of my professors, Dr. Louis Stone.

Dr. Stone was a lifelong serial entrepreneur and real estate investor, and he held (and still holds) an aversion to anything that cramped his freedom. In other words, he was a natural small and mighty real estate investor! Dr. Stone became my mentor, friend, and eventually an investor in my real estate business. After my class with him ended, I decided to jump into real estate investing full time, but I stayed in touch with Dr. Stone along the way.

---

6 John Schaub, *Building Wealth One House at a Time* (New York: McGraw Hill, 2016)

I spent my entire first year as a new real estate entrepreneur intensely studying and practicing the craft of finding good property deals. In a later chapter, I'll also teach you how to build this valuable skill. But even though I could find deals, my business partner and I didn't have enough money or credit to consistently buy them. That's when Dr. Stone reentered my life as a private lender.

Dr. Stone and a few other individuals made us loans or partnered with us to buy the real estate. We were able to make a profit without much of our own money, and these investors were able to earn a profit without doing much active work. In Chapter 20, I'll teach you the specifics of these strategies so that you can use them for yourself. But in our case, it was a match made in heaven. Dr. Stone called himself the "old lion," and we were the "young pups."

By 2007, as I've mentioned, my business partner and I had grown at a much faster pace. We got so good at finding deals and then creatively finding the money through private loans, seller financing, and other sources, we were able to expand quickly. But fortunately for us, Dr. Stone advised us to slow things down. He told me:

> Chad, you're doing an excellent job of taking care of me and my money. You pay on time, you communicate well, and you always put the safety of my money first. I trust you and appreciate your attention to detail.
>
> But I'm worried what will happen if you have too many investors like me. If you have thirty investors instead of three, will you still be able to give your investors excellent, personalized service? And if we receive worse service, isn't it possible you could get less money from each investor as a result? Wouldn't it work well for everyone if you just focused on being better, not bigger?

First of all, Dr. Stone showed that he understood human psychology. He wrapped his most prickly advice in a lot of sweet sugar so that I could swallow it! But second, his advice was sound. We were at a crossroads in our business where we could either grow out of our problems—like most traditional businesses—or we could focus on being small and mighty real estate investors who succeeded with quality, not quantity.

As you've guessed by now, we decided to serve a smaller number of investors, tenants, and buyers with excellence instead of scaling our business even more. And this turned out to be a successful financial decision. We not only survived the Great Recession of 2008–2009 but we thrived.

You can also think of this "quality over quantity" approach as a craftsman mindset. In his book *So Good They Can't Ignore You*, Cal Newport describes a craftsman as someone who obsessively focuses on becoming better at a craft.[7] (And when I say craftsman here, I mean any gender.) Cal Newport adds that by focusing on mastering the mundane details of real estate or any craft, you then become "so good that they can't ignore you."

In real estate investing, this means you become excellent at the core skills of the business, including acquisitions, deal analysis, financing, construction and remodeling, bookkeeping, and property management. It should be no surprise that these are also the core skills I'll teach you in this book. And by mastering those skills, you'll become "so good" that wealth, cash flow, and financial freedom can't help but flow into your life.

But you may also find another hidden gem of becoming a craftsman. As you deepen your knowledge and skill, you may unearth joy in doing meaningful work that matters. Even if you only work a few hours a week on your craft (my current real estate schedule), you'll get to experience a lifelong profession that uses your skills and makes a positive impact on your community, customers, investors, and vendors.

But one of the common temptations that will steer you away from the joy of your craft is overuse of debt. And that's the topic of Rule No. 5 of the small and mighty investor.

RULE NO. 5: DEBT IS A TOOL, NOT A RELIGION

Do you want to know something amazing? You can begin with little or no money, buy a group of properties, and within ten to twenty years be a multimillionaire who has incredible amounts of freedom and control over your life. This is exactly what I did, and debt (aka leverage) made it possible.

In the physical world, common tools like wheelbarrows, bottle openers, crowbars, shovels, and hammers use the principle of leverage. They allow you to lift, move, or exert forces on much larger objects than you could on your own. The same applies to *financial leverage*.

---

7 Cal Newport, *So Good They Can't Ignore You* (London: Piatkus, 2016), p. 37.

In real estate investing, you can "lift" a large financial "object" like a $250,000 rental house without having all the money yourself. By using debt, you need only a down payment to buy the property. The lender provides the rest of the money in the form of a loan (aka a mortgage). I'll explain many specifics about real estate loans in this book, but just know for now that it's entirely possible to only spend between $12,000 and $50,000 of your own money to buy a $250,000 rental property.

But the leverage gets even better because your tenant helps you pay back the loan. Each month you collect rent and use it to pay for property expenses like taxes, insurance, and maintenance. And if you follow what I teach in this book, you'll also have enough left over to pay your mortgage plus some cash flow for yourself.

The math of becoming a millionaire in this way is very simple. Just buy four $250,000 properties, rent them, and pay off their debt over time. In the end, you'll own four properties, free and clear of all debt, with a likely value of $1,000,000 or much more.

MILLIONAIRE WITH FOUR RENTAL PROPERTIES

Property	Value	Down Payment	Debt (Beginning)	Debt (End)	Net Worth (End)
Property 1	$250,000	$50,000	$200,000	$0	$250,000
Property 2	$250,000	$50,000	$200,000	$0	$250,000
Property 3	$250,000	$50,000	$200,000	$0	$250,000
Property 4	$250,000	$50,000	$200,000	$0	$250,000
Total	$1,000,000	$200,000	$800,000	$0	$1,000,000

Clearly, debt is a powerful tool. If you're comfortable with it, I highly recommend that you use it as a small and mighty investor. But I also recommend that you don't make it more important than it really is. Unfortunately, a lot of real estate investors are so enamored with the power of debt that it becomes like a religion.

In this "perpetual debt religion," more debt is better. If debt works well as a tool on four properties, then why not use it on fifty or five hundred? And because debt in this religion is sacred, paying off debt is sacrilegious. The debt priests remind you that it's *crazy* to pay off debt with a cost of only 4 percent interest when you could invest that money into something that pays you a return on investment of 10 percent or more.

The problem with the debt religion is that it focuses only on one almighty metric: growth. Using leverage is certainly the right tool to maximize growth, but I'll reiterate that growth isn't the only thing that matters in investing or life. As you learned with the big business beast, growing too fast can eat all your free time and flexibility. And debt also increases your risk of losing money or even going out of business.

In the 1980s, famous financial personality Dave Ramsey was a successful real estate agent and investor. At the early age of 26, he had already accumulated investment properties worth over $4 million. He owed about $3 million of debt on these properties, which means he had a net worth of over $1 million. In today's dollars, that means he had wealth of over $2 million at a very young age!

But then something changed. The banking industry had a crisis, which led to his old friendly bank getting sold to another bank. The new bank wasn't impressed with Dave, and they told him to pay back $1.2 million of his loans within ninety days! If he didn't pay them back, the banks threatened to foreclose on his properties.

After three years of struggle, Dave and his wife finally had to file bankruptcy.[8] The humiliation and pain of this bad experience with debt led Dave to begin helping others to control their finances and avoid his mistakes. He now teaches millions of people through his radio show and other platforms about how to pay off debt, cut up their credit cards, and never get into debt again.

---

8 Susan Drury, "The Gospel According to Dave," nashvillescene.com, May 31, 2007, https://www.nashvillescene.com/news/the-gospel-according-to-dave/ article_19d2e1d8-297a-5dab-b871-55cd7e61e76f.html.

It's easy to discount Dave's story or say, "that'll never happen to me." But the risk of bankruptcy or loss from taking on too much debt is real. I personally knew investors during the 2008–2009 recession who went out of business for the same reason. Even major businesses like Goldman Sachs and General Electric had to get bailouts from Warren Buffett because they overextended themselves with debt during the Great Recession.[9]

You don't have to eliminate debt altogether like Dave Ramsey, although that's fine if it's your preference. My point here is that small and mighty investors simply have a healthy respect for both the power and the risk of debt. They *carefully* use it as a tool to build massive wealth, but then they put the tool away or use it less often when it's not needed anymore.

Warren Buffett once said not to risk something you have to get something you don't need.[10] That's the main point of being careful with debt. And speaking of appreciating what you already have, Rule No. 6 reminds us not to wait and defer your life until it's too late.

RULE NO. 6: DON'T DEFER LIFE

By 2009 my business partner and I felt secure that we would financially survive the Great Recession. Because housing prices crashed, we were not particularly wealthy on paper. And our cash flow certainly wasn't enough to be financially independent. But we were happy not to be sinking financially like many individuals and businesses at that time.

During this same period, I was also personally exhausted. For the prior seven years, I had basically been sprinting forward nonstop with my real estate business. I was like a driven maniac, climbing full speed up the wealth-building mountain without taking a rest. My legs, lungs, and spirit were gasping for oxygen!

As a result, my wife and I came up with the idea of saving money to

---

9 Alex Crippen, "Warren Buffett Casts Vote of Confidence in General Electric With $3B Investment," cnbc.com, October 1, 2008, https://www.cnbc.com/2008/10/01/warren-buffett-casts-vote-of-confidence-in-general-electric-with-3b-investment.html.

10 Marcel Schwantes, "Warren Buffett Says These Simple Habits That Most of Us Ignore Separate Successful People From Everyone Else," Inc.com, June 21, 2018, https://www.inc.com/marcel-schwantes/6-common-sense-things-warren-buffett-says-you-must-do-to-be-happy-successful.html.

take a long-term trip to Spain and South America. This would be more than a vacation, where you relax for seven days and then come back to a mountain of anxiety from all the work you missed. This would be a four-month mini-retirement that essentially pressed pause on life. It would be like stopping my high-speed mountain climb to camp on a comfortable plateau where I could rest and rejuvenate my spirit.

Ironically, it was on this same trip to South America that I quite literally learned the foolishness of sprinting up life's mountains. My wife and I were exploring the Colca Canyon in a remote, beautiful part of Peru. We decided one day to hike down 3,600 feet (about twice the height of the Empire State Building) to the base of the canyon. And then we decided to turn back around and hike up on the same day!

The hike down had gone well. At the bottom of the canyon floor, we even found a small "oasis" complete with a swimming pool, palm trees, and a store serving bottles of beer. After taking a brief dip in the pool, we bought some of the only food we could find in the store—sugar cookies—and began hiking back up.

We began walking with another group of tourists and their Peruvian guide, all of whom had become our friends during the hike. Wisely, their guide held them back to a slower pace as we quickly moved up ahead of them. My wife and I were both confident, fit hikers. At home and many times on this same trip, we enjoyed walking fast and steadily up steep inclines.

About halfway up the canyon trail, I was feeling so good that I looked back down the hill to catch the eye of our friends. I motioned with my hands "Come on! What's taking you so long?" I would shortly come to regret that message.

Not much farther up the path, I started getting light-headed and weak. My wife and our hiking companion were also very tired, but I was the one really dragging. Our pace up the path slowed to a shuffle. Every 25 feet we had to stop so one of us (mainly me) could rest and lean against the rock wall.

At each resting point, I looked back down. The guide and his clients were moving slowly but steadily. They even stopped to rest at times. But they continually got a little closer and a little closer. Eventually, the guide and his two clients walked right past us.

I was too exhausted to be humiliated. And the guide and his clients were too kind to turn the earlier joke back around on me. They disappeared up the path and were back in their rooms taking hot showers long before us. At nightfall, we finally stumbled back into the village at the top of the canyon.

Fortunately, this humbling experience taught me important life lessons. First, the four-month mini-retirement trip and this climb out of the Colca Canyon reminded me to sprint less and pace myself more. Like the story of the tortoise and the hare in Rule No. 2, slower is often faster in the end.

But I also learned (and I'm still learning) that life doesn't start at the top of the mountain. Most of your life happens during the climb! If you sprint so fast that you fail to savor and enjoy the climbs and the plateaus, you'll be missing out on most of life. You'll be deferring your happiness until it's too late.

Becoming a small and mighty investor can be a practical step to apply this lesson and force yourself to slow down and enjoy life more. You can certainly travel and take mini-retirements like my family and I did. But you can also just find ways to slow down your pace of work. Maybe you can leave work early or take more days off to enjoy your family, friends, or hobbies.

In either case, the goal is to eventually find a more balanced version of success. This is the hallmark of small and mighty investors. But to do this, you'll have to learn to measure success differently, which is the final rule of a small and mighty investor.

RULE NO. 7: MEASURE SUCCESS DIFFERENTLY

Edward Deci is a researcher and professor of psychology who is well known for his theories of human motivation. In his book *Why We Do What We Do*,[11] Deci explains that there are two basic types of human motivation—extrinsic (external) and intrinsic (internal). Common extrinsic motivators are money, fame, and beauty. Common intrinsic motivators are meaningful relationships, personal growth, and contribution to a community.

---

11 Edward Deci, *Why We Do What We Do* (New York: Penguin Books, 1996).

There is nothing inherently wrong with either type of motivation. Both influence all of us to some extent. But Deci found that if someone's extrinsic motivators were more influential than their intrinsic motivators, they were more likely to have poor mental health. And in contrast, someone with dominant intrinsic motivators was more likely to be content, feel better about themselves, and have positive psychological health.

Think about today's popular culture. What types of "successful" people do you see the most in public or on social media? It's popular to show famous people or influencers who have extrinsic symbols like wealth (fancy cars, big houses, hundreds of investment properties), fame (millions of social media followers), and beauty (six-pack abs, supermodel bodies). But are the people behind these external symbols really happy? Do they have strong, meaningful personal relationships? Are they making contributions to their communities that they can be proud of?

I'm not judging here. Maybe they are happy with their lives, maybe they aren't. More than likely, we'll never truly know. Yet we feel envy toward these people's accomplishments. We measure our self-worth (or lack thereof) based on their external symbols of success compared to our own. I'm not pointing fingers, because I am guilty of it myself!

It's possible to measure success differently. That's the goal of small and mighty investors. They still enjoy extrinsic motivations like wealth, popularity, and beauty as they come. They still count cash flow and the number of properties they own. But they keep these external measures in perspective. They take to heart the quote "not everything that counts can be counted, and not everything that can be counted counts."[12]

Ultimately, the things most of us want in life—fulfillment, peace of mind, and happiness—aren't externally measurable at all. Therefore, success for a small and mighty investor is really a means to an end. We measure and build wealth in multiple currencies: time, money, and mobility. But the ultimate purpose of these tools is simply to give you personal freedom. And with that freedom, you get to create your own authentic success—the kind that only you can measure.

---

12 William Bruce Cameron, *Informal Sociology* (New York: Random House, 1963), p. 13.

CHAPTER 3
THE SMALL AND MIGHTY FORMULA FOR FINANCIAL FREEDOM

Author and investor John Schaub, whom I introduced in Chapter 2, began investing in real estate in Sarasota, Florida, in the mid-1970s. Like my own story, Schaub began by dipping his toes in the "grow big, grow fast" approach to real estate investing. He once owned a motel, a restaurant, a wine and cheese shop, several apartment buildings and duplexes, part interest in a TV station, and many parcels of land.

But somewhere in the frenzy of growth, he realized that his big, complex business created more hassles and left him with less free time. It also turned out that his simplest investments—single-family houses—made him the most money and required the least work. These realizations led him to simplify and reduce the size of all he owned.

Schaub removed layers of business overhead, hassle, and headaches. Instead of hundreds or thousands of properties, he chooses to own 25 to 30 well-located single-family houses. These houses attract responsible tenants who pay on time, rarely call him, and stay for years.

The simplicity and stability of this approach have allowed Schaub to self-manage his properties while still having plenty of free time and flexibility. When not working, he travels, spends time with family, flies his airplane, writes, and teaches other investors. And far from "settling" financially, this simple strategy has built enough wealth that he has been able to donate large amounts of money and time to charities important to him, like The Fuller Center for Housing.

You don't have to invest in single-family houses exactly as John Schaub did to become a small and mighty real estate investor. For that matter, I don't recommend that you copy *anyone* exactly. Your unique approach will always look different than those of others. But if you want to maximize your personal freedom, I do recommend you embrace the core idea of Schaub's philosophy. It's the same idea that defines what a small and mighty investor is all about.

A SMALL AND MIGHTY INVESTOR, DEFINED

Borrowing from Schaub's philosophy, my definition of a small and mighty investor is this:

> Own the minimum number of investments that accomplish your financial goals.

Minimizing—not maximizing—is the goal of a small and mighty investor. Instead of 10×, you want to ½× . Your ideal financial destination isn't the most properties, it's to have *enough*. With enough, you can spend your time doing whatever matters to you.

This definition is similar to a principle in science and philosophy called Occam's razor. The principle says that if you have competing theories, you should always choose the simpler one. Scientific theories, which aim to understand how the world works, can easily become too confusing and complex. So scientists use this rule of thumb to simplify their theories enough to make them testable and practical in real life.

The definition of a small and mighty investor works the same way. It's a rule of thumb that makes your goals more practical and achievable. You *do* want to accomplish your financial goals, whatever those are. And at the same time, you want to do it in the simplest, most elegant way possible. Like a graceful athlete or dancer, becoming a small and mighty investor is an exercise in balance.

One part of that balance, of course, is accomplishing your financial goals. So, the next logical question is: How much money or wealth do you really need? How much is enough for *you*? To help you answer that question for yourself, let's start with something called your financial independence number.

YOUR FINANCIAL INDEPENDENCE (FI) NUMBER

Can you imagine your life when there's no more pressure to earn money? This happens when your investments (aka your wealth) are large enough to pay for your lifestyle without you having to go to work. This is called financial independence (FI), and it was the main topic of my first book, *Retire Early with Real Estate*.

Most small and mighty investors have the goal to achieve FI someday. If that's also your goal, I recommend quantifying it with something called a financial independence number. It's defined simply as the point where investment income is greater than your personal expenses. Here's the formula:

$$\text{Financial Independence (FI) Number} = \text{Investment Income} > \text{Personal Money Needs}$$

This is a simple formula, but figuring out your personal expenses is the part that requires a little effort. To make that process easier, I recommend thinking about your expenses and your FI number in three different categories:

1. **Lean FI:** Cover the basics you need to survive, such as housing, food, and health care.
2. **Regular FI:** Cover the basics plus other "nice-to-haves," such as vacations and eating out.
3. **Fat FI:** Cover all the basics and normal expenses plus luxuries or extra financial cushion.

The actual dollar amounts for these categories could vary widely, depending on your personal preferences. This is called *personal* finance for a reason, so plan to figure out your unique expenses. To help make this concept more concrete, I'll offer some real numbers that will give you a starting point.

According to the U.S. Bureau of Labor Statistics, the average annual spending of a U.S. household in 2020 was $61,334.[13] I like round numbers, so let's define regular FI for most people as $60,000 per year. Lean FI by my definition would be about half, or $30,000 per year. Fat FI would be double, or $120,000 per year.

Later in this chapter, I'll provide an exercise to help you determine your actual personal expenses and FI numbers. But for now, keep my recommended numbers in mind as we move on to the next step of a small and mighty real estate investor—figuring out how to pay for these expenses with real estate investments!

AN INCOME FLOOR USING REAL ESTATE CAN SET YOU FREE

Financial independence means being able to live off your investment income. But how do you turn your investments into something you can live on? And how do you know you won't run out of money before you run out of life? You'll hopefully have a lot of years of life to pay for, especially if you want to achieve FI earlier than normal.

One way to solve this challenge is to create an income floor.[14] An income floor is an idea I learned from financial blogger Darrow Kirkpatrick. It's simply a steady stream of income from reliable, passive sources.

Examples of reliable sources include pensions, social security income, stock dividends, interest, rental income, and some insurance annuities. This income stream becomes a floor because you have confidence that the income will keep coming in through good times and bad times, up markets or down markets. That steadiness allows it to become a solid foundation that you can build your financial independence upon.

Although you can build an income floor with other sources, I've found real estate rental properties to be the ideal solution. Quality income

---

13 "Consumer expenditures in 2020," bls.gov, December 2021, https://www.bls.gov/opub/reports/consumer-expenditures/2020/.

14 Darrow Kirkpatrick, "A Floor with an Upside: The Best Strategy for Lifetime Income?" caniretireyet.com, August 15, 2012, https://www.caniretireyet.com/a-floor-with-an-upside-the-best-strategy-for-lifetime-income/.

properties that are conservatively financed produce steady income that you can depend on. And because the income is steady, it's simple to calculate how many properties are enough to cover your personal expenses.

Just as importantly with real estate, both the rents and the values of your properties will likely increase over time if you follow the lessons in this book for picking the right locations and properties. This means that if your real estate portfolio pays for your FI number today, it has a good chance of increasing enough to pay for your expenses in the future, even if those expenses increase with inflation.

This allows you to simplify your real estate planning. Instead of predicting your exact future financial needs, your job is simply to build enough quality income streams from real estate to pay for your expenses *today*. The math is actually quite simple.

HOW MANY RENTAL PROPERTIES DO YOU NEED TO BE FREE?

Let's assume your *fat* FI number is $120,000 per year. That's how much investment income you need to comfortably cover all your personal expenses plus a big cushion for extras. How will you use real estate investments to pay for that?

As you'll see in this book, there are many different ways to do that. But one simple example is to own a small number of rental properties, free and clear of all debt. This means you buy the properties and eventually pay off the mortgages. Let's ignore for now whether you *should* pay off your debt; some of you may not want to do that, and that's fine. Later in this chapter, I'll give you another example of someone who achieved FI while still having debt on his rental properties.

The point I want to make now is that a small no-debt portfolio of rental properties would make an excellent income floor. It would be a very safe and stable way to achieve your FI number. Even if rents were to drop during a deep recession or depression, you could drop your rental rates without risk of negative cash flow or a bank foreclosure. And both the value and rents from your properties would have a good chance of increasing during inflationary times.

To make this more real, let's assume your small portfolio has ten properties. Although the actual numbers will vary depending on your location and your personal income tax situation, it could look like this:

10 DEBT-FREE RENTAL PROPERTIES

Property	Rent	Net Operating Income/ Month	Mortgage Payment/ Month	Positive Cash Flow/ Month	Positive Cash Flow/ Year
Property 1	$1,800	$1,000	$0	$1,000	$12,000
Property 2	$1,800	$1,000	$0	$1,000	$12,000
Property 3	$1,800	$1,000	$0	$1,000	$12,000
Property 4	$1,800	$1,000	$0	$1,000	$12,000
Property 5	$1,800	$1,000	$0	$1,000	$12,000
Property 6	$1,800	$1,000	$0	$1,000	$12,000
Property 7	$1,800	$1,000	$0	$1,000	$12,000
Property 8	$1,800	$1,000	$0	$1,000	$12,000
Property 9	$1,800	$1,000	$0	$1,000	$12,000
Property 10	$1,800	$1,000	$0	$1,000	$12,000
Total		$10,000	$0	$10,000	$120,000

Net Operating Income = rent − operating expenses
Operating Expenses = taxes + insurance + management + repairs + vacancy

Pause and think about what this means. Using a small number of rentals, you've built an income floor that could pay for $120,000 of expenses. You've hit your fat FI number!

Now I know you probably have other questions about how to accomplish this. The rest of this book will teach you the details of how to find properties like this, run the numbers, collect rent, and even pay off your debt. But for now, just focus on the financial results of these ten simple rental properties.

How would those results change your life? What would you choose to do with your time? What would you choose *not* to do? It's exciting to think about. And it's also exciting to know that only ten rental properties can make you financially independent!

Of course, your number doesn't have to be ten rental properties. You can increase or decrease the number of rental properties based on your FI number. The math works either way.

For example, if you feel more comfortable with $240,000 per year, you could choose to own twenty debt-free rental properties instead of ten. (Twenty cash-flowing rentals at $12,000 per property = $240,000.)

Alternatively, if you simply want to cover your lean FI number—let's say it's $30,000 per year—you'd only need three debt-free rental properties using the numbers in this example. (Three cash-flowing rentals at $12,000 per property = $36,000.) That would be an extra-small but mighty portfolio!

To show you one example of how this concept works in real life, I want to share a story of a couple I know who built a real estate income floor to retire.

FINANCIAL PEACE USING REAL ESTATE

Karen and Bob recently moved to the location of their dreams in Portugal. After years of high-stress jobs, mainly in the technology sector, they describe their current life as peaceful. Income from their small portfolio of rental properties pays for their lifestyle, and other investments in stocks, bonds, and cash give them diversification. They now plan to travel and explore, while also spending time on long-neglected hobbies like astronomy, photography, clothing design, and cooking.

Diverging from the Traditional Approach to Retirement

For many years, Karen and Bob dreamed of pursuing these life goals, but the goals finally became real possibilities a few years ago when they determined their FI number. In their case, $60,000 per year was what they needed to cover their regular personal expenses. But the uncertainty of how to safely pay for those expenses using their investments still put their dreams on hold.

During their careers, Karen and Bob faithfully set aside money in 401(k) retirement plans. This made sense because their employer matched their own savings up to a certain percentage. The match and the tax savings increased the amount of money they were ultimately able to save and invest. But this traditional strategy also created challenges. Here's how Karen describes it:

"Putting all our savings into our 401(k)s led to most of our retirement savings in stocks, which as the market fluctuated was stressful. Over the last few years, we've withdrawn money from our retirement accounts, paid the taxes, and invested the full remaining amount into real estate. Now when the market tanks, we don't worry, knowing that at least half of our net worth is diversified into real estate. In order of percentage, we are diversified across real estate, stocks, bonds, cash, art, and personal items."

Karen and Bob decided to diversify their retirement investments into real estate. Specifically, they've used their real estate investments to create an income floor to pay for their $60,000/year regular FI number. Now at 65 years old, this gives them the confidence and peace of mind to actually pursue their life goals. And in a few years, things will get even easier when they began drawing their $3,000/month social security pension.

The Real Estate Retirement Strategy

When they began, Karen and Bob spent a few years learning the real estate business and searching for their ideal strategy. Ultimately, they liked the small and mighty approach that they learned in my online course. So they made a goal to purchase ten rental units in the Upstate region of South Carolina.

To purchase these ten properties, they paid cash that was withdrawn from their retirement accounts. Because there was no debt, these properties easily paid for their $60,000 per year FI number. They also hired a local, trustworthy property manager so that they would have the time and flexibility to travel and live anywhere in the world.

Financial Peace

After reaching this financial plateau, Karen was relieved.

"Our portfolio has brought us so much peace knowing we are not impacted by stock market swings, like many retirees. Also having the portfolio 100 percent paid off gives us peace because if a property or two or three are unoccupied we aren't really affected apart from a small loss of income. No worries about making the mortgage."

Karen and Bob's main focus now isn't real estate. Their focus is on living their lives to the fullest. But their small and mighty portfolio of real estate and other investments made it possible. They've now covered 100 percent of their personal expenses and have a nice financial cushion.

In Karen and Bob's example, the real estate income floor pays for *100 percent* of their normal FI number. Eventually, this is a great goal to reach for anyone, but the downside is that it could take years to build enough wealth to get there. So many small and mighty investors make a short-term goal to achieve lean FI. As you'll see, this can still give you an incredible amount of freedom and flexibility.

LEAN FI AND FREEDOM EARLIER IN LIFE

Let's again assume your fat FI number is $120,000 per year, but right now, you only receive $36,000 per year with three debt-free rental properties. While not your full goal, this may still cover your most essential expenses, like housing, food, transportation, and health insurance. And that alone relieves a lot of financial pressure!

As I explained earlier in the chapter, covering the basics like this is known as "lean FI." And reaching this milestone is what propelled me and my wife to take our four-month mini-retirement journey to Spain and South America in 2009. We weren't fully financially independent, but by partially building our income floor, we were able to make important life changes *now* instead of later.

But taking sabbatical trips isn't the only flexibility lean FI can give you. If you have young kids, one of the parents could choose to stay home to spend more time with them. You could quit a job you no longer like and take a better one, even if it pays less. Or you could finally pursue a dream of entrepreneurship, start a nonprofit, or partake in some other professional venture that seemed too risky before.

The point here is that you don't have to wait until regular or fat financial independence to cash in on your freedom. In fact, it's usually better *not* to wait! Remember Rule No. 6 of small and mighty investors? Don't defer life! Don't wait on the important things in life if there's a responsible way to do it now.

In my case, the responsible way was to build a *partial* income floor with rental income and then to fill the gap with other sources like consulting and house flipping. In other words, I combined multiple streams of income, some more active and others more passive, to pay for my personal expenses. And I've noticed many other small and mighty investors do the same.

THE FI COUPLE FINDS PARTIAL FREEDOM IN THEIR EARLY THIRTIES

One of my favorite examples of partial financial independence comes from Ali and Josh Lupo, aka @theficouple on Instagram. They began their financial journey in their twenties as a social worker and a counselor with more than $100,000 of student debt. They both had grueling schedules and emotionally draining jobs. This led them to begin saving money to pay off their student debt while also investing in real estate using a strategy called house hacking.

Within four years, they paid off their student debt and accumulated several small multi-unit rental properties using owner-occupant loans with small down payments. These properties produced some cash flow, but not enough to meet their normal FI number. That small real estate income floor, however, did cover some of their essential expenses, like housing. And using that solid foundation, Ali and Josh also started a new side business in the social media space. That business grew and now produces enough income to fill the gap of their personal expenses. As a result, they've been able to leave their jobs and work on something that's more rewarding.

Josh and Ali continue to buy more properties, but real estate investing hasn't *yet* made them fully financially independent. Unlike Karen and Bob, they don't have debt-free rental properties, and they may never pay off all their properties. But real estate investments have helped them *quickly* make real, tangible progress toward their life goals. By combining their small and mighty real estate strategy with multiple sources of income, they've experienced freedom and flexibility earlier than they ever thought possible.

Now let's look at one more example just to see the variety of paths small and mighty investors take. In this case, the investor quit his job and started a small business as a real estate entrepreneur.

THE SMALL AND MIGHTY ENTREPRENEUR

While still in his twenties, Anthony Petz began his professional career in a sales job. From the beginning, however, he had a strong desire to become an entrepreneur and control his own financial destiny. So, he studied books, classes, and audio recordings to learn how to flip and rent investment properties.

At 25 years old, Anthony bought his first residence in his hometown of Bellingham, Washington. Two years later, he and his new wife, Michaela, bought and moved into one side of a duplex. They rented the other side of the duplex, and they also rented out his first house. Unfortunately, other than those early purchases, progress wasn't easy at first for Anthony. In fact, he almost quit real estate during those early years:

> "It probably took me five years of long hours and very hard work with very little reward in real estate before things took off. Honestly, I was on the verge of giving up just before everything finally came together."

Anthony's primary frustration was finding properties that met his conservative criteria for rentals or flips. He couldn't find many good deals at first. But fortunately, he maintained an "unrelenting dedication to his goals" and also sought out education and answers from more experienced investors. Finally, the results came.

Quitting His Job at Age 30

In 2010, Anthony quit his job at age 30. It was a bold move because he and his wife knew they had to cover personal expenses of $3,000 per month, or $36,000 per year. And when they soon had kids, that number increased to $5,000 monthly. Their goal was to cover $2,000 of expenses with rentals, and Michaela would continue to work to cover the rest. But the reality was a little different, as Anthony explains:

> "I didn't actually have $2,000 in passive income when I left the workforce. I had 4 rentals (6 units) when I decided to quit my job. But I wanted so badly to work for myself and could feel the acquisition momentum picking up. I'd spent the better part of the

last decade intensely studying books, seminars, and local investors while also putting in the work to apply what I'd learned. So, I
believed I was ready and that if I were able to dedicate more time
to real estate investing, I could start making major progress in the
direction of my goals."

Financially, their plan combined a small amount of rental income,
Michaela's job salary, and Anthony's goal to quickly generate active
real estate income. They also saved six months of cash in case Anthony
couldn't generate money fast enough. And according to Anthony, they
got down to a few weeks of cash before things got better!

The Entrepreneurial Path

Like my own journey, Anthony's story represents the entrepreneurial,
more aggressive, version of the small and mighty investor story. Unlike
Karen and Bob's more traditional route working jobs, Anthony took a
big leap by using real estate to earn a living. Anthony also didn't diversify
much into stocks, bonds, or traditional investments to build wealth. He
focused most of his energy, money, and time on real estate.

Anthony's entrepreneurial path meant that he bought more properties
than other small and mighty investors. He also took more risks than
people are willing to take. But I like to share stories like his because
both the entrepreneurial and traditional approaches to small and mighty
investing can be legitimate paths. In the end there is a similar result—
financial independence.

The Reward of the Journey

A couple of years after Anthony quit his job, Michaela and he passed
$2,000 per month of passive rental income. And within five years, their
passive real estate income surpassed their normal FI number of $5,000
per month. Today, at age 42, they own twenty-five rental units that produce over $10,000 per month of income, and they don't have plans to
grow significantly. Although Michaela continues to work at a job she
enjoys and Anthony occasionally flips houses and manages the properties, they are technically financially independent with rental properties.

Here's how Anthony reflects back on the journey:

"Eventually, with time, the rental portfolio took over and became a substantial source of income that more than covers our basic needs. That initial five-to-ten-year period was by far the most challenging of my life, but it was also the most rewarding. Originally my primary goals were financial, but honestly, the greatest rewards were personal. I grew so much as a person, and my wife and I grew so much as a couple and in our partnership."

Every journey of a small and mighty investor is unique. As you saw from Karen and Bob, Ali and Josh, and Anthony and Michaela, it's possible to begin at different ages, own different numbers of properties, grow at different paces. But in all three cases, they had a deliberate focus on their financial goals. They then worked backward from those goals to build the right-size real estate investing business that met their needs. Now they all have more *freedom* to spend time doing what's most important to them. And that's the main point!

To end this chapter, I want to give you an exercise that will help you do the same thing they have done.

EXERCISE
Your Small and Mighty Rental Property Goal

This exercise will help you get clear on your FI number and how many rental properties you need to own to reach it. Think of this as your personal small and mighty rental property goal! If you do each of these recommended steps, you'll have clear short-term and long-term goals to aim for as you read the rest of this book.

If you're in a hurry, feel free to borrow my average FI numbers of $30,000/year (lean FI), $60,000/year (regular FI), and $120,000/year (fat FI) to plug into the questions below. But to get the most out of this exercise, I recommend you figure out your actual personal expenses. If you're a budget nerd (like me!), you probably already have spreadsheets showing exactly what you spend right now. But if you've never done this before, take some time to sit down and figure it out. After all, this is *your* life and financial independence.

If you need help categorizing your personal spending information, I've got a "Personal Expenses Spreadsheet" you can download for free in the book resources at www.biggerpockets.com/smallandmightybonus. You can also use free software online (I've used Mint.com) to track your expenses over time.

Now complete each of the steps below:

1. Determine your "Lean FI" number

My annual ESSENTIAL personal expenses are: _____

_____

As you learned before, your lean FI number is the amount of investment income that would cover your most basic personal expenses. Remember, this isn't luxury living. These are the absolute basics that simply help you to survive.

2. Determine your "Regular FI" number

My annual REGULAR personal expenses are: _____

_____

Repeat the same process as question No. 1, only this time determine your regular FI number by adding some nonessential expenses. For example, this could include adding a larger eating-out budget and money for vacations. This may also be the same as the personal expenses you're spending right now.

3. Determine your "Fat FI" number

My annual FAT personal expenses are: _____

_____

Repeat the same process as questions 1 and 2, only this time determine your fat FI number. Take your regular FI number, round up, and give yourself an extra cushion. This cushion could account for unknowns, extra luxuries, or extra savings (like for your kid's college or for charitable donations). If you're not sure how much to round up and you want a rough goal, just double your Regular FI number.

4. Determine the net operating income of an average rental in your area

The median monthly rental price in my area is: _____

_____

Google "median rental price [YOUR ZIP CODE]" to find the median rental price for a single unit in your likely investment area.[15] Keep in mind that a house is one rental unit, a duplex is two rental units, and so on. So, even though you may buy a multi-unit building, for this exercise the rent is for each individual unit, not for the entire building.

The estimated annual net operating income of a rental unit is:

_____

_____

For now, just take your median rent from the previous answer, multiply it by 12 to get an annual rent amount, and then multiply that answer by 0.55. This will give you a rough estimate of the income your rental will produce *after* operating expenses like taxes, insurance, management, repairs, and vacancy.
   For example:
- Median monthly rent = $1,800
- Annual rent = $1,800 x 12 = $21,600
- Estimated net operating income = $21,600 x 0.55 = $11,880

---

15 The BiggerPockets rent estimator is a great resource for this; you can search by zip code or for individual addresses to get rent averages. Find it at www.biggerpockets.com/insights/property-searches/new.

5. Determine your rental unit goal

The point of this final step is to give you a rough target for the number of rental units you'll need to buy to achieve your financial goals. The idea is to keep this process simple. So, here are two disclaimers that help with that:

Disclaimer No. 1: It's not important to get the number of properties exactly right. Life and your real estate plans will certainly change, and you'll have plenty of time to adjust your goals along the way. As former U.S. President Dwight Eisenhower said: "Plans are worthless, but planning is everything."[16] This step counts as planning, and it'll give you a big-picture goal to work toward.

Disclaimer No. 2: To determine this goal, I'm assuming you'll eventually own rental properties free and clear of debt. Remember the income floor? I use this assumption because it makes a lot of sense. But of course, you don't have to own debt-free rentals to reach financial independence. If your preference is to keep debt on properties, just **multiply the number of units in your answers below by three.** You'll need more leveraged properties to produce the same amount of income, so this is a rough adjustment that'll give you a reasonable goal.

To determine the number of rental units you need, complete the steps below.

My goal for number of units for LEAN FI is: _____

_____

Divide your lean FI number by the estimated annual net operating income (NOI) of a single rental unit.

---

16 Dwight D. (Dwight David) Eisenhower, 1890–1969, United States. Office of the Federal Register, and United States. President (1953–1961: Eisenhower). Dwight D. Eisenhower: 1957: Containing the Public Messages, Speeches, and Statements of the President, January 1 to December 31, 1957. Washington: Office of the Federal Register, National Archives and Records Service, General Services Administration, 1958.

For example:
- Lean FI number = $30,000
- Estimated NOI of a single rental unit = $11,880
- Lean FI rental unit goal = $30,000 ÷ $11,880 = 2.53 units = 3 units (rounded up)
- (For leveraged rentals goal) 3 debt-free units x 3 = 9 leveraged units

My goal for number of units for REGULAR FI is: _____

_____

Use the same process as the prior step, but use your regular FI number instead of the lean FI number.

For example:
- Regular FI number = $60,000
- Estimated NOI of a single rental unit = $11,880
- Regular FI rental unit goal = $60,000 ÷ $11,880 = 5.05 units = 6 units (rounded up)
- (For leveraged rentals goal) 6 debt-free units x 3 = 18 leveraged units

My goal for number of units for FAT FI is: _____

_____

Use the same process as the prior steps, but use your fat FI number.

For example:
- Fat FI number = $120,000
- Estimated NOI of a single rental unit = $11,880
- Fat FI rental unit goal = $120,000 ÷ $11,880 = 10.1 units = 11 units (rounded up)
- (For leveraged rentals goal) 11 debt-free units x 3 = 33 leveraged units

CONCLUSION TO PART I

The point of the first part of the book was to help you understand more clearly what a small and mighty real estate investor is and why you should become one. Hopefully I've convinced you, and you're ready to continue! You now have a goal for the number of rental units you'd like to own, so that'll give you a big-picture target to aim for as you read the rest of the book.

But keep in mind that this goal is the *end* destination. If you're anything like me or most small and mighty investors, the path to get there won't be a straight line. For example, you may buy fifteen or twenty properties, sell some of them, and end up with ten once you reach financial independence. Or you may buy a few properties to start, and then, like Karen and Bob, use your retirement funds to buy enough properties to reach your goal.

For now, don't worry too much about the details of how your plan will work five or ten years from now. In the last part of the book, I'll give you some strategies to pay off debt, clean up your portfolio, and win the financial game. For now, I recommend focusing on the practical next parts of the book, where I teach you the best techniques I know to buy, finance, and manage good real estate deals. If you get good at these key skills, hitting your big-picture goals will be much easier.

Let's now move on to the next chapter, where I'll help you pick the right real estate strategy and get focused on the next steps of your small and mighty investing journey.

PART II

THE JOURNEY OF A SMALL AND MIGHTY REAL ESTATE INVESTOR

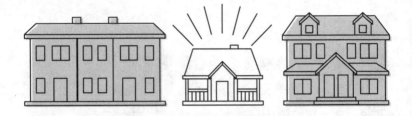

CHAPTER 4
THE JOURNEY STARTS HERE (STARTER PHASE)

I n the first few chapters of this book, we focused on your mindset as a small and mighty investor. I tried to convince you that you don't need a massive number of properties to achieve financial freedom. Instead, you can get big enough to meet your financial goals while staying small and simple enough to maximize your free time and mobility. Then I took you through an exercise to figure out your long-term goal for how many rental properties you need to achieve financial freedom.

The rest of this book will be about the nitty-gritty details of real estate investing. You'll learn how to find, negotiate, finance, buy, manage, and automate your rental properties. These are practical lessons and examples that you can use immediately to grow and improve your rental property business.

But before you learn those details, this part of the book is about taking a step back to understand the journey you are about to take. Before you go on a long trip, you usually look at a map to figure out where you are and where you need to go. In the same way, you can figure out where you are as an investor and understand what lies ahead. To start this process, I want to explain the difference between goals, strategies, and tactics.

REAL ESTATE GOALS, STRATEGIES, AND TACTICS

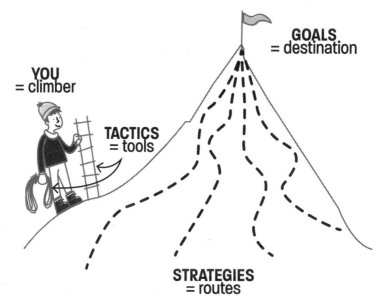

Your journey as a real estate investor is a lot like climbing a mountain. To navigate, you need goals to aim for. For example, Fat FI is the equivalent of the peak of the mountain for many investors. And Lean FI and Regular FI are major milestones or plateaus along the way. As you climb, you periodically look up toward these destinations to guide you. But most of the time you're focused on more practical things, like your strategies and tactics.

A strategy is a plan to reach one of your goals. You can think of it as a route going up the mountain. Your job is to choose the strategy that fits your situation and that will take you toward your goal in the safest and fastest way possible. I'll share more about real estate strategies later in this chapter, but they include house hacking, short-term rentals, long-term rentals, private lending, wholesaling, and fix-and-flips.

A tactic, on the other hand, is a specific method that you use while applying a strategy. For climbers, these would be shoes, warm clothes, ropes, and other tools that help you safely get up the mountain. In real estate, tactics are the specific skills or tools you use to successfully buy, finance, manage, or sell your properties.

Real estate tactics include financing techniques like private money loans, seller financing, or the BRRRR method (buy, rehab, rent, refinance, repeat). They include deal-finding tactics, like the marketing and negotiation lessons I'll teach in later chapters. And they also include property ownership tactics, like tenant screening criteria, technology systems, and rental debt snowballs to pay off your debt sooner. You'll learn these tactics and more in the rest of this book.

But there is one big takeaway lesson here. As you progress in your real estate journey, your goals, strategies, and tactics will need to change. A hiker on a 1,000-foot hill doesn't have the same goals, routes, or tools as a professional climber on Mt. Everest. In the same way, a beginner real estate investor won't have the same goals, strategies, or tactics as someone approaching financial independence.

The trick is figuring out which goals, strategies, and tactics *you* should focus on now. And to help you do that, I want to explain the three phases of a real estate journey.

THE THREE PHASES OF A REAL ESTATE INVESTING JOURNEY

I once heard a great teacher named Pete Fortunato explain that real estate investors pass through three phases on their journey to financial freedom. Those phases are:

1. **Starter:** A beginner whose goal is to get started with real estate investing.
2. **Wealth Builder:** An intermediate or advanced investor whose goal is to build wealth and accelerate their progress.
3. **Ender:** An advanced investor whose goals are to push toward the finish line of financial freedom and to enjoy the benefits.

To help you figure out which phase you are in, I'll explain each one in more depth and share real-life stories. I'll also share goals and strategies that are most relevant to your phase of the journey. There are too many tactics to list them all here, but the entire book will be filled with dozens of tactics and techniques that you can use no matter which phase you are in.

PHASE NO. 1: STARTER

When I met Michael, he was in his mid-twenties. He had found some professional success as a freelancer creating and editing online videos. This career paid for his lifestyle and gave him flexibility for his favorite hobby of traveling the world.

One day, he heard me on a podcast interview with the blogger the Mad Fientist, an expert on financial independence. In the podcast, I talked about using real estate investing to achieve financial independence. He was intrigued. Specifically, he was intrigued by a discussion I had about using house hacking to get into real estate with a small down payment to pay for your living expenses.

Michael took a course with me to learn how the real estate business worked. He didn't own a home yet, and he had no prior real estate experience. Michael also did not have enough cash yet to buy his first property in the metro Philadelphia area.

Over the next twelve months, Michael built his knowledge, his cash savings, and his network. In the end, he got preapproved for an FHA first-time home buyer loan. And with enough cash in the bank for a down payment, repairs, and reserves, he began making offers on small multifamily properties.

After nine rejected or failed offers, Michael was frustrated and almost gave up. I had a call with him, and I could sense he didn't think real estate investing was going to work for him. He was ready to move on, focus more on his job, and get back into traveling.

But I encouraged him to stick with it. I reminded him that as a new investor, it's normal to look at a lot of properties and make many offers before your first deal. In the end, Michael agreed that he would make at least five more offers to see what happened.

A couple of offers later, Michael got his first property under contract! It was an older duplex that he negotiated to purchase for $105,000. One apartment was already rented for $850 per month. With the help of his brother, Michael used his cash savings to spend about $25,000 on cosmetic repairs and then moved into the other side.

With the $850 of monthly rental income from the second unit, Michael received enough to pay for his mortgage payment, taxes, and insurance. Since then, he's also bought a second multifamily unit, and his confidence is soaring.

Who Is a Starter?

Michael was clearly a Starter; he was a beginner investor in the first phase of his real estate journey. While not in financial distress, most Starters have less than $100,000 in wealth to invest. I define "wealth to invest" as your net worth not counting a personal residence or personal property. And although timing can vary, the Starter phase usually lasts until you've done a few deals or have been in the business for a few years.

As a Starter, you often lack knowledge, confidence, money, or a network of people to support you. For that reason, your main priority at this stage is learning and gaining experience. You will likely make mistakes, and that's okay. If we choose to learn from them, mistakes can be our most valuable teachers.

Goals for Starters

Although a Starter dreams of someday achieving financial independence, that goal is too far on the horizon to be practical. A mountain climber who just started climbing wouldn't aim at the peak. Instead, they would make a goal to reach a reasonable point further up the mountain.

As a real estate Starter, you can do the same thing. A good short-term Starter goal is to buy between one and four properties. Those first properties will get you moving in the right direction.

The first properties are also your real-world education. In the process of buying and owning these first properties, you can test the theoretical strategies and tactics against the reality of your local market. Some tactics won't work for you, and others will. Keep using what works and put the others back in your toolbox for later.

The real goal of this stage is to build your confidence and momentum. Although it would be nice to make a big profit on every deal, don't beat yourself up if your first deals aren't home runs. As long as you avoid the biggest mistakes, which I'll teach a lot about in this book, your first deals will be a solid foundation to build upon.

Strategies for Starters

Because you don't have as much knowledge or cash to work with as Starter, not every real estate investing strategy will work. Based on my own journey and my experience helping hundreds of other investors, I have found certain strategies that do work well for Starters. As you begin or continue your journey, I recommend you choose from the following list:

- **Traditional House Hacking:** With this strategy, you live in a house or small multi-unit property and rent out extra bedrooms or units. The rent can pay for some or all of your housing expenses while you learn the rental business. And you can keep the property as a rental if you move out later.
- **Live-In-Then-Rent:** Most people sell their house when they decide to move. With this strategy, you just keep your former primary residence as a rental. It does require thoughtfulness to buy the right house and right numbers that could later work as a rental.
- **Live-In Flip:** If you like fixer-upper projects, you can move into a house that needs work, live in it for at least two years, and later sell it for a tax-free profit if you follow the IRS rules. This strategy is a great way to quickly grow your wealth and learn how to fix up and own properties.
- **Turnkey Long-Term Rentals:** Long-term rentals are the bread-and-butter strategy of small and mighty real estate investors. And as a Starter, it's easiest to start with turnkey long-term rentals, meaning properties that don't need repairs before renting.
- **Fixer-Upper Long-Term Rentals:** While turnkey rentals are easier, I do know plenty of Starters who began with fixer-upper rentals. If you buy the property below its full value, you can also use the BRRRR method (buy, rehab, rent, refinance, repeat). When done well, your refinance can pay you back some or all of your original cash in the deal.
- **Short-Term or Medium-Term Rentals:** With turnkey or fixer-upper rentals, you can also choose to rent to short-term (for example, vacationers, like through Airbnb) or medium-term (for example, traveling nurses, digital nomads) tenants. With the right property, these strategies can generate more cash flow than long-term rentals, although they also require more intensive management because tenants move out more often.
- **Wholesaling:** This is a strategy where you find and resell deals quickly to other investors. If you are willing to spend a lot of time making offers and looking for deals, this can be a strategy to earn extra cash without owning properties.

In Chapter 7, I'll share real stories from small and mighty investors who used these strategies. The real-life details will help you understand how each of them works. You can also check out podcasts, YouTube, and the BiggerPockets bookstore for more in-depth education on each strategy.

Pitfalls and Challenges for Starters

The biggest risk for a Starter is quitting. Unfortunately, I've met many potential real estate investors who never stuck with it long enough to find success. Getting started is not easy. Progress can feel slow, like pushing a boulder uphill. Unless you are committed, you'll never make it through this tough early phase.

Starters also face the biggest obstacles inside their own heads. Fear and lack of self-confidence are loud and hard to overcome. "Who do you think you are trying to invest in real estate? It might have worked for other people, but surely it won't for you. You'll probably fail and end up worse off than before."

If you let those inner voices take control, they can derail even the best plans. In my experience, the remedy is small, positive action. Figure out the next tiny action you need to do today, and then do it. Then do it again and again. It's hard to overthink and second-guess yourself when you're in motion.

With enough tiny action, you'll find yourself making progress right into the next phase of a Wealth Builder. And that's the topic of the next chapter.

CHAPTER 5
HOW TO GROW YOUR WEALTH (BUILDER PHASE)

By the time I met Travis, he was in his early forties, married with two kids, and already owned a couple of rental properties. He lived in Oakland, California, and he invested in two single-family houses in the nearby town of Vallejo. Neither of these deals were home runs, but they got him started. He learned a lot, and he was itching to make more progress.

After listening to my podcast, Travis took coaching with me to get help with his next steps. Travis had a high-earning job in a freight brokerage, and his wife had a good job in the local education system. Their salaries plus good savings habits meant that he had plenty of cash to buy his next deals. But he wanted to pick a target market with more cash flow potential, and he wanted to build a real business that could consistently find good deals.

During the first few months, Travis hit some dead ends, including exploring a market that didn't produce any immediate results. But Travis stuck to a plan and invested his time and money into building his team, networking with other investors, and marketing to find good deals. Eventually he found a breakthrough and ended up buying several townhouse rentals in Chattanooga, Tennessee.

Travis put 20 percent down and got fixed-interest, thirty-year conforming mortgages. The properties produced positive cash flow from day one. He had some trouble with his property manager and has since taken over management duties from a distance. But he now has a solid foundation to continue buying more properties and building more wealth.

Who Is a Builder?

Travis was a Wealth Builder (or Builder) because he already had a base of knowledge, money, and experience. In the Builder stage, you can save money consistently, so your focus has shifted to compounding and growing that money. In most cases, you have wealth or a net worth of between $100,000 and $1 million.

The Builder phase is often a little messy as you experiment with new growth strategies. And you rarely travel in a straight line toward your goals. My experience of buying too many properties in 2004 to 2007 is a good example. In 2008 and 2009, I had to clean up some of the messes I had made buying bad deals. But luckily, I survived financially and learned from my mistakes. Being able to learn from these messes is one of the reasons I recommend you grow at a slower, more deliberate pace.

Goals for Builders

As a Builder, your goal is to build your wealth until it's large enough to support you financially. If you haven't done it already, I recommend the exercise in Chapter 3 for determining your FI number and the number of properties that will give you financial independence. This will give you a clear goal to shoot for as a Builder.

You can also set a goal for a certain net worth. In the long run, a net worth goal makes a lot of sense because you can turn your wealth into income by selling or rearranging your assets. Just be careful using this metric if most of your wealth is in your home or in highly leveraged real estate. This may make you feel rich "on paper," but it can be hard to use or access this type of wealth in the short run.

Strategies for Builders

As a Builder, you're still in the middle of climbing the wealth-building mountain. You need to turn the wealth you already have into a much larger amount of wealth that will help you reach financial independence.

Therefore, the strategy you choose should be one that safely grows your wealth as quickly as possible.

Luckily, there are many choices of strategies for you. I'll give you a list of suggestions here, and then I'll share real-life stories of investors who've used these strategies in Chapters 7 and 8.

- **Any of the House-Hacking strategies:** If traditional house hacking, live-in-then-rent, or live-in flips appeal to you, you can also choose them as your strategy in the Wealth Building stage just like you did as a Starter.
- **Turnkey Long-Term Rentals:** Long-term rentals are still the bread-and-butter strategy of small and mighty investors. Even though I recommended turnkey rentals for Starters, they can still work as a Builder. You can use the lessons you've learned to start buying them at better prices and in better locations.
- **Fixer-Upper Long-Term Rentals:** Finding deals that need repairs is still a good strategy as a Builder. But in addition to fixer-uppers, look for other ways to add value to properties, like improving management, raising rent, or reducing expenses on multifamily properties. When you buy properties below their full value, it can accelerate your growth and allow you to safely use more leverage to conserve your cash.
- **Short-Term or Medium-Term Rentals:** Turning your properties into short-term or medium-term rentals can still make sense in this phase. Some of the Builders I know who've reached their income goals the fastest have used this strategy for some or all their properties. For example, I share a story in Chapter 8 of a woman who replaced her job income with just four short-term rentals.
- **Rental Cash Flow Compounding:** If possible, save all the cash flow you earn from your rentals and reinvest it into down payments for more properties. This also means keeping your property loans on the longest amortizations possible (thirty-year loans or interest only) to keep your payment as low as possible. Avoid paying off debt until the next phase.
- **Trade-Up/1031 Tax-Free Exchange:** As you accumulate properties, you can accelerate your growth by "churning your equity" and selling a property to invest in another. You can "trade up" by using a special technique known as a 1031 tax-free exchange. It allows you

to defer taxes on the sale and reinvest all your money in the next deal. It's a fantastic way to compound your growth if done well, and I explain it more in Chapter 24.

- **Private Lending/Note Investing:** Instead of owning properties, you can own the financing by making loans or offering seller financing. Like banks, this allows you to earn steady interest income while still having the security of real property. My favorite vehicle to loan money is a self-directed retirement account. Certain retirement account companies specialize in this type of transaction, which allows you to earn all your interest tax-free and compound your growth as much as possible.

The approaches to finding, buying, financing, and owning properties with all these strategies are pretty much the same. So whichever strategy you choose, the chapters in the rest of this book will help you learn the tactics and techniques you need. The main exceptions are private lending and short-term rentals.

To loan your own money as a private lender, you'll need to study additional resources outside of this book, like the BiggerPockets book *Lend to Live* by Alexandria Breshears and Beth Pinkley Johnson.[17] I've also personally benefited from an online course called Hard Money Lending,[18] which is taught by Dyches Boddiford, one of my mentors.

For the short-term or medium-term rental strategies, most of what you'll learn in this book will be very helpful. I'll teach you about finding, buying, and financing properties, which is the same for these strategies. But I won't go into detail on short-term or medium-term property management. You can read BiggerPockets books or study free online information to get more details on that.

Pitfalls and Challenges for Builders

Growth always has risks. The tools of growth, like debt leverage, are double-edged swords that can give and take away wealth. In my experience, your biggest challenge in the Builder phase is managing these risks.

---

17 https://www.biggerpockets.com/lendtolive.

18 You can find more details about the course at https://assets101.com/events/hard-money-lending-online/ or just visit his main website, assets101.com, for an updated schedule of classes.

In a later chapter on financing, I'll teach how you can safely finance your real estate by taking the fewest risks. Pay close attention to these lessons. I've known more investors who went out of business because of debt problems than from any other cause.

Another challenge of the Builder stage is burnout. Even a short journey through the Builder phase could be three to five years, and a longer journey could be one or two decades. This journey is like an ultramarathon. Pace yourself, play the long game, and don't forget to enjoy the plateaus along the way.

The length of the Builder phase is one of the reasons I wrote Rule No. 6 of a small and mighty investor: Don't defer life. Although wealth building is a fun game, the whole purpose is to support your life. So don't let an obsession with long-term goals take you away from enjoying your life and the people around you during the journey.

If you can make it through the Builder phase, you'll then find yourself in the Ender phase. That's the topic of the next chapter.

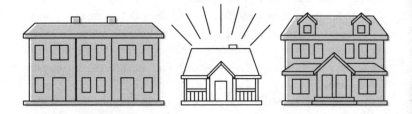

CHAPTER 6
HOW TO FINISH THE FINANCIAL JOURNEY (ENDER PHASE)

I met Sean and Heather when they were recently married, in their twenties, and in the Starter phase. Sean had a job in financial services, and Heather was an engineer. They earned good money, had good savings habits, and were eager to learn. I got to participate as a teacher as they bought their first deals and built a solid foundation.

We stayed in touch as Sean and Heather grew into Builders. They found their niche in the Charlotte, North Carolina, market with long-term rentals, and they grew their portfolio to well over ten properties. They used their good credit and income to get long-term, fixed-interest loans at good interest rates. And they saved income from their jobs and from recycling rental cash flow to buy more properties.

Along the way, Heather decided to stay home with the kids as they started a family. Their solid foundation allowed them to make this move financially. And Heather continued to participate in the acquisition and management of their properties.

In 2021, about eleven years from when they started, Sean and Heather had already hit their limit of ten conforming loans. This means the lenders who provided conforming thirty-year investment mortgages would no longer make them loans. To continue expanding their portfolio, they began using private loans to acquire good deals. With their decade of knowledge and experience, they knew how to find and perform well on these deals.

But as Sean and Heather grew to a total of twenty-one properties, some questions started to nag at them. Why were they buying more properties? What was the goal they were trying to accomplish? And didn't they already have enough to achieve their long-term goals?

In the end, they decided to sell nine of their properties. After paying taxes, they used the cash from those sales to pay off debt on some of the remaining properties and to pad their cash reserves. And they now have a goal to pay off the rest of the debt on their small and mighty rental portfolio in the near future. Using the excess cash flow from their job and rental income, they plan to quickly pay off mortgages using the rental debt snowball technique, which I'll talk about in the final part of the book.

Who Is an Ender?

Sean and Heather had clearly crossed the threshold between the Builder and Ender phases because maximizing growth was no longer their main priority. That doesn't mean they no longer wanted to grow. It just meant that their priorities had changed.

In the Ender phase, you've built a large net worth, usually $1 million or more. And you're either near your financial independence goal or you've hit a milestone and you're ready to slow things down to enjoy life more. The priorities for Enders are increasing income, reducing risk, and freeing up your free time to do things that matter.

Goals of an Ender

Here's how many Enders turn those priorities into goals:

1. **Income:** Build an income floor where your investments produce cash flow to pay for your FI number, whether that's Lean, Regular, or Fat FI.
2. **Reduce risk:** To paraphrase Warren Buffett, don't lose what you have trying to gain something you don't need. In other words,

manage and reduce risk so that you don't lose the hard-earned wealth you built.

3. **Reduce hassle:** Time is the most rare and precious asset in life. Simplify, outsource, and optimize your investment business to free up more of your personal time.

As I said in the beginning of this book, real estate and your finances are just tools to help you live your best life. Most Enders don't "retire" and do nothing once they achieve their real estate goals. Instead, they spend their time working on the most fulfilling activities possible, whether they make money or not. They get "paid" in joy, fun, and purpose instead of worrying about trading hours for dollars. These goals make that reality possible.

Strategies for Enders

One of the hardest transitions for Enders is to put the Builder tools back in the toolbox. Those tools served you well for a time, but they no longer serve your goals now. Here is a list of my favorite strategies for Enders. I've also added a few techniques that I'll cover in more detail in Part VI of the book (How to Win the Real Estate Game).

- **Long-term rentals:** Whether you have turnkey or fixer-uppers, using long-term rentals is still an excellent strategy for Enders. But many Enders switch or trade up to higher-quality properties that attract long-term tenants.
- **Short-term or medium-term rentals:** This strategy can still work as an Ender, but to reduce hassle, you may want to hire a third-party property manager.
- **Private lending:** Fund deals for Starters and Builders to earn passive interest.
- **Note investing:** Sell some of your properties with Seller Financing to receive more passive principal and interest over a long period of time.
- **Joint ventures:** Provide capital for the long-term deals of Starters and Builders. You're now the person with money who can help them start and grow. See Chapter 20 for examples of this technique.
- **Syndications:** Invest in larger deals as a limited partner via a technique called syndication. Before investing money, study resources

like *The Hands-Off Investor* by Brian Burke to understand the complexity and the process of deals.

- **Prune the portfolio:** Sell off excess or undesirable properties to clean up your portfolio. Use the cash from sales to pay off debt or reinvest in better properties. See Chapter 24 for more details.
- **Trade up:** Sell underperforming or high-intensity properties for higher-quality, more passive properties. Use a 1031 exchange to defer taxes, if possible. See Chapter 24 for more details.
- **Strategic refinancing:** Pay off dangerous, high-interest, or high-payment debt with better debt to reduce risk and increase cash flow. See Chapter 25 for more details.
- **Rental debt snowball:** Use excess cash flow to quickly pay off one debt at a time until some or all your portfolio is free from debt. See Chapter 25 for more details.
- **Optimize:** Improve systems, paperwork, asset protection, and team members so that the investment operations run as smoothly and hassle-free as possible. See Chapter 22 for more details.

Many of these strategies, like long-term rentals or joint ventures, are also used in the Builder phase, just in a different way. As an Ender, you want to leverage your time as much as possible by letting your capital do the work. With your time freed up, you can focus on doing whatever is most important to you.

Pitfalls and Challenges for Enders

One of your biggest challenges as an Ender is your own psychology. To build wealth successfully, you had to focus intensely on maximizing growth. But growth can become an addiction that's hard to shake. The goalposts for success will constantly move, and you can find yourself on a manic treadmill for the rest of your life.

To use a poker metaphor, the challenge for Enders is to take chips off the table. You've got to plow back some of your wealth into techniques that won't always maximize growth but will optimize your resiliency. To do that, you've got to convince yourself that you're playing a different game now. You're not in a race to make more than everyone else. Instead, your goal is to have the financial resources you need to live your best life.

Another challenge for Enders is finding purpose, meaning, and excitement after you've reached a large milestone. You may have been pushing for this goal for decades, and when you finally achieve it, you can ironically experience a void that leads to depression.

This is a personal journey, so I can't tell you how to address this for yourself. In my own case, however, I started working on my next thing well before becoming an Ender. I found a passion project in online education that has fulfilled me even more than real estate investing. It's the reason you're holding this book in your hands! My hope is that you find one or more "next things" and passion projects for yourself before you become an Ender.

MINI-CYCLES FROM STARTER TO BUILDER TO ENDER

I've presented the phases of a real estate investor as one long path that you travel on until the end. But during my own journey, I traveled from Starter to Builder to Ender in more frequent mini-cycles. These mini-cycles formed a sort of upward spiral rather than a straight line. And they were also a lot more fun than one long, grinding journey!

My business partner and I began as Starters in 2003. Within two years, we were clearly on the path of Builders, using leverage and growing fast. But then 2007 and the Great Recession hit. We had to quickly pivot and focus on survival in a changing market. Part of our pivot was reducing risk, selling properties where possible, systematizing our operations, and increasing income.

By 2009, we were nowhere close to full financial independence. But we had stabilized our portfolio and created a reasonably steady base of income. And the end of that mini-cycle allowed me and my wife to take a mini-retirement for four months to Spain, Peru, Chile, and Argentina. We used cash savings to pay for most of our trip.

Then in 2010, we had to become Starters again and figure out the new real estate and lending market. But we quickly got back into the Builder phase, and between 2010 and 2016 we used private and commercial loans to buy the best deals of our career, including several multifamily apartments. By late 2016 and 2017, we slowed down that mini-cycle into more of an Ender phase with a focus on income, risk reduction, and systemization.

That's when my wife and I took our 3- and 5-year-old kids on a seventeen-month mini-retirement to Ecuador in South America. Rental and interest income paid for 100 percent of our expenses while living abroad. And we had excellent systems and managers back at home that allowed me to work only a couple of hours per week from another continent.

Since I returned from that trip, another mini-cycle has continued during 2018 to 2022. As I write this book at the end of 2022 and beginning of 2023, I'm living abroad again with my family, this time in Spain. We're squarely in the Ender phase now. And while there is always room to improve, I feel better about the income, risk profile, and systems of our business than ever before.

Every journey is different. The only thing I know for sure is that yours won't be exactly like mine. But I do recommend looking for opportunities to create your own mini-cycles. Becoming an Ender sooner and more often builds plateaus during your journey. You take chips off the table, reduce some risk, and then continue your journey upward. Eventually you get to better and better places financially, but you get to enjoy the journey along the way.

THE JOURNEY CONTINUES

I've personally been on the journey as a real estate investor for over twenty years. I vividly remember the excitement, anticipation, and fear in those early days as a Starter. Those were also some of the most fun times in my life.

I also remember the rush and sometimes frantic sensation of being a Builder. Particularly when the 2007–2008 recession hit, I felt like I was holding on for dear life to a galloping horse! But with a combination of good luck and pulling hard on the reins, I slowed the horse down and made it out of that phase safely.

And now I am enjoying the fruits of the Ender phase. Having flexibility, free time, and options is amazing. At least for me, the payoff in the end was worth the sacrifice during the journey.

My motivation and drive for writing this book is the image of you getting to experience those same fruits of financial independence. I can't tell you how long your journey will be because we all start with different circumstances and face different challenges. But I firmly believe you can successfully make the journey. Helping you do that is why I wrote this book!

Before we leave the topic of real estate phases and strategies, I want to tell you some stories. In the next two chapters, I've collected stories from real small and mighty investors who used different strategies in their personal real estate journeys. As you read these stories, think about which strategy makes the most sense for you. If during this part of the book you can find a particular strategy you'd like to focus on, it will make the techniques in the rest of the book even more helpful.

CHAPTER 7
STORIES OF SUCCESSFUL REAL ESTATE INVESTING STRATEGIES (PART 1)

The next two chapters are a collection of real stories about the strategies that small and mighty investors have used during their real estate journeys. This chapter will focus more on strategies I recommended for Starters. And the next chapter will focus both on Builder and Ender strategies.

I hope you find the stories helpful and inspiring. I also hope you'll use them to pick a strategy for your own real estate journey. When you focus on one strategy, it will make everything else that you read in this book easier to implement.

The first few stories are all from my journey as a Starter real estate investor. And the first is about how I got into house hacking when I was 24 years old.

HOUSE HACKING ADVENTURES IN MY TWENTIES

In 2004, when I was 24 years old, I bought my first home to live in. It was a three-bedroom, two-bath single-family house that I still own today as a rental. I was able to buy it with owner financing and a very small down payment. But about six months after buying this house, I knew I had made a mistake.

My First Home Was a Mistake

I was a brand-new, full-time real estate investor with no guaranteed income, yet my payment on this house was about $800 per month including principal, interest, taxes, and insurance. And when the house needed maintenance, which it always did because it was old, I spent even more money. Bottom line—this house was eating money that I didn't really have.

When a friend of mine told me about a vacant four-unit property in my hometown of Clemson, it sounded like an opportunity. It was a bank-owned property, meaning a local bank had foreclosed on the previous owner and now wanted to sell it. It wasn't officially on the market yet, but the friend who brought it to me told me the bank wanted to sell it for $80,000.

My Best Christmas Present Ever

I quickly went out to visit the property, and the first thing that greeted me was a large message, spray-painted across the front of the building, "Merry Christmas." I didn't know whether to open my gift or run away, because the property was a mess! It smelled horrible, and its style was straight from the 1970s, including orange shag carpet, mustard yellow appliances, and brown wall paneling. But my mentor, Dr. Stone, who you may remember from earlier, convinced me this was the perfect opportunity.

I made an offer and negotiated with the bank. After a little back and forth, I was the proud owner of this ugly building for the low price of $70,000. I borrowed 80 percent of the price from a local bank, and Dr. Stone gave me a private loan for most of the $14,000 down payment and $45,000 of repair costs at 10 percent interest. I then paid contractors to paint everything and install new decks, windows, central heat and air, flooring, and kitchen appliances.

Living for Free in My Twenties

After the repairs, I moved into unit 2, and I rented the other three units to grad students from nearby Clemson University. My tenants loved the updates and the convenient location along the bus line to the university. And I loved the fact that their total rent of $1,200 (or $400/unit) covered *all* my monthly expenses on the property. After refinancing with a long-term mortgage, I was living for FREE. I had stumbled into an amazing real estate strategy that hadn't even been named yet. It's now known as house hacking.[19]

LIVE-IN-THEN-RENT: HOW I TURNED MY HOME INTO AN AMAZING RENTAL

In the previous story, I told you about my first *traditional* house hack. But I've used a second variation of house hacking called *live-in-then-rent* more often. This strategy just means keeping your home as a rental instead of selling it once you're ready to move. As you'll see, it's a simple strategy that almost anyone can use.

Turning a Mistake into an Investment

As I mentioned in the previous story, I bought my very first home at 24 years old. It turned out to be too expensive for me at that stage of my life. I could have stayed and used house hacking to rent the other two bedrooms out to cover most of my costs. But instead, I chose to rent the entire house for $950 per month.

I then moved into one unit of the recently remodeled four-unit property. Eighteen years later, I still own this original house. Not only does it now rent for almost $1,600 per month, but the value has also increased from my purchase price of $110,000 to more than $250,000 today. Renting out my first house turned into a very good decision!

---

19 Thanks to my friend and fellow BiggerPockets author Brandon Turner for coming up with a catchy name for this very cool strategy that investors have been using successfully for years. And to another friend of mine, Craig Curelop, who leveraged house hacking into financial independence in a few short years and wrote a book on it, *The House Hacking Strategy*.

Our Baby's First Home Was a Fixer-Upper!

After living in the four-unit house hack for several years, in 2009, my wife and I were ready to have kids. The small 700-square-foot apartment was a little cramped. So, we bought a fixer-upper house in a good neighborhood near Clemson University for $130,000. The seller agreed to finance the house to us with a $4,000 down payment, and we invested about $40,000 in new wiring, plumbing, windows, a heating and air system, new sheetrock, a remodeled kitchen, and two remodeled bathrooms.

Our total investment was over $170,000, and the value of the house at the time was probably less than our total investment. It didn't seem like a great deal at first. But it was a nice place to live, the repairs made it a low-maintenance home, and our payments to the seller were affordable at $400 per month.

Another Baby, Another House

We lived in the house for two years and enjoyed life with our new baby. But just before we had our second baby, we bought a larger house in town (that's Home No. 4 if you're keeping score!) that would give more space to our growing family. We moved into the larger house and kept the old house (Home No. 3) as a rental for $995 per month.

An Excellent Long-Term Rental

Now, ten years later, the old house's rent has increased to $1,550 per month, and the value has increased to $240,000. We self-manage the property, but because of its good location, it is incredibly easy to find excellent tenants. And because of our upfront repairs, it's also very easy to maintain.

As for cash flow, our seller financing payment is still $400 per month, and other expenses like taxes, insurance, maintenance, and rental licenses are $400 to $500 per month. And most months we have between $650 and $750 of cash flow to put in our bank account. Like my first house, this began as a residence, but it is now one of my best long-term rental properties.

The Best Strategies Are Simple

The live-in-then-rent strategy is so simple it can be deceiving. But like me, you could do this only a couple of times and build an enormous amount of wealth and cash flow. The trick is to avoid large, expensive, high-maintenance residences that wouldn't also work as a rental. This will give you the flexibility to rent the house if you decide to move someday. Also, be sure to run the numbers up front on your home as if it were a rental. You can use deal analysis formulas that I share in a later chapter to be sure it will produce a positive cash flow.

HOW I MADE $180,000 ON MY FIRST RENTAL PROPERTY BY BEING PATIENT

When I was 24 years old and still living in my four-unit house hack, my business partner and I bought our first pure rental property. At the time, we were also flipping and wholesaling houses to make a living, but we thought this single-family house was a good long-term rental opportunity. It was a cookie-cutter-style house that had only been built a few years before we bought it. And it was in a location we liked in a small city called Easley, South Carolina.

The Details of Our First Rental Purchase

We paid a price of $94,050 for the house. Our down payment was $6,150, which meant we owed a balance on our financing of $87,900. We were able to get this much smaller down payment by using a seller financing technique called buying subject-to the mortgage. I'll cover that and other alternative financing techniques in a later chapter.

The seller called me about her property after seeing my magnetic car sign that said "I Buy Houses." She had recently married, and she and her new husband now owned two houses. Money was extremely tight making two mortgage payments, and they were not interested in becoming rental landlords. We could make the purchase quickly to alleviate their problem before they missed any mortgage payments.

The house was worth about $105,000 at the time of our purchase, so we were able to buy it with a discount from the full value of about $10,000. When we bought it, we estimated the house would rent for between $795 and $895 per month. Our mortgage payment was $575 per month (principal and interest), so we had between $220 and $320 per month to pay all our operating costs like taxes, insurance, and maintenance. We didn't run the numbers very well on this first deal, but we thought the income after expenses would at least cover our mortgage payment or perhaps give us a small cash flow.

Rental Property Reality Wasn't as Good as We Imagined

As it turns out, we had negative cash flow of over $300 per month during the first few years. First, we were too optimistic about the rent value. We were only able to get $750 per month. Second, we had a tenant who constantly had difficulty paying the rent. And as rookie investors, we let this bad situation get worse by not requiring the tenant to leave sooner.

But eventually, we learned from our mistakes, and we screened to find well-qualified tenants. Our income became more reliable, and our cash flow finally turned *slightly* to the positive. But during this time, we also experienced the Great Recession and property market crash. If we had tried to sell our rental, the value would have been $100,000 or less. That meant we had very little, if any, equity in our rental.

Up to that point, this long-term rental strategy wasn't working very well! But the best strategy for a long-term rental in a good location is patience. And our little house became a better investment over time as the rents and market prices began increasing after the recession.

Time Heals Rental Property Mistakes in Good Locations

Today, eighteen years after we bought the house, the market rent is over $1,500 per month. The property has a positive cash flow of over $500 per month, or $6,000 per year. And the market price has increased to more than $230,000, which gives us over $180,000 in equity when you subtract our remaining $50,000 mortgage balance. I've run the numbers on this property, and we've earned a return of about 20 percent a year on our investment, even including the negative cash flow in those early years.

This first property is certainly not the best investment I've ever made. But it shows the power of using the long-term rental strategy as a small and mighty real estate investor. My long-term rental purchases have gotten much better over time, and they've helped me become financially independent. By applying what you'll learn in this book, you can do what I've done or even better.

FROM $33,000 IN STUDENT DEBT TO LIVING FOR FREE WITH A HOUSE HACK

Sarah Wilson graduated from college with a degree in journalism. She had accumulated $33,000 of student debt in the process, but she soon got a job at a local newspaper. It didn't pay much, but it was a good start.

A Difficult Start to a Career

Then the unexpected happened. Sarah got laid off. She soon found herself sinking financially, living off unemployment, and deferring her large student debt with no hope of paying it back. In her own words, "It was a terrifying time."[20]

Sarah eventually found another newspaper job earning $26,000 per year, and she slowly started climbing her way out of a financial hole. But she decided to never allow herself to be in this situation again. She learned how to live frugally on a budget of $1,600 per month, she found ways to generate income on the side, and she even started a YouTube channel (@budgetgirl) to document her journey of paying off debt. Three years later, Sarah had completely paid off her debt, thanks to these new financial habits.

Renting Before Buying Can Be a Good Strategy

Throughout her debt payoff journey, Sarah had always been a renter. She began with a $200 per month basement apartment in an old house. Then she rented "a $400 per month rental apartment in sleazy part of town."[21] Finally she moved to College Station, Texas, for a new job and found a $665 per month apartment. Sometimes she had to live in places that weren't that nice, but they all fit into her strict budget. And without down payments or house repairs to worry about, she was able to save all her money for paying off debt.

With her debt finally paid off and $10,000 in the bank as an emergency fund, Sarah entered a new phase. Instead of trying to financially survive, she was able to *save* money and start *building* wealth. When her apartment owner decided to raise her rent from $665 to $900, she decided it was time to own a home and try house hacking.

---

20 "How Budget Girl Paid Off $30k of Debt & Bought 2 Rentals While on a Low Income," *Real Estate & Financial Independence* podcast, last accessed on September 20, 2022, https://www.coachcarson.com/budgetgirl/.

21 Ibid.

Sarah Discovers House Hacking

Sarah immediately liked the idea of living in a small multifamily property more than a single-family home because it was "just less risky." The idea of paying more each month than she already paid in rent "didn't sound sexy or fun."[22] Sarah shopped for small multifamily properties for a year, and then in the beginning of the COVID-19 pandemic, she finally found and bought a duplex she liked.

The property was a five-minute drive from Sarah's work at Texas A&M University, and it had two units, each with three bedrooms and two baths. It was only twenty years old and still in excellent condition. The price of $240,000 was within her budget, especially given that it came with a tenant who already paid $1,050 per month in rent. She used an FHA loan program to buy the house with a 3.5 percent down payment of $8,400. She also used an extra $3,000 for cosmetic repairs and $10,000 as a rental property reserve fund.

House Hacking Results

Eventually, the original tenant moved out, and after a light remodel, Sarah now rents the unit for $1,250 per month. She also charges $500 rent to her boyfriend, who lives with Sarah on her side of the duplex. Combined, that rent pays for most of her mortgage, taxes, and insurance on the property with the result that Sarah only spends about $150 per month to live there!

Although there have been rough moments, like when she had to pay out of pocket for water runoff issues, Sarah's house hacking experience has been extremely positive. In fact, after reflecting on the experience, she says, "This has been a fantastic property and I wish I could buy every other one on this block." Sarah has now become a real estate investor!

HOW A COUPLE USED THE LIVE-IN FLIP TO START INVESTING IN REAL ESTATE

Mindy and Carl Jensen didn't mean to flip their first home. It was just the practical thing to do. They were getting married, and they each had their own home. Mindy had a condo that was smaller and not as nice, so they decided to flip it and move into Carl's house.

---

22 Ibid.

$25,000 Profit on Their First Flip

Before selling, they replaced the ugly old linoleum floor with tile. They did the work themselves after reading DIY books. Then, after adding a fresh coat of paint, they sold the condo for a $25,000 profit.

Because Mindy had bought the condo as her residence and lived there at least two of the last five years, she made all that profit tax-free. In fact, she could've made up to $250,000 tax free as an individual or $500,000 tax-free as a couple, thanks to section 121 of the U.S. tax code.[23]

The Benefits of Live-In Flips

The first live-in flip was a lightbulb moment for Mindy and Carl. They learned that they had the skills to make money with their house. And they also learned that this could be a valuable, repeatable wealth-building strategy. In an article about live-in flips,[24] Carl explained several other benefits that he learned to love about the live-in flip strategy:

- **Low risk:** The flipping shows on TV are high risk because they need to sell quickly and their holding expenses are high. But you can take your time with live-in flips.
- **Tax savings:** To earn $100,000 *after* taxes at your job, you have to earn a lot more—$150,000, even $200,000 in some cases. But with one live-in flip, you could earn $100,000 and keep 100 percent of the profits.
- **No rush:** You'll want to stay in the home for at least two years to get the tax benefits, so you can do the repairs or hire someone to do them at your leisure.
- **You don't have to sell:** You may decide that you love this fixed-up house and you want to make it your forever home. Or you could keep it as a rental instead of selling it. In that case, you still have three years to change your mind and sell it with the tax-free benefits.

Doing More Live-In Flips

For all those reasons and more, Mindy and Carl decided to repeat the

---

23 26 U.S. Code § 121 - Exclusion of gain from sale of principal residence, Legal Information Institute – Cornell Law School, https://www.law.cornell.edu/uscode/text/26/121.

24 "Getting Rich with the Live-in House Flip," Coach Carson Blog & *Real Estate & Financial Independence* podcast, last accessed on September 24, 2022, https://www.coachcarson.com/getting-rich-live-in-flip/.

strategy. They continued to buy ugly but livable houses to live in. Then they fixed them up to resell at least two years later.

Nine houses later, they've become experts at remodeling and flipping homes. But instead of $25,000 profits, some of their later houses produced well over $100,000–200,000 of tax-free profit. And the profits they generated, especially early on, were a nest egg that grew and eventually allowed them to achieve financial independence.

As documented on their blog 1500days.com, Mindy and Carl now have a net worth of over $4.3 million! They've diversified their investments into stock index funds, individual stocks, and real estate investments. But it all started with their live-in flips.

Tips to Make Live-In Flips Work Well

Carl has a few tips for any of you considering the live-in flip strategy.[25]

- **You can do the work:** When Carl and Mindy first started, they didn't know how to do any repairs. To learn how to tile, paint, or install a toilet, they checked out books from the library and carefully followed instructions. These days, you have YouTube, which has videos that teach how to do any repair you want to make.

- **Start with a couple of basic skills:** You don't have to do it all. If you can hang cabinets and tile, you can create a beautiful kitchen. Start small with a couple of jobs and hire out the rest. You can add more skills as you go.

- **Know when to hire it out:** In some cases, it's cost- and time-effective to hire a pro. For example, Carl doesn't do rough carpentry, drywall, or big concrete jobs. I'll add that I don't do *anything*! I hire it all out.

- **Look for homes that are cosmetically ugly:** With house flips, you need a vision. Lime green carpet is your friend. A sinking foundation is not. Carl and Mindy seek out homes with cosmetic flaws but level floors, solid mechanical systems, and a dry basement.

- **Have fun with it:** This is your opportunity to be creative! Enjoy the process and let your personality shine through with small touches that make a big difference.

---

25 Ibid.

If you have the desire to make ugly or worn-out homes beautiful again, the live-in flip is the perfect strategy for you. While it may require living in a dusty home for a while, the satisfaction and the profits in the end could be well worth the trouble. And it's another excellent way to dip your toe into the real estate investing game before you go all in.

HOW A NEW INVESTOR USED WHOLESALING TO REPLACE HIS JOB

In 2008 Nasar El-Arabi had a full-time job in Charlotte, North Carolina, working for a call center in the banking industry. He was interested in real estate, so he bought two rental properties using traditional loans. But he dreamed of leaving his job to become a full-time entrepreneur. He didn't want to be an employee for the rest of his life.

Getting Started as a Wholesaler

To make that goal happen, Nasar spent his nights and weekends learning new real estate skills and networking with successful real estate investors. Along the way, he heard that the strategy of wholesaling was a method to earn quick cash in real estate. So, he decided to give it a try.

In 2010, Nasar began working every spare hour to find deals. He used the same deal-finding strategies you'll learn later in this book, like Driving for Dollars, direct mail, and networking with other investors. He also built a list of other investors who had cash and were willing to buy good deals if he found them.

He Finally Found a Deal

Unfortunately, for eight months Nasar bought no deals despite all his efforts. But then one day he got a call back from a tired landlord. This man owned a lower-priced rental house, and he recently had to evict a tenant. The property had become a headache, and the man was ready to get rid of it. He wanted to retire from the rental business after thirty years of investing in real estate. He told Nasar to make him an offer.

It may be hard to believe today, but this property in 2010 in a lower-priced area of town was worth about $30,000 fixed up. And it also needed about $15,000 of repairs. Nasar decided to make an offer of $15,000. The owner accepted.

No Buyers Want My Property!

Nasar got the property under contract with a long due-diligence period. During this due-diligence period, Nasar could inspect the property and still back out if he needed to. As soon as he got it under contract, Nasar emailed every investor he knew to see if they wanted to buy it. But no one wanted it for his asking price, which was his contract price plus a small markup for a profit.

But Nasar wasn't ready to give up. He used a marketing company to build a mailing list of other investors. The list included anyone who had bought properties for low prices during the past six months in that area. Nasar mailed all of them postcards about the property, and he finally got some calls back from interested investors.

Renegotiating to Make a Deal

Nasar eventually had to renegotiate with the seller because he and the other investors found additional problems with the property. This led to a lower contract price of $11,000. And he also finally found a cash buyer willing to pay $13,000 for the house. So Nasar assigned his contract to this buyer for a $2,000 assignment fee. The other investor then bought the property for $11,000, did the repairs, and rented it out.

Is $2,000 Worth the Trouble?

You might ask whether $2,000 was worth all that effort and trouble. Here's what Nasar had to say:[26]

> "$2,000 is in no way a lot of money. But all I wanted was a proof of concept. That was priceless to see that it works. I was 90% sold [on wholesaling] before, but now I was like 110% sold."

The $2,000 didn't change Nasar's life financially. But the confidence and knowledge he gained from the transaction made all the difference in the world. It led to many more wholesale deals that did make a lot more money.

---

26 "From No Job to a 7-Figure Real Estate Investing Business — Interview with Nasar El-Arabi," *Real Estate & Financial Independence* podcast, last accessed on September 30, 2022, https://www.coachcarson.com/realestatedoru/.

Becoming a Full-Time Wholesaler and Flipper

Then in 2012, Nasar lost his regular job at the bank. While this could have been a time to feel bad for himself, Nasar saw it as an opportunity. The situation just forced him to make the leap to being a full-time real estate entrepreneur, which he always wanted to do anyway. And because of his preparation and training as a wholesaler, he successfully made that transition.

Ten years later, Nasar now makes more than $1 million a year wholesaling, building, and flipping properties. In the process, he's wholesaled and flipped dozens of properties. He also owns a small and mighty rental portfolio with sixteen units. Because of his success wholesaling and flipping properties and then sharing what he's learned, Nasar has become known online as the Real Estate Doru. He's also become financially independent.

FROM LIVING IN AN RV TO SHORT-TERM RENTALS IN AN EXPENSIVE MARKET

Joe Jimenez graduated from college in 2011 with a degree in civil engineering. With the economy still reeling from the Great Recession, few firms were hiring rookie engineers. Without work as an excuse, Joe decided to pursue a dream of hiking the entire 2,190-mile Appalachian Trail. It was an experience that changed the trajectory of his life.

Life on the Appalachian Trail

On the trail for hours at a time, Joe had time to think about what mattered and what he wanted his life to look like. He realized that the prototypical American Dream of working a job, accumulating stuff, and chasing future happiness wouldn't work for him anymore. The simplicity and rawness of his trail experience "ruined" his ability to pursue a conventional life path.[27]

Minimalist Lifestyle in an RV

Joe eventually did return to his career, and he got married to his high school sweetheart, Katie. But they brought the minimalist trail lifestyle

---

27 "Meet the Dirtbag Hiker Who Just Bought Two House Hacks in Montana," *Real Estate & Financial Independence* podcast, last accessed on October 9, 2022, https://www. coachcarson.com/montanahousehacks/.

into their life together. For example, they bought and lived in an RV, which allowed them to live inexpensively for a few hundred dollars per month. Joe also biked to work each day, giving him exercise and avoiding the need for a second car. Neither Joe nor Katie was used to having much money, but because they lived frugally, they were able to save a lot of the income they earned at their jobs.

Beginning Their Real Estate Journey

Eventually, Joe and Katie also became interested in real estate investing. When they decided to move to Kalispell, Montana, to be near Glacier National Park, they bought a duplex apartment. Initially they thought it would make a good house hack to live in, but since both sides were rented to long-term tenants, they just financed it as a rental property instead of a personal residence. For a temporary home, they continued living nearby in their RV.

But with the cold Montana winter looming, Joe and Katie knew they needed a more permanent residence. So they found another duplex apartment, and they moved into one side as a house hack. They then decided to furnish and fix up the other side to rent for short stays on Airbnb. After hearing about the large potential cash flow of short-term rentals, they were excited to try it out.

The Results of Their First Short-Term Rental

They had hoped things would go well, but Joe and Katie's first season with a short-term rental exceeded their expectations. Their unit was rented for most of the summer and fall, and because the property is relatively close to a ski resort, it was also popular during winter. In their first season, the one unit averaged $3,000 per month of rent. This compares to the $1,800 per month the unit would have produced as a long-term rental.

To show you their overall numbers, their purchase price was $430,000, and they paid $86,000, or a 20 percent down payment. They also spent $20,000 for repairs and furniture, which they put on a credit card with a zero percent introductory rate for the first nine months. Their monthly expenses were $1,930 for a mortgage payment, which included taxes and insurance, and about $1,000 for utilities, maintenance, and advertising.

Altogether the expenses were about $3,000 per month, which they covered 100 percent with the rent from the short-term rental!

Settling into Their Long-Term Home

After some time, Joe and Katie bought and moved to a small house that better suited their long-term needs. The new house also has an ADU (accessory dwelling unit, small guest house) that rents for $950 per month. With their former duplex now rented on both sides as a short-term rental, it produces $6,000 per month of rent and a positive cash flow of about $3,000 per month. With the addition of the positive cash flow from their original duplex, Joe and Katie could cover their basic living expenses (aka lean FI) from their small and mighty portfolio of five rental units! But now they're hooked on the process, and they're searching for their next short-term rental to purchase!

MORE STORIES OF REAL INVESTORS

I chose these stories to demonstrate how the Starter phase can look different for every investor. It's not easy to focus, pick a strategy, and build momentum as a new investor. But I hope these real small and mighty real estate investors have inspired you and have given you some ideas about your own journey.

In the next chapter, we'll continue with more stories about the strategies used by small and mighty investors. But now I'll mix in more Builder and Ender phase stories so you can see how strategies evolve over time.

CHAPTER 8
STORIES OF SUCCESSFUL REAL ESTATE INVESTING STRATEGIES (PART 2)

I n this chapter, I share more real-life stories from small and mighty real estate investors. While the last chapter focused more on the Starter phase, this chapter will focus on the Builder and Ender phases. You'll see that some of the specific strategies, like long-term rentals and short-term rentals, are the same as in the Starter stories. But pay attention to how the investors use them in different ways to grow and eventually live off their rental properties.

I'll begin again with one of my favorite real estate stories about a friend of mine. Beginning with very little money, she was able to climb her way to a debt-free rental property portfolio.

FOURTEEN NO-DEBT RENTAL PROPERTIES AFTER STARTING WITH A WAITRESS SALARY

In 2009 during the depths of the economic crisis, Ashley Hamilton was working as a waitress in Detroit, Michigan. As a single mom with two kids, she was doing what she could to pay the bills while earning less than $20,000 a year. Luckily when she filed her tax return that year, she learned that she would receive a refund of $6,300.

The Best Way to Invest Your Tax Refund!

Ashley had a choice of what to do with that tax refund. Her friends used their money to take trips, buy clothes, or pay the rent. And she could certainly think of some practical uses for that money, like buying a better car that wouldn't break down so much. But Ashley decided to use the money to buy a foreclosed house, which during the housing crisis in Detroit was selling for less than her tax refund amount (yes, prices there were ultra-cheap).

After some plumbing work, paint, and carpet, Ashley and her kids moved into the house during August of 2009. She also had to save money for a few more months to buy a furnace before the cold Detroit winter. But as Ashley settled into her new home, a lightbulb went off in her head. She was no longer paying $700 per month in rent, and this home could provide financial security for her and her family forever. And beyond that, she could save her money and do it again!

The Lightbulb Moment: Buy More Real Estate

Ashley began saving $500 a month, and by the next year when she received another tax refund, she had enough money to buy another house. She rented it to a family and kept it as a long-term rental. And now with her combined job income, rental income, and tax return, she was able to save enough money to pay cash for at least one or two houses per year for the next ten years.

A Debt-Free Rental Portfolio in Ten Years

By 2019, Ashley had a portfolio of fourteen investment properties with no debt that paid her enough income to be financially independent. Instead of working as a waitress, she had investments that were now working for her. In total, these long-term rentals paid her $8,000 per month in cash flow and represented wealth of over $800,000.

Ashley took a couple of years to enjoy her success. But then she decided to grow a little more and bought eleven additional properties in one year using some leverage. She now has twenty-four long-term rental properties that are producing cash flow and building more wealth for her.

HOW ONE WOMAN QUIT HER JOB WITH JUST FOUR SHORT-TERM RENTALS

Antoinette Munroe never planned to build a small and mighty real estate empire. When Antoinette was growing up in Dade County, Florida, her mom never made more than $15,000 a year as a bus driver, and her dad didn't do much better as an air-conditioning technician. Finances were tough, and Antoinette vividly remembers as a kid when her parents filed bankruptcy and didn't have enough money to go around.

The Entrepreneurial Itch to Buy Real Estate

When she became only the second person in her family to graduate from college, Antoinette simply wanted to be independent. She didn't want to have to go back to the financial situation she came from. And a well-paying corporate job at PepsiCo gave her that independence.

But a few years into her corporate career, an entrepreneurial itch that had started during a real estate internship in college began to reappear. Antoinette decided to buy a 1950s-era, two-bedroom, one-bath house for $169,000. It was the cheapest house she could find in a nice neighborhood in Orlando, and it needed a lot of work! With the help from friends and YouTube how-to videos, Antoinette spent four months fixing the house up before moving in with her partner.[28]

Building an Extra Room for Extra Income

But Antoinette was motivated to reduce her housing payment as much as possible, and she had the idea of using rent from roommates to help her do that. She decided to build a one-bedroom addition to the house. It was essentially a separate suite with its own kitchen and a separate entrance.

---

[28] "How to Leave Your Corporate Job & Become Financially Independent," *Real Estate & Financial Independence* podcast, last accessed on October 11, 2022, https://www.coachcarson.com/antoinettemunroe.

The addition cost an extra $95,000, and she had to stretch her credit to its limits to finish the project. But in the end, the house was worth almost $400,000. And she was able to live in the one-bedroom unit and rent out the other side to short-term guests on Airbnb.

Airbnb and the Short-Term Rental Strategy

This Airbnb experiment turned out to be a game changer. The first month Antoinette made $3,500 in rent, the second month $4,500, and it kept getting better from there. Because her mortgage payment was only $1,500 per month, the rent from her Airbnb guests paid for 100 percent of her housing costs and more! She used the excess rental cash flow plus savings from her job to quickly pay off all her debts from the remodel. And as the dust settled, Antoinette began to realize she had found a new path as a real estate investor.

Over the next few years, Antoinette built her own small and mighty portfolio of four houses. One of them was even a new construction house that she moved into. But she was sure to also build a garage apartment that she could rent on Airbnb to cover her housing costs!

Short-term rentals had started as a financial tool that allowed Antoinette to live for free. But now it had become a tool that generated enough income to let her leave her corporate job at 36 years old. Today, Antoinette has a net worth of over $1 million, she's taken amazing trips around the world, and she's figuring out what the next exciting challenge in her life will be.

USING THE BRRRR METHOD TO BUY EIGHT LONG-DISTANCE RENTALS FROM NEW YORK CITY

Eitan and Noga Sella moved from Israel to New York City in 2020 during the heart of the COVID-19 lockdown. Noga had enrolled in a PhD program for occupational therapy, and Eitan was able to work virtually with his cybersecurity job. They decided to invest in real estate in the United States, and that's how I first met them.

Picking a Strategy

When Eitan enrolled in my online class, he was technically in the Starter phase. He had experience with one rental in Israel, and he also had a healthy amount of cash and stock investments. But he had no local experience, tax returns, or credit history in the United States. He also lived in metro New York City, one of the most expensive markets in the country.

Eitan was interested in house hacking in New York City, but he ultimately decided to start with long-distance rentals in a cheaper market. By purchasing less expensive properties, he could use his cash savings to buy a couple of properties without a loan. But his plan was to use the BRRRR method (buy, rehab, rent, refinance, repeat) to refinance and pull his cash back out to do more deals.

Picking a Long-Distance Market

Eitan's more immediate challenge, however, was finding a place to invest. He used online resources, my target market criteria (see Chapter 10), and local agents to explore different markets. Then he narrowed his choices down to a couple of regional markets in Texas and another in Rochester, Minnesota.

Like many new investors, Eitan risked getting stuck with analysis paralysis at this stage. But he decided to just roll the dice and invest in the first deal he could find that made sense. When you're a Starter, decisions like this can seem heavy and consequential. But as most experienced entrepreneurs know, some of your first successful steps are random. You've just got to decide something.

Creating a Buy Box

Eitan's first deal ended up being in Rochester, Minnesota. He originally heard about the market on a podcast, and after exploring it more, he liked what he saw. Rochester was a growing but relatively small market with about 120,000 people, which meant less competition from large institutional investors. It had a solid job base with the Mayo Clinic hospital system and a growing tech sector highlighted by a recently opened Google research and development center.

Eitan hired an investor-friendly agent (visit www.biggerpockets. com/agent to match with an investor-friendly agent yourself) to be his guide on the ground. And together, they chose to focus on three solid neighborhoods near the Mayo Clinic with houses that averaged about $220,000 in value. Eitan defined his "buy box" (see Chapter 14) as single-family houses with three beds, two baths, and a cute yard. Ideally the house would also have "expandability" potential, like cosmetic repairs or an unfinished basement that he could fix up and add value to the house.

The First Deal

Eitan scoured leads sent by his agent each day, and finally one paid off. He bought a house for $200,000 using all cash. It had an existing tenant who paid $1,350 per month and moved at the end of their lease the next year. Eitan originally estimated that with a remodel cost of $10,000 the house would rent for $1,600–$1,650 and have a value of $220,000. But after the tenant moved, he and his property manager decided to spend $25,000, estimating that the value could be $240,000 or higher.

After the dust cleared, the house appraised for $290,000! Eitan admits he had some tailwinds from an unusually strong market in 2021, but his initial strategy was working. He refinanced the property for 80 percent of its value ($232,000) using a local bank that was a commercial lender who liked rental property loans. This BRRRR method deal allowed him to pull out 100 percent of his original cash.

The Builder Phase Continues

Eitan quickly built on the momentum of his first deal and jumped into the Builder phase during the next few months. He purchased three more single-family houses in the same general location, and like the first deal, he successfully used the BRRRR method on each of those properties. Then in the next year, he also bought a small multifamily rental in Rochester and a vacation rental in the Poconos region of Pennsylvania. Now, two years after his first purchase and three years after deciding to start investing, he has eight properties and ten rental units in total.

Here's what Eitan had to say about his rapid journey:

> "It's been a wild ride since we started investing in the U.S. housing market. We own eight properties and ten doors in total, most of them in the Rochester area. We had four successful BRRRRs, where we pulled out all of our equity back, and I am very proud of our achievement. But none of that matters.
> **This entire time only one thing mattered: learning.** When

you're just starting, every decision seems critical, but most of these decisions don't matter. Learning, on the other hand, helped me play the long game and focus on the big picture.

Before any acquisition, I would also write down my thesis about that property and numbers. When the property was finally renovated, rented out, and refinanced, I would go back to the thesis and compare it to the reality and improve toward the next purchase. Yes, the rehab budget was always off. Yes, the holding costs were higher than expected. Yes, it was stressful, but I'm far more experienced now.

It also made things more fun: Whenever I listened to a podcast and caught a new idea about what kind of countertops to install in the house or a negotiation tactic, I would just try to implement them, just to see if they worked because, well, why not? More often than not they even worked."

LONG-TERM RENTALS IN A HIGH-PRICED MARKET STARTING WITH A $16,000-PER-YEAR SALARY

At 23 years old in 2007, Joe Breslin was living in Washington, D.C., and paying his bills as an SAT tutor and weekend music DJ. As Joe remembers it, he made about $16,000 that year. But as a single, young person who valued the freedom of not having to work a regular 9-to-5 job, he kept his expenses very low so that he could live off that income and still have a little money left over.[29]

House Hacking to Lower Expenses in a High-Cost Area

One way that Joe kept his expenses low was house hacking and renting spare bedrooms to roommates. But he used a unique approach. Instead of buying a property, he rented a four-bedroom house and subleased three of the bedrooms to the roommates. After collecting all their rent, he only had to come out of pocket $80 a month. This freed up the rest of his income to save for investing and for paying off student debt.

---

29 "From Scratch to 15 Multi-Unit Properties in Washington, D.C.," *Real Estate & Financial Independence* podcast, last accessed on October 18, 2022, https://www.coachcarson.com/15-multiunit-properties-washington-dc/.

The Best Early Investment Was Education

Joe had become interested in real estate investing after observing his older brother Walt investing in another city. Driven by a hunger to learn and to build on his freedom, Joe intensely studied the craft of real estate. He bought books and took courses that taught him how to run the numbers, evaluate properties, and pay for buildings with little or none of one's own money. Joe later said this early investment of time and money in education was the best investment he ever made.

One of the key lessons Joe learned was that you don't need your own money to buy a deal if you can find truly excellent deals. This was critical for Joe, because with properties starting in the $700,000 to $1 million price range, he didn't have enough money on his own to buy deals. So, Joe spent 100 percent of his spare time and effort on growing his skill at directly marketing to homeowners and negotiating to buy their properties.

Using Direct Mail to Find His First Deal

Joe paid $200 to an online direct mail company for a list of all the owners of properties in his area with two units or more. He then began sending these homeowners personal letters introducing himself and expressing his interest in buying their building. Most of his letters either never garnered a return call or got a "no thank you" type of response. But a small number of owners did have promising situations, and Joe eventually found his first deal.

For Joe, a good long-term rental deal was, first of all, in an excellent location. But second of all, it had to have extra value from day one, above and beyond his purchase price. This meant that he either was buying it at something like 75 percent of its current value, or that he could do something to the property, like adding an extra apartment, that would increase its value.

Because Joe's first deal met these criteria, he was able to ask another investor who had the money and credit to partner with him to buy the property. Joe's contribution was finding and managing the property, while the money partner's contribution was putting up the money and credit. In a later chapter on how to buy with little cash, I'll explain the mechanics of how you can do deals like this too.

Growing to Fifteen Properties and Financial Independence

Although Joe didn't begin with much money, he admits that he was lucky to start investing during the recession of 2007 to 2009. During this time of economic turmoil, he was able to find even more long-term rental properties that made sense. Within about ten years, Joe owned all or part of fifteen multi-unit buildings in Washington, D.C., and his portion of the income was over $200,000 per year. Starting with none of his own money, he was now financially independent using rental properties in a higher-priced market!

Now in his late thirties and married with a young daughter and an infant son, Joe has enjoyed using his financial independence to slow down. After both children were born, he got to spend time with them and help his wife get more sleep and enjoy motherhood. Joe loves using his free time to exercise, read, and explore hobbies such as flying airplanes. He now also has ambitions to expand his entrepreneurship into social causes and the nonprofit space. In particular, he wants to help house, serve, and connect local homeless people with others who have more advantages and resources.

The final story I want to share with you in this chapter is about another amazing person who started from scratch and used long-term rentals to achieve financial independence.

FROM HAIRSTYLIST AT 18 TO FINANCIALLY INDEPENDENT WITH LONG-TERM RENTALS AT 33

Myra Oliver grew up in a rural part of Kentucky. At 18 years old, she went against her parents' advice and skipped college. Instead, she became a hairstylist and moved to Texas (the land of big hair!), where she worked three jobs to pay for hairstylist school. Shortly after, she found a retiring barber who sold his business to Myra for $5,000, with $1,000 down and $4,000 on an owner financing contract.

The Early Days of Entrepreneurship Are Tough

Although Myra was motivated, things weren't easy. She typically worked twelve- to fourteen-hour days charging $5 for haircuts. But she was driven by a desire to be independent, and she didn't want to repeat some of the money stresses she had observed with her parents. She lived frugally, shopping at discount stores instead of the name-brand stores where her friends went. She was able to save up enough money to pay off the barber and a family loan within two years.

A few years after moving to Texas, Myra met and then married Rick, who was a police officer. He would often get deals for little or no rent in apartment complexes, which allowed them to save additional money. Together they decided to buy their first home in the late 1980s when Myra was 22 years old.

The First Home Purchase

The price of that first house was $35,000, and the owner agreed to finance the property at zero percent interest! They went on to pay off the property in five years, and eventually they kept it as a long-term rental after they moved out. They still own the property today, and it's worth more than $200,000 and has paid them more than $300,000 in rent over a thirty-year period!

The First Rental Property Purchase

But at 22 years old, Myra spent most of her time standing behind the hairstylist chair each day. She dreamed of owning a business that paid her without having to show up for work. That led her and Rick to buy their first rental property.

Myra saw a newspaper ad for a simple house in a lower-priced neighborhood for a price of $18,000. Rick wasn't excited about the location because of nearby crime issues, but it was the only type of property they could afford. They made a down payment, got a bank loan, and began renting the property.

Eleven Years, Ten Long-Term Rentals

Over an eleven-year period, Myra and Rick accumulated a total of ten long-term rental houses. The process was very similar with each property. They saved up the down payment, got a bank loan, and then began saving again for the next one. They both kept their jobs during this time to pay the bills and to help them save for investing. And they learned to manage and repair the properties themselves to keep things simple and to save money.

At the end of that eleven-year period when Myra was 33, those ten properties produced over $5,000 per month of cash flow. This was plenty for Myra and Rick to live on, so they were financially independent!

But rather than leaving their jobs right away, they kept working for a little longer and used all their cash flow to pay off the debt on those ten rental properties. Now they had a debt-free rental portfolio. Instead of just financial independence, they also had financial peace.

CONCLUSION TO PART II

The purpose of this part of the book was to explain the journey of a small and mighty investor. Whether you are a Starter, Wealth Builder, or Ender, you can't shortcut the process. You've got to figure out the strategies that make sense for *you* at this phase of the journey, and then start where you are.

In the next part of the book, we will get into the nitty-gritty details of becoming a small and mighty investor. Now that you have a map of the journey, it's time to hit the road! And because real estate is a people business, that road begins with how to build your all-star real estate team.

PART III

HOW TO BUY PROFITABLE INVESTMENT PROPERTIES

CHAPTER 9
HOW TO BUILD AN ALL-STAR REAL ESTATE TEAM

As the head basketball coach at UCLA, John Wooden won a record ten NCAA national championships in his last twelve seasons. Of course, a big part of his success was recruiting star athletes like Kareem Abdul-Jabbar and Bill Walton to play for UCLA. But perhaps more impressive, Wooden was able to convince these star players, along with everyone else on the team, to work together so that they could win championships.

Wooden would explain to his star players that "the main ingredient of stardom is the rest of your team."[30] Coach Wooden knew these players had potential, but he also knew that even star players couldn't succeed by themselves. Basketball, like most things in life, is a team sport. And both the star players and the supporting players would only reach their full potential if they worked together as a team.

---

30 John Wooden with Steve Jamison, *Wooden: A Lifetime of Observations and Reflections On and Off the Court* (New York: McGraw Hill, 1997), p. 66.

In Part III, you will learn how to buy profitable real estate investments. These are the same strategies and techniques I've used over the past twenty years to buy properties that now pay for my financial freedom. Specifically, you will learn how to pick the best locations and properties, how to run the numbers like a pro, how to find and negotiate excellent deals, and how to confidently handle due diligence and closings.

But like Coach Wooden's team of star basketball players, you won't succeed at buying properties without the right team members. Real estate investing is a team sport, and the main ingredient of your success as a small and mighty investor will be the rest of your team. That's why this chapter is all about how to build a real estate all-star team. I'll teach you what team members you need, and how to find them. And we'll begin with something called the three circles of your team.

THE THREE CIRCLES OF YOUR TEAM

In the book *The Millionaire Real Estate Investor*, authors Gary Keller, Dave Jenks, and Jay Papasan explain that millionaires leverage their network, aka the people around them, to find financial success[31]. And they focus on strengthening three different categories of their network:

1. **Inner circle:** personal relationships like spouses, partners, or mentors
2. **Support circle:** long-term, often fiduciary business relationships
3. **Service circle:** short-term, transactional business relationships

As a small and mighty investor, you also need to leverage your network, which I'll call your team. And you can divide your team members into these same three categories of inner, support, and service circles. Next, I'll unpack each of the specific team members within each category, one at a time.

INNER CIRCLE

Think about your inner circle as your most trusted council of advisers. These are the people you regularly share your personal thoughts,

---

31 Gary Keller, Dave Jenks, Jay Papasan, *The Millionaire Real Estate Investor* (New York: McGraw Hill, 2005), p. 159.

struggles, and victories with. Your inner circle could look different than mine, but in my experience, here are the key members of the inner circle.

Spouse/Partner

If you are married or have a committed long-term relationship with someone, that person is at the center of your inner circle. Because your investment decisions will impact both of your lives, you need to be on the same page. And even if your spouse or partner isn't as active in real estate investing as you are, it's still critical to involve them in decisions and get their support.

In my case, my wife has not been active in our investing business because she has other professional interests. But we work together on our personal budget, and we make decisions together before investing a large amount of our money in something new. I also value her support, perspective, and counsel. It's particularly helpful because she has more distance from the decisions and can often see them more clearly.

Business Partner

If you have a business partner, this is a key part of your inner circle. For some of you, this might be the same person as your spouse. For others, like me, this will be a different person.

I've had a business partner from the very beginning of my real estate investing journey. We were friends at first, and after going to a few real estate classes together, we decided to start our investing business together. He was a person I trusted wholeheartedly, and we also had different, complementary skill sets. Importantly, we also aligned with our long-term goals and style of investing. Luckily, we both wanted to be small and mighty real estate investors!

Mentor

A mentor can be a critical member of your inner circle. A mentor is someone who has hard-earned experience in life and business. They also care about you as a person, and they want to see you succeed in the long run. Through regular communication, a mentor can offer you much needed wisdom, encouragement, and perspective during your journey.

Finding the right mentor may not come easily at first. It's critical that a mentor is supportive of your overall life and investing goals. For example, there may be family members who care about you deeply, but they don't understand or support what you're doing. They may even criticize you for your efforts.

If you're lucky enough to already have a supportive mentor, be grateful and take advantage of their advice. I was fortunate to have a father who also invested in real estate. I could call him and get help and advice throughout my career.

But I also met another mentor who was the professor in a business class I took at a local university. I began the relationship with simple questions and conversations, but over time I found ways to also add value to him financially by borrowing money from him for my deals. He appreciated being able to passively earn income from my efforts, and as a natural byproduct, I received his mentoring during our regular conversations.

I've also had other mentors through books, courses, and paid coaching. John Schaub, who I've talked about in this book, is someone I consider a mentor. For almost twenty years, I've paid for his live events, home study courses, and a monthly newsletter. And over time, I've been able to reach out to him and stay in touch for advice and feedback.

Accountability Partner(s)/Mastermind Group

An accountability partner is someone who provides you with feedback and urges you to be responsible with your real estate investing. But unlike a mentor, who is further along on their financial journey, an accountability partner is in a very similar place to you. You're taking the journey together and supporting and encouraging each other along the way.

The best place to find accountability partners is at real estate meetups or local REIA (real estate investing association) groups. Search on the BiggerPockets forums or on Google to find local meetups in your area. You can also find accountability partners while taking online or in-person classes. For years now, I've regularly met virtually with two friends whom I originally met at a real estate class.

A close cousin of accountability partners is a mastermind group. I learned about the concept in the book *Think and Grow Rich* by Napoleon Hill. The author told the story about billionaire Andrew Carnegie, who credited his entire fortune to his small group of peers who met regularly to give one another support and advice. You can form your own small mastermind group, which I have done over the years. Or you can join paid mastermind groups with a mentor you trust, which I have also done.

SUPPORT CIRCLE

Think about the support circle as the next circle after your inner circle. They are also trusted advisers, but their advice or skills are focused on a particular craft. Your relationship with support circle members is often long-term in nature, and in some cases it's a fiduciary relationship. This means they owe you a special duty to act for your benefit with their advice, and not for the benefit of themselves or other clients.

Real Estate Agent

A real estate agent should be a key member of your team. In addition to bringing you potential deals, an excellent agent can be your guide to the inner workings of a local real estate market. They can help you make good decisions about which locations will make the best investments and which properties have the most value. They can also help you understand price trends and assist you in making an offer on your potential deals.

If you are a long-distance investor, a real estate agent can also be your on-the-ground resource to study a property and a neighborhood before making a purchase. Although you can buy a property without ever visiting it in person, *someone* you trust (or multiple people) must visit the property and evaluate it carefully before you spend hundreds of thousands of dollars. Your real estate agent should be one of those people.

There are various ways to formally have a relationship with an agent. As a new, long-distance investor it can make a lot of sense to have an exclusive agency relationship with the right agent. This usually means they will earn a commission on any deal you buy. You'll be using them as a resource from beginning to end of your purchase.

As a local investor who quickly built experience, I used a different approach. I typically worked with agents on a deal-by-deal basis for investment purchases. This meant I paid them a commission when they brought me a deal, but I didn't work with them on other deals that I found. I simply stayed in touch with multiple agents and considered every deal as they brought it to me.

But I also work closely with one carefully picked agent at a time to *sell* my properties, when needed. This agent helps me decide which repairs or cleanup to do before selling, and they even pick out materials and paint colors for me. They take professional photos, help decide a price, market the property, and get it sold. This service is well worth the commission in my experience.

For an investor, the best type of agent is one who is investor-friendly and understands your goals and desired return and investment parameters. These types of agents have skill sets and connections that standard residential agents may not have. You can find investor-friendly agents on BiggerPockets at www.biggerpockets.com/agent/match.

Property Manager

A property manager is another key member of your team. In our own small and mighty real estate business, we communicate with and rely on our property manager on a weekly basis. They are our eyes, ears, and representatives for everything with our rental properties.

If you use the house-hacking strategy, you may not feel the need to use a property manager because you'll be living on-site. Some of you who use the short-term or long-term rental strategies may also choose to self-manage instead of using a property manager. My mentor John Schaub still manages his own properties after more than forty years of investing, and with his self-reliant, single-family-house tenants, it does not take much of his time.

But for those of you who have more time-intensive rentals (like college student rentals in my case) or who just want a more passive rental experience, a property manager is an excellent choice to handle the day-to-day affairs. They typically handle leasing, turnover between tenants, maintenance, rent collections, and basic bookkeeping. In exchange, they receive a commission as a percentage of the rent collected and sometimes also a large portion of the first month's rent.

Beyond day-to-day rental management, an underappreciated value of property managers is their assistance when you buy a new property. Property managers typically know more about the trends and actual rental rates in your market than anyone else because they often manage hundreds or thousands of units at a time. I rely on this expertise when I buy a new property. I ask my managers to tell me what the property will rent for and what repairs I need to do before renting it.

To give you an example of how valuable property managers can be, let me tell you a quick story about how I almost didn't buy the best deal of my career. My property manager, who is also a real estate agent and investor himself, brought me a potential multifamily rental deal in my town. He just happened to know the seller, so it wasn't even on the open market.

The asking price was just over $1 million, and based on the current rents, I thought it was overpriced. I offered much less, but the seller wouldn't budge. My property manager then told me I was underestimating the rent. I had estimated raising rents a couple hundred dollars per unit, but he convinced me that by spending about $10,000 per unit on repairs, I could raise the rents even more. At these higher rates, the deal made a lot more sense.

In the end, I met the seller at his price, and I'm extremely happy I did. My property manager handled the entire process of remodeling and finding new tenants, and within a year, all units were rented for what he had estimated. This has easily been one of the best investments we've ever made. The property had a positive cash flow after the first year, and we've since had offers from other investors for many times what we paid for it.

Handyperson/General Contractor

In real estate, you're in the business of buying and owning "sticks and bricks," or physical pieces of real estate. At some point, every piece of real estate breaks down and needs to be repaired. Because of that, you need a trusted general repair contractor who can handle a variety of these repairs.

A handyperson is a type of contractor who can physically do a variety of skills. With smaller projects, you can give them a punch list of items to do, and the handyperson can do them all. Especially with rental properties, you need to have a handyperson on your team. I like to have one or two I can trust and call on regularly. If you have a property manager, they will often have their own go-to handyperson that you can use.

For larger remodel projects, you'll need a general contractor. This type of contractor is typically licensed in your state. They can pull required permits from local governments, hire other subcontractors to do work, and manage the process and budget of the overall project. If you regularly purchase major remodels to rent or to flip, you need a trusted general contractor on your team.

Real Estate Attorney

Although real estate is about the physical "sticks and bricks," it's also built on a legal foundation of contracts, title law, landlord tenant law, and a maze of other regulations. For this reason, your team must include a competent attorney who specializes in real estate. Early on, you may rely on this attorney to help you with contracts or to form a legal entity (like a limited liability company). But you should also keep the attorney on call for advice on any situation that comes up related to legal matters.

Title Company or Closing Attorney

A title company handles the money, details, and paperwork of your real estate purchase, sale, or refinance transactions (aka closing). Importantly, they also perform an in-depth search of the title of the real estate to ensure there are no legal problems with ownership. Then they give you a guarantee and an insurance policy for further peace of mind. I'll talk more about this process in the chapter on contracts, due diligence, and closings.

Some states require that attorneys, not title companies, handle the closing transaction. In that case, you'll need a team member known as a closing attorney. There could be some crossover between this attorney and your real estate attorney.

Insurance Agent

Real estate is a large financial purchase. If disaster strikes, like a fire, tornado, or major water leak, it could cost you tens or hundreds of thousands of dollars to repair or replace your property. And as a business that interacts daily with customers and vendors, you also have potential legal liability. This means someone could sue you for money if problems arise, such as an injury while on your property.

Because of all of this, you must get good hazard insurance (in case of losses from fire, wind, water, etc.) and liability insurance (in case of a lawsuit). And your insurance agent is the team member who can help you navigate the right insurance products. Most investors get what's called a landlord insurance policy, which includes hazard and liability insurance. But also consider an additional liability policy called umbrella insurance, which can cover losses above and beyond your standard policy. A competent, *investor-friendly* insurance agent can have a detailed discussion with you about all of this.

Certified Public Accountant (CPA)
Real estate investing has numerous tax benefits, but the rules are complicated. A certified public accountant (CPA for short) is a professional who can help you navigate your tax obligations. Not only will they assist you in all the steps of filing your federal and local tax return documents, but they are also an invaluable resource for tax *planning*.

I regularly contact my CPA throughout the year. Sometimes it's a simple email question asking for help with paying my quarterly estimated taxes. And other times, it's a more in-depth email or call for advice on how a potential sale of a property will impact our taxes. I can confidently say that I've not only saved thousands of dollars in taxes because of my CPA but I've also had much more peace of mind because of his help.

Banker/Lender (For Business Accounts, Commercial Loans, HELOCs)
You can't collect money or pay bills without a business bank account. You will need to have a business banker on your team. But this relationship is much more important than simply opening your account. A helpful business banker can also be your contact for future commercial real estate loans, including loans for remodeling or construction. They can also be your source for other loans, like reward credit cards, unsecured loans, or a home equity line of credit (HELOC).

I personally like using local or regional banks for my business banking. I've found with smaller banks you can build long-term relationships easier than with big, conglomerate-style banks. That relationship is key so that you have a real person to contact. For example, I regularly contact my banker for small matters, such as a fee that shouldn't have been added. And I also contact my banker for larger matters, like help with a wire transfer or a loan for a remodeling project.

Lender (For Traditional Mortgages)

If you plan to get loans to buy real estate, you'll need a lender on your team. Your prior team member, the business banker, can often be a source for commercial loans. But commercial loans often have terms that are less attractive, like a balloon payment in five years where you have to pay back 100 percent of what you owe.

Traditional residential mortgages, on the other hand, have much better terms, such as a fixed interest rate for thirty years. So you also want to have a lender for traditional residential mortgages. This lender can help you with owner-occupant loans, like for a house hack and rental property loans. I'll talk more about the specifics of these loans in a later chapter.

The right mortgage lender has experience closing mortgages in a variety of situations. They are organized and clearly communicate their expectations up front. Mortgage lenders are notorious for being overly optimistic and overpromising, so I like one that's more realistic with the potential roadblocks up front. You'll also want to ask how much experience they have with your particular loan program. If you're house hacking and want, say, an FHA (Federal Housing Administration) loan, ask how many of those loans they've closed.

Sometimes you'll find these traditional lenders as separate branches of your bank. Other times they'll be independent mortgage lending businesses. There are also a larger number of online mortgage lenders now, so these can also be a good option.

Lender (For Investor Mortgages)

In 2010, the U.S. Congress passed new lending laws to protect owner-occupant consumers from the risky subprime loans that partially caused the 2008–2009 financial crisis. The new laws divided residential mortgages into two categories:

1. **Qualifying:** Meets the strict requirements of these new regulations
2. **Non-qualifying:** Does not meet the new requirements

Although the law was primarily focused on owner-occupant consumers, new types of *investor* loans emerged within the non-qualifying category that benefit the small and mighty real estate investor. These types of mortgages are different than traditional mortgages, which often require in-depth qualifying procedures. Instead, qualifying for these new investor mortgages is easier and based more on the property income itself. At the same time, lenders still offer attractive terms like thirty-year, fixed-interest rates, which make excellent long-term rental loans.

To find these lenders, search for "non-qualifying mortgages" or "DSCR mortgages," which stands for "debt service coverage ratio." The lenders usually specialize in offering investor mortgages. The same lenders also often offer remodel loans, which I'll cover next.

Lender (Private/Hard Money Loans)

Instead of going to a traditional lender for loans, you can get a loan from a private lender. This is usually an individual or a small company that loans their own money. The interest rates are sometimes higher on these loans, but they will quickly loan money on properties even if they need repairs. And they're usually more interested in the value of the hard asset (thus the term *hard money loans*) than strict credit or income requirements for the borrower. For this reason, investors often use private or hard money lenders for fix-and-flip or BRRRR (buy, rehab, rent, refinance, repeat) deals.

The prior category of investor lenders can be good sources of hard money loans, also known as rehab or bridge loans. You will also find smaller hard money lending companies at local real estate meetups or REIA (real estate investment association) meetings. I'll talk more about finding your own individual private money lenders in the part of the book on financing. Private lenders have been the primary way I've funded my own investment properties over the past twenty years.

SERVICE CIRCLE

This is the final, outer circle of your team. While these team members are still very important, you can often fill these positions easily with the help of your support circle team members. For example, a general contractor or property manager can recommend their own trade contractors. But to make sure you know the types of people you'll eventually need, I'll list them briefly below.

Trade Contractors

Trade contractors perform a variety of physical repair tasks at your property. This is not an exhaustive list, but they could include the following:

- Plumber
- Electrician
- Heating and air specialist
- Pest control company
- Mold and moisture control company
- Lawn and landscape maintenance
- Painter
- Sheetrock/wall repair specialist
- Carpenter
- Flooring contractor
- Carpet cleaner
- Tile installer

Surveyor

This team member evaluates the physical land and shows you exactly where the corners and boundaries of your property are. Although problems are rare in established subdivisions, a survey is a good idea to avoid conflicts with neighboring properties. I've had a couple of properties for more than twenty years for which I didn't get surveys; a survey would have saved me a lot of money and headaches.

Inspectors

When you buy a property, you want someone to physically evaluate the condition of the property to identify any unknown or costly problems. You'll find several different categories of inspectors to use, including:

- **General inspector:** evaluates the structure, electrical, plumbing, roof, and other building systems to identify any problems.
- **Moisture and termite inspector:** evaluates the building for excessive moisture levels that can cause mold, rot, and decay. This inspector also checks for the presence of termites or other wood destroying insects.
- **Radon inspector:** tests for the presence of radon, a naturally occurring radioactive substance that can cause lung cancer.

- **Asbestos and lead paint inspector:** checks for the presence of asbestos and lead-based paint, both of which are found in older houses and can cause health problems.

WHERE TO FIND THE BEST TEAM MEMBERS

Now that you know which team members you need, the next question is, where can you find *excellent* team members? The biggest shortcut is to find one or two key team members, like your property manager or real estate agent, and ask them for referrals for the rest. You can also ask for referrals from other investors in your target market.

Where do you find those initial team members or other investors? Here are a few of the best places I've found.

- **Local real estate meetups/REIAs:** I've been a member of my local real estate investor association for twenty years now. I've made friends with other investors at monthly meetings, and I can always ask this network for referrals to build my team. Most cities have multiple real estate investor meetups; do a search online.
- **BiggerPockets:** The online forums at BiggerPockets are an excellent place to network with other investors and investor-friendly team members (property managers, real estate agents, lenders, etc.). BiggerPockets also has an agent referral service that can help you find investor-friendly local agents.
- **Facebook groups:** Search on Facebook for real estate and real estate investor groups in your target market. You'll quickly notice who the active investors, agents, and other team members are within these groups.
- **Google search:** Just search for the type of team member you want in your location and sift through the results. Read reviews and then reach out to the ones who seem best.
- **Driving your market:** When all else fails, just drive around your neighborhoods and target market, and look for signs of likely team members. Call real estate agents, check out for rent signs, look for contractor trucks, and just talk to people. You'll learn a lot and possibly build your team in the process.

HOW TO PICK THE BEST TEAM MEMBERS

Once you find potential team members, you then need to figure out if they're a good fit. I've mostly worked with excellent team members in my twenty years of investing, but I've also had some bad ones. Knowing what I know now, here are the main criteria I look for in excellent team members.

Competency

Competency means the person knows what they're doing. They're excellent at the skills of their craft. They've demonstrated that they can deliver on the outcomes you need from them.

You can begin testing competency by asking them questions. How many years of experience do they have? If they're an agent, how many transactions have they done? If they're a property manager, how many properties do they manage? If they're a contractor, do they have examples or pictures of their past work?

You can also test competency by talking to references. Online reviews are a good start, but also look for other customer stories. With a property manager, for example, ask to communicate with an existing property owner client.

Unfortunately, you sometimes learn about *lack* of competency by getting burned. I've had a couple of team members who made repeated errors during their services for me. I should have let them go earlier, but to be nice, I held on too long. As a result, it cost me money, hassle, and even some reputational points because it reflected poorly on me with my customers. We all make hiring mistakes, but once you recognize one, move on quickly. It rarely gets better with time.

Trustworthiness

If you have the best, most competent team members, but they're not trustworthy, you will get burned. Trust is the glue that holds any relationship together. You must do your best to figure out if you can trust a potential team member.

As a fellow human being, you already know most of what you need to determine trustworthiness. Are their words congruent with their actions? Are they too slick? Too fast-talking?

Someone once told me that when you play with snakes, you're likely to get bitten. I happen to like snakes in real life, but this means don't deal with snakes in business. Untrustworthy people, or snakes, will bite you. It's just a matter of time. Avoid having them on your team.

Attitude

Attitude is an intangible but extremely important quality I look for in team members. A negative, unhelpful attitude weighs down your business relationship. On the other hand, a positive, helpful attitude can make everything fun and productive.

You can evaluate attitude simply by having a conversation or visiting them in person. Listen carefully to the way they talk to and treat people around them. Observe their energy and the feeling you get around them. This will tell you a lot about their attitude.

Alignment

Alignment has to do with both the values and the goals someone has. You want to find team members whose values and goals align with your own. This means you're moving in the same general direction.

My business partner and I luckily were very well aligned. We both valued hard work, having fun, and keeping our business small and mighty. Our goals have evolved over time, but we've had continuous conversations to ensure that we're moving in a similar direction.

This is another criterion you get from conversations with a potential team member. Ask what's important to them. Ask where they hope to be in five years. This level of personal question may not be appropriate for every team member, but the closer to your inner circle this person is, the more you want to have this conversation. Getting *into* a close business relationship is a lot easier than getting *out* of it.

HOW TO KEEP THE BEST TEAM MEMBERS HAPPY

Most of this chapter was about finding new team members. But in the real world, you need to keep your best team members happy so you can avoid having to find more team members! Here are a few tips on how to keep your best team members around for a long time.

Pay Quickly

When someone bills you for their service, pay them quickly. I know other entrepreneurs who drag out payments to their vendors, making them wait 30 days to get paid. Whatever benefit the entrepreneur gets, they're damaging their relationship with these team members.

My team members know that I pay quickly. It's the same way I would want to be paid if I were in their shoes. And I believe it moves me up their priority list when I need their service again.

Pay Fairly

We are all in business to make money. But you don't want to nickel-and-dime your way into profitability. I've been cheap with contractors before, trying to negotiate their rate down too much. It backfired because they either moved on to someone who paid better, or they worked with a bad attitude.

With my best team members, I try not to do much negotiating on pay rates. I do expect them to be fair with me, and I'll price check with competitors. But I now realize that the cheapest paid workers aren't always the best.

Be Clear and Decisive

Some of my biggest problems with team members have come from being unclear. For example, on several remodel projects I didn't set clear expectations about how I wanted a contractor to complete the job. In the end, I was upset, the contractor was upset, the work wasn't right, and it all could have been avoided.

Thought leader Brené Brown says that "clear is kind. Unclear is unkind."[32] In my problems with contractors, I wanted to be too nice. This caused me to avoid being clear and having tough conversations up front. But it would have been kinder to be clear in the first place. Especially if it's a tough conversation, I now try to have it up front and get everyone's expectations in writing.

---

[32] "Clear Is Kind. Unclear Is Unkind." brenebrown.com, last accessed on November 4, 2022, https://brenebrown.com/articles/2018/10/15/clear-is-kind-unclear-is-unkind/.

Be a Servant Leader

With a long career in sports and business, I've seen a lot of "dictator style" leaders. They let everyone know who is in charge, and they rule with an iron fist. Even when this style of leadership "works," it leaves a lot of damaged relationships in its wake.

An alternative approach is to be a servant leader. Your *position* as a leader doesn't make you the authority. You *earn* authority by demonstrating that you are a true leader. You treat people with respect. You serve them as much as they serve you. You're firm when needed, but you always show that you care. People *choose* to follow servant leaders, and everyone is better because of it.

CONCLUSION

You now know who needs to be on your small and mighty team, and you know how to get started building that team. Remember that your members are the number one ingredient of your success as an investor. Identifying and recruiting the right team members should be one of your top priorities at any stage of your investing career.

Now let's continue to the next chapter and learn about the right investment locations for small and mighty investors.

CHAPTER 10

THE BEST LOCATIONS FOR REAL ESTATE INVESTING

Y ou now know how to put together an all-star real estate team. But remember, you're still the star and captain of this team. If you want to buy profitable investment properties, you will still need to make the most important decisions yourself. And the first decision you'll need to make is where to invest. Even more than the investment property itself, your property's *location* will determine the profitability of your investment.

That's why in this chapter I will teach you what it means to invest in the right location. I'll give you a checklist of criteria that you can use to pick a new market or evaluate your current market. These criteria will be both on the larger, regional scale and on the local, neighborhood scale. I'll also teach you what to do if the market where you live isn't ideal for your investing strategy.

To get started, I want to share two stories from my own real estate investing experience. In the first story, I bought a rental property with an excellent location. In the second story, I bought a property less than ten miles away, but it had an awful location. The first property made lots of money, the second property lost money. Location made all the difference.

PROPERTY WITH AN EXCELLENT LOCATION

You may remember this first property from my Live-In-Then-Rent story from Chapter 7. It was the third personal residence I ever bought, and it was the house that my wife and I bought to start a family. Our prior residence in the four-unit house-hack apartment was too small.

We Overpaid

Before we could move in, this house needed a lot of work! The landlord who owned it did not take care of property maintenance for years. We paid for new plumbing, new wiring, a brand-new kitchen, brand-new bathrooms, new sheetrock, painting, and more. Between our $4,000 down payment and over $40,000 of repair costs, we needed about $45,000 of cash. This used all our own cash, and then we had to borrow money from a private lender to finish the job.

The purchase price of $130,000 plus our repair costs of $40,000 gave us a total cost of $170,000. We bought the house in 2009 during the depths of the recession, and we would have been lucky to sell it for even $165,000. I remember an investor friend telling me skeptically that we had overpaid.

How the Location Saved Me

My friend was right. But let me tell you about the location and how it saved me. The house is an easy walk to nearby Clemson University and to the South Carolina Botanical Gardens, which is one of the most beautiful places to visit in our area. Although the neighborhood did have several college student rentals, it also had a significant number of long-term owners. Overall, it was a quiet and safe place to live for a young family.

The location was also closely tied to the success of a major research institution of higher education. As Clemson University did well and grew, the demand for living in this location would also grow. And in a small town of seven square miles where most of the land was already built on, it wouldn't be easy or cheap to build new houses like mine. There would be a limited supply of competition.

Our Home Becomes an Excellent Rental

As a result of this excellent location, the property became an easy rental after we moved out. Every time we advertise it for rent, we quickly have multiple applications from highly qualified tenants. This allows us to be picky and find tenants who pay on time, take care of the house, and stay for a long time.

And as I explained in Chapter 7, the financial results for this property have been excellent. Thirteen years later, the price and the rent have increased significantly. Because of the excellent location with high demand and low supply, the house has slowly become a very profitable and easy long-term rental property. Even though we "overpaid" for the purchase price, our wealth and cash flow have increased. This is the power of picking the right location.

PROPERTY WITH AN AWFUL LOCATION

Unfortunately, my track record for picking the right locations hasn't been perfect. One of those bad picks is a story I want to share with you. I call it my "unforgettable loser rental."

The Mill Hill

In 2007, my business partner and I bought a two-property package deal. It was located on a "mill hill," which is the name people used for old neighborhoods around abandoned textile factories in our part of the southern United States. Once thriving communities, many of the neighborhoods have deteriorated from neglect over time. And the worst locations have become centers of crime and drug use.

The package deal included one small two-bedroom, one-bath house built in 1925 and a nearby single-wide mobile home built in the early 1980s. Both were in decent condition for older properties, but the neighborhood was even worse. Nearby neighbors had mean-looking dogs chained to trees, multiple cars on blocks, and tough-looking guys glaring from their front porch all day.

"Good" Price and Terms

Why did we buy these properties? The short answer was price and terms. We thought a "low" price and good financing terms would make up for the neighborhood problems.

The combined purchase price was $43,500, and with closing fees, our total cost was $45,000. The seller was a burned-out landlord who was tired of the business, and he agreed to owner-finance the property with just $1,000 down. We owed him a mortgage of $42,500 with 7.25 percent interest, and our interest-only payment was $256.77 per month.

Our plan was to either rent the properties or resell them with owner financing to someone who would live in the house. The house rented for $400 per month and the mobile home rented for $300 per month. We thought $700 per month was plenty to cover all our mortgage and property expenses. But we were wrong.

How Things Went Bad

First, we made a mistake underestimating repairs and other expenses for an older house. But that is another topic I'll cover in detail in the chapter on how to run the numbers. Second and most important, we made the mistake of picking the wrong location. If we had picked a better location, the rising rents and prices could have bailed us out from our other mistakes. That's what happened with the house my wife and I bought in the first example. But in this case, our location worked against us.

From the beginning, we had a hard time attracting and keeping good tenants. The tenants we could attract didn't pay on time and eventually had to move or be evicted. This was traumatic for everyone, and it also cost us a lot of money. The only thing going for this property was its affordable rent price, but many good tenants did not want to deal with the problems in the neighborhood. We couldn't control or fix those problems, yet they affected our investment in a big way.

For seven years, these properties put us through a roller coaster of up and down cash flow. One year we'd have positive $3,500 cash flow, and the next year we'd have negative $8,000. The negative years were a result of vacancy, eviction costs, turnover costs, and repair costs. By the end of 2014, these properties were no longer fun to own, and they did not seem to be getting better. So we decided to sell them.

Let's Sell Them!

By 2015 when we decided to sell, the overall housing prices in our South Carolina market had recovered and even grown. But our little mill hill seemed to be frozen in the past. Even after some cosmetic repairs, our real estate agent recommended that we list the house for only $39,000.

Even at that price, however, we received little interest and no offers. So, after dropping the price to $30,000, we finally received a cash offer from an investor for $22,000. Even though this didn't cover the cost of our mortgage, we swallowed our pride, pulled out our checkbook to pay the difference, and agreed to sell.

We held on to the single-wide mobile home for another six years, but in 2021 we also sold it for a price of $12,000. Combined, we sold these properties for $34,000 after buying them for $45,000 more a decade before. We did end up slightly positive on rental cash flow in the end, but overall, we still lost over $10,000 on these two properties after fourteen years of work and trouble.

Now you see why I call this deal my "unforgettable loser rental." And you also know why I'm so adamant about picking good locations! In the rest of this chapter, I'll teach you how to pick the right location for your investment properties so you don't make the same mistake.

WHAT MAKES AN EXCELLENT LOCATION TO INVEST?

When I was a brand-new investor, I bought properties without thinking much about my target market. But after experiences like those I explained in the prior stories, I decided to study the exact criteria that make good investment locations. I learned that you can understand real estate locations by zooming in and out, just like you do on Google Maps.

When you're zoomed all the way out, you can see the large scale, regional picture of a location. This means you evaluate large metropolitan areas (often called an MSA—metropolitan statistical area) to see whether the region would be fertile for real estate investing. Then once you pick a region, you zoom in to the local level. With this more neighborhood-level perspective, you evaluate the potential for real estate investments street by street, just as a tenant or buyer would.

What follows are the key criteria I recommend you evaluate for your market on both the regional level and the local neighborhood level. Think about these criteria as a checklist. No market will be perfect and meet every single criterion, but the more criteria you can check off, the more promising that market will be for real estate investing.

LARGE SCALE, REGIONAL-LEVEL CRITERIA
1. Jobs
Whether you rent or sell your property as an investor, your customers (aka your tenants and buyers) provide the income for your business. And these customers can only pay you if they have good jobs. Therefore, you want to pick regions of the country where the job market is growing, pays high salaries, and is projected to be strong into the future.

2. Population Growth
Your rental properties fill a fundamental need for housing. The more people who move to an area, the more in-demand your properties will be. This means you should pick regions of the country with strong population growth now and in the future.

3. Affordability/Price-to-Rent Ratio
The price-to-rent ratio roughly indicates the housing affordability of a region. In less affordable regions, the price-to-rent ratio is higher. In more affordable regions, the price-to-rent ratio is lower.

In the less affordable regions, it's also harder to find positive cash-flow investments. For example, a 2022 study by SmartAsset[33] showed that San Francisco has one of the highest price-to-rent ratios. Therefore, it's also one of the worst potential markets for cash flow.

In the study, the average home price in San Francisco is $1,461,917. The average annual rent is $39,152 ($3,263 per month). To calculate the price-to-rent ratio, divide $1,461,917 by $39,152. This gives you a price-to-rent ratio of 37.34.

On the other hand, the same study shows that Detroit has one of the

---

33 "Price-to-Rent Ratio in the 50 Largest U.S. Cities – 2022 Edition," smartasset.com, last accessed on October 24, 2022, https://smartasset.com/data-studies/price-to-rent-ratio-in-the-50-largest-us-cities-2022.

lowest price-to-rent ratios. The average home price there is $75,667. And the average annual rent is $13,007 ($1,084 per month). To calculate the price-to-rent ratio, divide $75,667 by $13,007. This gives you a much lower price-to-rent ratio of 5.82.

I want to say here that low prices don't automatically make a good real estate deal. Remember my loser rental property! I'll show you other criteria that matter just as much. But the price-to-rent ratio is an important criterion to keep in mind if cash flow is important to you.

4. State Rental Laws

Every state has its own laws to regulate rental properties. Some states' rules are more tenant-friendly and others are more landlord-friendly. If you have a choice, pick states that are more landlord-friendly for your investments.

Google "landlord-friendly states" or "tenant-friendly states" to do your research. Some of the criteria you want to look for are whether the state:

- Makes it easy or hard to evict tenants who don't pay
- Puts restrictions on security deposits or tenant applications
- Has rent-control laws that limit the rate landlords can charge for a rental

5. Small Cities and "Surban" Centers

Although large cities can be good locations for real estate investments, I've found that small and mighty real estate investors thrive in smaller cities or towns that are near big cities. The nearby big city ensures there are plenty of well-paying jobs. But the smaller cities and towns ensure that prices are more affordable and that competition from large institutional real estate investors is less of an issue.

I think of a small city as a metro area of 500,000 or less, but you can also find excellent small "surban" towns within large metropolitan areas. *Surban* is a term coined by real estate consultant John Burns in his book *Big Shifts Ahead*. It refers to smaller, more affordable towns that mimic urban living but are in the suburbs of large cities. These surban towns typically have thriving, walkable, livable city centers, and they are my personal favorite places to live and invest in.

LOCAL, NEIGHBORHOOD-LEVEL CRITERIA

1. Romance

One of my first real estate teachers, Greg Pinneo, always said that "romance" was his No. 1 criterion for an investment property location. Romance is the "it factor" that makes a place special. It's that fuzzy yet very real emotional attraction that makes people want to live somewhere.

The choice of where to live is always emotional. Discover the unique attractive forces in an area like a park, a cute downtown, or a body of water. Find the things that tug on people's emotional strings. Then buy as close to these attractive forces as possible.

2. Convenience

If romance is the central force of your area, you want your investment location to be as convenient to that force as possible. You also want an investment location convenient to jobs, shopping, and other necessities. Your tenants' lives will be busy, and as a result they'll prioritize convenience and pay more for it. Ten miles or less from a major job or entertainment center is my cutoff for convenience, but the closer the better.

3. Safety/Crime

Everyone wants a home that's safe. So pick investment property locations with both real and perceived safety. You can do plenty of searches online, but it's best to visit a location yourself at different times of the day and week.

Look for signs of crime, such as protective cages over HVAC units, bars on windows, and boarded-up houses. Talk to longtime residents. And talk to other landlords and property managers. But be careful of your biases that cause you to write off a location just because it's not where you would want to live. There are plenty of safe, nice locations that may not be a high-dollar, luxury place to live.

4. Transportation

Transportation infrastructure can make or break your investment. Traditionally this means automobile transportation. But I personally love investments in neighborhoods with good public transit and pedestrian and bike infrastructure. This means there are well-lit sidewalks or bike paths that connect residential to commercial areas. Plus, it helps if there are interesting things along the way, like sidewalk shops, public art, and green spaces. Check out the book *Walkable City* by Jeff Speck for a strong explanation of what walkable places look like.

This has become such an important topic for me that I co-founded a nonprofit in my hometown of Clemson, South Carolina, to build more walking and biking paths. Like many towns or cities that grew since World War II, our town is built around cars. I couldn't push my daughters in a stroller to the local park a quarter mile away without risking our lives. Like an entrepreneur, I decided to do something about it! It has also occupied a lot of my time after financial independence.

5. Schools

For families with children, locations with good schools are a top priority. This preference especially impacts housing markets in suburban areas where families with children often settle down. If you want to maximize your pool of customers in those areas, pick properties in school districts with good reputations. You can begin your research online at websites like greatschools.org. But also do more local research with actual parents and community members to get the true story.

6. Insurance Rates

Landlord insurance can be one of your larger costs with a rental property. Often regions or states that are prone to such natural disasters as hurricanes, tornadoes, or earthquakes have higher insurance rates that can reduce your cash flow. For example, hurricane-prone states Florida and Louisiana have much higher insurance rates. Google "landlord insurance rates by state" or ask your local insurance agent for help on this research.

7. Property Tax Rates

High tax rates can significantly hurt the cash flow of your investment property. And every state and local municipality approaches property taxes differently. Therefore, study the property taxes in your location to understand how they work. The most comprehensive place to study this information is the local government's Annual Comprehensive Financial Report. You can also search for the local treasurer or tax collection agency.

When you do your research, you want to learn the overall tax rates, whether investment properties are taxed differently, and whether taxes are on the rise. To give you a local example, my state of South Carolina does not tax rental investors and owner occupants in the same way. A house owned by a rental investor can have taxes three or four times higher than those of an owner occupant. The investor tax rates are still competitive with other states, but the owner-occupant tax rate is unusually low.

8. Local Government
Beyond property taxes, you also want to evaluate your local government to understand whether it's landlord-friendly. On the extreme side, rent controls or prohibitive short-term rental laws can make or break your investment. On the less extreme side, rental licensing laws can be an extra cost and hassle that you need to be aware of.

9. Neighborhood HOA/Covenants
Like restrictive local government laws, some neighborhood rules (known as CC&Rs or covenants, conditions, and restrictions) can create unfriendly investing locations. For example, some may prohibit you from renting your property. Your closing agent or attorney should be able to look these up for you when doing a title search.

Also be sure to check the financial condition and future plans of any HOA (homeowners association) or condo association. I knew an investor who bought a condo as a rental, only to be surprised when the HOA assessed (charged) all owners a several-thousand-dollar fee to replace a roof. He could have probably learned of that problem by doing more research.

THE NEIGHBORHOOD ABCS
In addition to the criteria above, you should study the ABCD classification system of your market. In the investment real estate world, there is an informal system of rating both local and regional locations. Class A locations are the most desirable and highest priced and Class D locations are the least desirable and lowest priced.

Why Investors Use a Rating System

The rating system is useful primarily because it allows you to compare one location to another when evaluating potential investments. Investors perceive Class A locations to be lower risk, and they often project that these locations will appreciate more in price over time. That's why they typically pay higher prices there. But the lower prices in Class D locations often lead to higher cash flow, which can be desirable for other investors. There is always a trade-off.

By knowing what classification you're looking at (A, B, C, D), you can apply slightly different formulas and evaluation criteria to each location. For example, you might pass on a deal in a Class D location if it doesn't give you at least $300 per month of cash flow. But in a Class A location, you might accept much less cash flow at first. I'll talk a lot more about formulas to evaluate deals in the chapter on running the numbers.

An Informal, Unofficial Rating System

When it comes to this ABCD classification system, you should know that there is no official book or organization that rates locations. This is an informal rating system that can vary from investor to investor and from market to market. Despite that, it's still widely used when promoting and evaluating properties.

You should also know that ABCD ratings can apply both to locations and to buildings. Brand-new buildings, for example, are usually a Class A. Older, worn-out buildings that need major upgrades are usually a Class D. But in this chapter, I'll just be explaining the ABCD system for locations.

Now let's look in more detail at how to evaluate your locations' ABCs.

Class A Location

This is the best, most desirable location in your real estate market. The easiest way to identify a Class A location is by the real estate prices and rents. The highest rates in your market will always be in the Class A locations.

For example, I invest in the small college-town market of Clemson, South Carolina. One of my Class A locations is right next to the university campus and the downtown restaurant/bar district. This allows the students, employees, or residents to walk to activities on campus and to the fun activities downtown. But in addition to proximity, this location also has the "romance" factor I talked about earlier. There are old oak trees lining the streets, beautiful old buildings, and a lakefront park that give the location character.

We don't own many properties in my Class A location because it's difficult to find properties that make sense as an investment. The resale prices for single-family houses in this location range from $500,000 to $1 million or more, which is above the median price for our area. And multifamily or commercial properties, if you can find them for sale, sell at very high prices compared to the rents. We plan to keep the few properties we have managed to buy in this location as long-term holds because they've done very well.

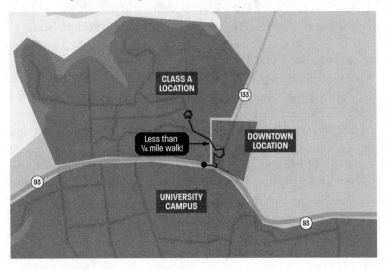

Class B Location

Class B is one notch below Class A, but it's still a very attractive location. The prices and rents are usually at or above the median price ranges. Although there are more rentals in this location than in a Class A, most properties are still owner-occupied.

Again, using my investment market of Clemson as an example, my Class B location is not quite as convenient as the A. It's a one to one-and-a-half-mile walk or bus ride to the university campus and downtown district. Over the past few years, this has been my favorite investment location. The properties have produced decent cash flow, and they've also grown at good rates because the demand is high and the supply of new housing is low.

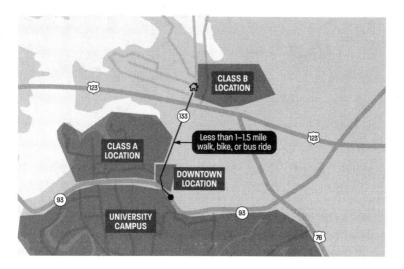

Class C Location

The residents of Class C locations are usually more working-class or blue collar. The neighborhoods and properties are often older, and sometimes they used to be Class B or A. You'll typically find a higher percentage of rentals in this location, often 50 percent or more of the properties. The resale prices will be at or below median for the area, and the rents will be lower than Class A or B.

In my local market, my Class C locations have been my best cash-flow properties. I own small multifamily properties, houses, and a small mobile home park that produce good income each month. As you can see in the map below, my Class C location is farther away from the core downtown and university district.

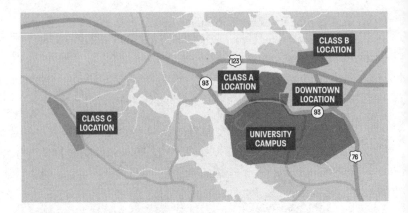

I've found some of my best overall investment deals in Class C locations that are "in the path of progress." Although these locations are currently priced as Class C, they often have qualities of Class A or Class B, like walkability, character, and convenience. If you patiently buy and hold on in these locations, your Class C location can improve to a Class C+ or B over time. This can produce both excellent cash flow and a lot of growth and wealth building for you as an investor.

Class D Location

There is a fine line between Class C and Class D. Sometimes Class D is a pocket within a Class C area, and other times the entire neighborhood can be Class D. You'll typically find these locations to be mostly rental properties with very few owner occupants. The lowest prices in your area will be in Class D locations.

Unfortunately, one common theme in Class D areas is crime. I have owned properties in Class D areas that were vandalized several times. My story about the awful location at the beginning of the chapter was a Class D location.

I want to emphasize that there are many good people who live in Class D locations, often out of necessity. Some investors see these locations as an opportunity, especially if they can buy several properties together or turn around an entire block. By proactively improving the neighborhood, these investors turn a Class D location into a Class C. But to make this work, you need to understand your neighborhood very well and have a strong management plan.

HOW TO CHOOSE YOUR TARGET MARKET

Now that you understand what makes a good market, it's time to focus on *your* target market. If you've already chosen a market, then just go through this exercise to evaluate the market you're already in. But if you're not sure where to invest, this process will help you pick a location. As you follow these steps, be sure to think on both the regional and local level about choosing your target investing market.

Step No. 1: What's your strategy?

In Chapters 4, 5, and 6, I suggested different real estate investing strategies, like house hacking, long-term rentals, or short-term rentals, depending on whether you're a Starter, Builder, or Ender. The goal was to help you pick the right real estate investing strategy for your situation.

Your chosen strategy can help guide you to a particular location. For example, if you chose house hacking, you'll probably want to invest where you already live and work. Or if you chose short-term rentals, you'll want to invest in a location that has strong Airbnb demand and friendly laws for short-term rentals. And long-term rentals are flexible and can work in a lot of locations, but if you are focusing on cash flow, you'll want to pick locations with lower price-to-rent ratios.

Step No. 2: What can you afford?

How much cash money do you have to invest? In which regions or in which local neighborhoods can you afford a down payment on an average property? This personal affordability question can guide you to certain regions of the country or certain neighborhoods within your region.

If you can't afford properties in the location you're considering, you have three choices:

1. Wait until you've saved enough
2. Partner with someone else to get enough money
3. Pick a different region or neighborhood that you *can* afford

If you do need to pick a new target market, consider Step No. 3 and follow in the footsteps of others who've done market analysis homework for you.

Step No. 3: Follow in the footsteps of giants

When you play video games, there's usually a secret cheat code that makes the game much easier. Similarly, here's a cheat code for picking an investing location. Follow in the footsteps of giants! This means pick the locations where larger investors or businesses are already going.

On the regional level, pay attention to the regions where institutional investors and builders invest. Big publicly traded real estate investment trusts (REITs) share their activities openly with current and potential shareholders. You can read and study this information to learn where they are investing regionally and why.

You can Google "single-family house REITs" or "publicly traded REITs" to find a list of them. As I write this, one of the biggest REITs in the single-family market is Invitation Homes (ticker symbol INVH). While you may not want to invest in the *exact* same location as these big investors, you can often pick smaller cities or towns near the big cities where they are investing.

If you're particularly looking for good cash-flow regions, you can follow in the footsteps of turnkey investors. Turnkey investing is a real estate investing niche where companies find, fix up, and rent properties that they then sell "turnkey" or ready-to-go to other investors. These companies do a lot of research to find markets with good cash flow and growth potential. I'll talk more about turnkey investing in the chapter on finding good deals. But you can also use them to help you pick a region to invest.

On the local level, look for activity from other remodelers and investors. For example, when you drive in a C neighborhood and see a lot of dumpsters and active remodel projects, that's a good sign. It means other investors are already putting money into that area. I also like to study the available rentals on the market. When you pay attention to all the rentals in your location, you'll find patterns of which locations tend to be better investment neighborhoods than others.

Step No. 4: Find your farm neighborhood

The best small and mighty real estate investors focus intensely on particular neighborhoods in a local market. They study, cultivate, and regularly work in a location like it was their farm. I recommend that you do the same thing.

As a new investor, it's okay to start very small. Even a neighborhood of fifty properties can become a good mini-farm. By studying every sold property, every rental property, and every for-sale property, you'll quickly become the expert in this location who can recognize good deals. And when you've exhausted your opportunities there, you can add a new neighborhood to your farm list.

You can also diversify your farm neighborhoods over time between A, B, C, and D locations. For example, when I first started, my business partner and I focused mainly on Class C locations because they were affordable and produced positive cash flow. But over time, we've added Class B and Class A farm areas as well. We built our cash-flow base with Class C properties, and now we've added in lower-hassle, higher-growth properties in Class B and A areas to give us a more diverse portfolio.

SHOULD YOU LEAVE YOUR HIGH-PRICED MARKET TO INVEST LONG-DISTANCE?

If you live in a high-priced market, you're probably wondering whether you should invest long-distance. You may love where you live, but the prices have risen so much that it seems impossible to invest there. You're torn between trying to make it work locally and starting an entirely new investing venture in another market.

Anytime I coach someone personally on this topic, I start with their investing strategy. Every market has successful real estate investors. So don't automatically assume investing can't work where you are. But not every *strategy* will work well where you are. You first need to return to the lessons of Chapters 4, 5, and 6, where I recommended certain strategies for certain phases of real estate. But I'll also share some additional tips here that will help you if you live in a high-priced market.

Advice for House Hackers

If you're willing to house hack, it's usually a good idea to stay local. This is especially true when you're a new investor. You have to live somewhere, so why not pick a residence that can generate income to reduce your housing costs? But in a high-priced market, you may have to adapt house hacking to the types of properties you have.

In California, for example, a growing trend is to remodel or build accessory dwelling units (aka ADUs) on the same property as a single-family house. You essentially turn a normal house into a "duplex" because you can rent out this extra housing unit. Or if you want to save even more money, you can live in the ADU and rent out the house for more money!

Pick a Market You Can Afford

If your strategy is short-term or long-term rentals, then your market decision really comes down to what you can afford. If you can't afford properties in your market, then invest in another location. There are plenty of small and mighty investors doing that today.

Sometimes the right market for you could be thousands of miles across the country. But don't forget about the smaller markets only a short drive from home. For example, I had a student in Oakland who bought a $400,000 rental house in Vallejo, which is about twenty-five miles from his home. That price may not seem cheap for many investors, but for him it was more affordable than Oakland. He partnered with someone to split the down payment, and he understands and likes the long-term prospects of the market.

Properties in high-priced markets don't usually produce much cash flow at first. But if you pick the right location and if you're patient, your investment property can get *much* better over time. The same forces that made these locations high-priced—strong demand and low supply—can force your property value and rents to grow significantly. Investors in many areas of California or New York City, for example, benefited enormously by owning rentals like this over the past few decades.

As with any decision, the decision to stay local or invest long-distance is a personal one. But don't let it give you analysis paralysis. There are no perfect decisions. Consider the lessons you've learned in this chapter, do a little homework, and then decide. It's possible you'll spend a lot of time exploring a potential market only to later decide it doesn't work. That's okay! You'll learn more from that process than any book could ever teach you!

EXERCISE
Target Market Worksheet

All the information I've shared with you in this chapter has one purpose—to help you choose and analyze a target market. To help you continue the process, I've got a **Target Market Worksheet** that summarizes all the information from the chapter. You can download it for free in the book resources at **www. biggerpockets.com/smallandmightybonus**.

The worksheet will summarize and guide you through the concepts in the chapter. It will also prompt you to do additional research that can give you more clarity about your market. Once you've finished this exercise or if you've already chosen your target market, you can move on to the next chapter where we'll learn to pick the best investment properties!

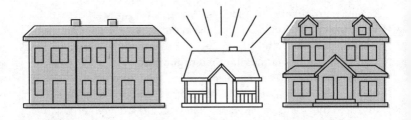

CHAPTER 11
THE BEST INVESTMENT PROPERTIES

Now that you've learned how to build the right team and pick the right location, it's time to learn about the investment property itself. An investment property is made up of the land and the physical building on top of the land. There are hundreds of different types of property you could buy, but in this chapter, we'll focus on the ones that make the best investments for small and mighty investors.

Specifically, I'll focus on single-family houses, multifamily apartments (small and medium-sized), condos, townhomes, mobile homes, commercial properties, and land. I'll also wrap up the chapter by describing my ideal rental property so that you'll have an example to start with. As with other chapters, the goal is for you to act on what you learn. To help with that, I'll leave you with an action exercise to get started identifying *your* ideal investment property type.

INSIST ON VALUE, BE FLEXIBLE ON PROPERTY TYPE

Before we get into the specific types of properties, I want to make an important point about real estate investing. There are investors who make money with *all* the property types in this chapter. Don't fall into the trap of thinking one type is automatically better than the others. For example, simply buying multifamily properties won't be your secret to cash flow and riches.

Instead, as an investor you should insist on value and be flexible on the property type. In other words, insist on good deals, which means buying a property in a good location with good financials (I'll cover how to run the numbers in a future chapter). Those criteria are nonnegotiable.

But beyond those criteria, be open to investing in any property type that makes the most sense in *your market* and for *your strategy*. Also be open to changing property types as the economy, local trends, and regulations change. If you keep an open mind, you'll be able to take advantage of unique opportunities in your local market.

Now I'll explain the pluses and minuses of each property type. Use this list to identify one or two property types that you would like to explore in your market.

PROPERTY TYPES
Single-Family Houses

A single-family house is a freestanding residential building. According to the 2021 U.S. Census,[34] single-family houses represent over 64 percent of all housing in the U.S. This means they're the most plentiful and widely available housing type for investing.

In *Building Wealth One House at a Time*, John Schaub says that "[a]fter 32 years of investing, I still buy houses instead of apartments or shopping centers. Why? Houses make me more money with less work than any other investment."

Houses have many benefits as investments, but here are some of the top ones:

- **Safe and Steady:** Even in down markets, a house in a desirable neighborhood is a safe investment. People always need a place to

---

[34] "American Housing Survey (AHS)," census.gov, 2021, https://www.census.gov/.

live, and houses are the most common type of property to live in. With houses, you'll have an easier time keeping your property full with tenants.

- **Hybrid Investments:** Some investors buy for cash flow. Others buy for appreciation or growth. Houses give you both. But unlike multifamily apartments or commercial properties, the value of houses doesn't depend on the income. Even if a house is vacant, it can still go up in value if someone is willing to buy it and live there.
- **Sell for Retail Price for Cash:** The U.S. federal government has a long history of subsidizing and supporting home buyers through tax incentives and loan programs. This means you can more easily sell houses at retail prices to buyers who can cash you out with their own financing.
- **Sell to Tenants:** When you're ready, you can sell a house to your tenant. This can save you money on commissions and closing costs while allowing them to become a homeowner.
- **Attractive Investor Financing:** Not only is it easier for your buyers to get loans on single-family houses, it's also easier for *you* as the investor to get loans on houses. Investment loans for houses are plentiful, as I'll explain more in a later chapter on financing.
- **Nonprofessional Sellers:** When you buy houses, it's possible to negotiate and buy directly from sellers. Unlike multifamily and commercial properties, these sellers aren't always professional investors trying to maximize profits. You'll find people selling for non-financial reasons, and if you help solve their problem, you can buy below market value and with attractive seller-financing terms.
- **Easier Tenant Management:** Tenants of quality houses tend to be more self-sufficient and stay longer than tenants of apartments or mobile homes. They also tend to pay on time. This makes your job as owner much easier and more profitable, whether you self-manage or hire a third-party manager.

On the downside, houses often have a worse price-to-income ratio than other property types. This means producing a positive cash flow from rents is more difficult. Strong cash flow with houses often comes many years later as your rent increases and/or your loan is paid off.

Small Multifamily Apartments (2, 3, 4 units)

I define small multifamily apartment buildings as two-units (aka a duplex), three-units (aka a triplex), and four-units (aka a fourplex). You can also find houses that fit into this category with rentable basement apartments, garage apartments, or ADUs (accessory dwelling units). Small multifamily apartments are one of the favorites for house hackers and other small and mighty investors because they share both the benefits of houses and of larger apartment buildings.

As with houses, attractive financing is abundant for small multifamily apartments. House hackers who move into these buildings can often get small down payments in the zero percent to 10 percent range, depending on the loan program. And most investors with good credit and enough income can get thirty-year mortgage loans with fixed-interest rates.

Like larger apartment buildings, small multifamily apartments have extra rentable units. This gives them a better price-to-rent ratio than single-family houses and means finding positive cash flow is easier. But unlike large apartment buildings, you can usually find this property type at a lower price. This makes it more affordable and an excellent choice to build your small and mighty investment portfolio.

I also love that small multifamily apartments are often located right next to houses. Especially in older neighborhoods built before the 1950s, it was natural to mix in houses with two-, three-, and four-unit buildings. These neighborhoods often have a lot of character and make amazing long-term investment locations.

Medium-Sized Multifamily Apartments (5–100 units)

There are no official definitions for apartment building sizes, but I call anything between five and one hundred units a medium-sized multifamily apartment. This is the property type that has made me and my business partner more money than any other. It does require more money and sometimes more risk, but the rewards in the end can be worth it.

Unlike with houses and small multifamily apartments, buyers for medium multifamily apartments are all investors. When you are a buyer, this can be a benefit because you're not competing with owner-occupant buyers who often buy on emotion, not on profitability. As a seller, however, this can be a negative. Your buyers always want to make a profit, and many of them are better at negotiating than you are!

My business partner and I made a lot of money with this property type using a technique called "value-add." With apartments and other commercial buildings, the price of a property is based on how much net income (cash flow) it produces. With value-add deals, you find ways to increase the net income (and the value) by increasing the rent, decreasing the expenses, or both. Once the value has increased, you can cash out with a sale or a refinance.

There's one more benefit I like about medium-sized multifamily apartments. This size property is usually too small for the big national apartment investors. It's not worth their time. But these properties are too big for most small, mom-and-pop style investors. This creates less competition for small and mighty investors who don't mind upsizing a little bit.

Keep in mind, however, that you'll need to pursue a completely different type of financing. With five units or more, you enter the commercial financing world. While there are still good investing loans out there, it's not as typical to get thirty-year, fixed-interest financing. And required down payments are usually 25 to 30 percent or more. I'll cover commercial financing in much more detail in a future chapter.

Condos and Townhomes

With both condos and townhomes, you own one unit that's part of a larger complex of units. Typically, a townhouse only shares two walls with a neighbor on the left and right, but you own your building and the small piece of land in the front and back of the townhome. With a condo, however, you typically just own the interior of your unit, and you share ownership of the land and common spaces with the other condo owners. Both townhouses and condos are governed by legal documents called covenants, conditions, and restrictions (aka CC&Rs), and these rules are enforced by an organization of the homeowners—the homeowners association (HOA) or condo owners association.

The main benefit of townhouses and condos is their affordability. Because they're less expensive to build, they are usually the most affordable housing units in your market. In a high-priced market, this might be your only affordable option for an investment property. Condos and townhomes can also have amenities, like pools, clubhouses, or common green spaces. But be careful about HOA and condo fees to pay for all these amenities. Excessively high fees can make it difficult to rent a condo or townhome with positive cash flow.

Many people also like condos and townhomes because there is less maintenance. With condos, the HOA charges a monthly fee that pays for landscaping, common area maintenance, and large capital expenses like roofs, exterior siding, and parking lots. With most townhomes, you're personally responsible for all maintenance and capital expenses, but with a smaller yard and smaller building, it can cost less than a house.

The main downside of condos and townhouses is the extra layer of due diligence required before investing in them. If an HOA is poorly managed, it could run out of money before major expenses are required. For example, if there's not enough money to replace a roof, the association can charge all owners a one-time extra fee or "assessment" that could cost thousands of dollars. Some CC&Rs are also restrictive to rental properties and limit whether you can rent your unit or whether you can rent in certain ways, like short-term rentals.

Mobile Homes on Land

A mobile home, also known today as a manufactured home, is a home that's built in a factory. After building the home, the manufacturer delivers and installs the home on a piece of land. Manufactured homes come in various sizes, including single wide, double wide, and triple wide. Because of the efficient construction process in a factory, the price of these homes is typically more affordable than comparable "stick built" homes that are constructed on site.

In the past, mobile homes had a bad reputation for poor quality. But in the United States after 1976, these homes were required to be built to the standards of the federal Department of Housing and Urban Development (HUD). This was about the same time that homes built in a factory began to be called manufactured homes instead of mobile homes. Over time, the industry has evolved to produce homes whose quality matches or exceeds that of stick-built houses.

Karen and Bob are the investors I featured in Chapter 3 who retired peacefully with ten long-term rental properties. Several of their properties were brand-new manufactured homes that became rentals. They first bought several lots in a neighborhood they liked that allowed manufactured homes. Then they bought the homes, which were installed on the land with permanent foundations (cement blocks and poured cement footers). Including land and home their cost was about $130,000, and their rent started at $1,400 per month. Because the homes are also in attractive rural locations near the city of Greenville, South Carolina, these have become excellent investments.

You need to carefully evaluate manufactured homes as an investment, just as you would any property. Older homes built in the 1980s, for example, may need more repairs than they are worth. I've had particularly bad luck with old metal roofs and siding that leaked regularly. You also have to study zoning regulations, because most local governments either don't allow manufactured homes or allow them only in certain zoning classifications.

But if you can find locations that do allow them, I think the stigma that prevents many people from buying a manufactured home is overblown. Yet because that stigma exists, you can sometimes have less competition for deals. And that can be to your advantage!

Mobile Home Parks

Instead of one home on a plot of land, mobile home parks have multiple mobile homes together. Parks can be small with only a few home lots, or they can be larger with hundreds or thousands of lots. As an investor, you may own just the land and lease the lots to mobile home owners, or you may own the land and the mobile homes.

My business partner and I own one small mobile-home park in a C location. The property has a house and three mobile home lots, one of which we rent to a person who owns their own mobile home. On the other two lots, we own older mobile homes that we rent to long-term tenants.

We bought this property during the 2009 recession for what seemed like a cheap price of $72,000. Because the house, mobile homes, and infrastructure were older, the property needed constant repair for the first years we owned it. If I had it to do over again, I would have torn down the 1980s-era mobile homes and bought new ones to rent. We would have made better cash flow in the end.

But ten years after the purchase, we paid off the owner-financing mortgage and now own the property free and clear. It now finally produces a solid cash flow. And because we keep the rents low, we attract long-term tenants.

In addition to the potential for strong cash flow, mobile homes can also be a wealth builder. If you own them in the path of progress, you can keep them as a rental until the market is good enough to redevelop the land. At that point you can develop the property into traditional housing lots, or you can sell it to another developer. The point is that the land underneath the old mobile homes can become your most valuable asset!

One of the biggest challenges of mobile homes and mobile home parks is financing. Not all lenders like lending money on mobile homes. This means you will need to either bring your own money, find private financing, or negotiate seller financing. In the case of our small park, we negotiated financing from the seller at an extremely low interest rate and a small down payment. We then invested in repairs and upkeep for the property using our own cash.

Another typical challenge of mobile home parks is management. Some of the best deals on parks have been mismanaged by the prior owners. When you buy them, it will take a lot of effort and hassle to turn them around. The cash flow and profits can be worth it in the end, but you need to be ready for that challenge with either your own management or an extremely competent property manager.

Commercial Property

Think about a local business in your hometown, such as a restaurant, pharmacy, or convenience store. In many cases, the businesses themselves don't own the physical piece of real estate. Instead, they pay rent to an investor who owns the real estate. If you choose to buy small commercial buildings, that investor can be you.

The commercial investing world has an enormous variety of building types and deal structures. But you can divide commercial real estate into the following basic categories:

- **Multifamily:** You learned about small and medium-sized multifamily rentals earlier in the chapter. But there are also large multifamily rentals with hundreds of units per apartment complex.
- **Office:** Office properties could be small, suburban buildings rented to attorneys or dentists, or they could be large skyscrapers rented to multinational corporations.

- **Industrial:** Buildings used as warehouses, light manufacturing, or heavy manufacturing are all considered industrial real estate.
- **Retail:** Retail buildings have businesses that sell goods to consumers. They can be as large as a big-box retail store or as small as your local pharmacy.
- **Hospitality:** This category is dominated by hotels and tourism and includes both local, mom-and-pop–style hotels and large luxury resorts.
- **Self-Storage:** People have a lot of stuff, and self-storage properties allow them to store this stuff easily and relatively cheaply.
- **Senior Housing:** This type of real estate provides housing and services to seniors, and it's typically divided by the level of service. In order of level, it includes independent living, assisted living, nursing homes, and memory care.

As a small and mighty real estate investor, you could focus on any one of these categories. But to find properties that you can comfortably finance and purchase, you'll want to focus on the smaller properties in each category. You'll also want to work on finding lenders, real estate brokers, and attorneys who specialize in these types of properties. There are many potential pitfalls as you get into commercial properties, so your all-star team will be more important than ever.

Commercial real estate has the same basic financial benefits as residential real estate, including cash flow, price appreciation, and tax benefits. But these types of properties are not nearly as popular or well understood by most small investors. This means there is often less competition compared to small residential properties if you're willing to hunt.

Another benefit of commercial real estate is that it can be much more passive. In commercial real estate, there is a concept called "triple-net leases." This means your tenant, the business, pays monthly rent, and then they are also responsible for the taxes, insurance, and maintenance of the property. With the right long-term tenant, a triple-net leased property can be an extremely passive investment.

Land Investing

With almost every other type of real estate, we've assumed you had a building on your real estate. But it's also possible to invest in land. There are a variety of sub-strategies within land investing, and they can all be profitable.

- **Flipping land:** My friend Seth Williams at REtipster.com has been flipping land for years. He markets to motivated sellers of land, buys it at low prices, and resells the land for a profit. I also know wholesalers who focus on buying lots in high-demand, urban areas (aka infill lots). They find these lots at good prices and flip them to builders.

- **Timberland:** This land provides wood for building, paper, and other industries. When you own timberland, it grows in value as the trees literally grow and mature. This is a long-term investment with its own set of risks, but it can be a lucrative investment. There are also REITs and investment funds that can make it more passive and diversified.

- **Farmland:** If you listen to interviews of Warren Buffett, he often discusses investing in farmland. He cites it as an example of a productive asset because the output is something useful for society that people literally eat or use. But you don't have to be a farmer to invest in farmland. You can also passively invest in land that you lease to other farmers. You can directly own land, or you can invest in REITs and investment funds that are more passive and in diverse locations.

- **Subdivision development:** If you buy land in the right location with the right zoning (or if you get it rezoned), you can subdivide the land into smaller pieces. You can then build on this land yourself or sell it to another investor or builder. The cumulative value of the smaller pieces can be much more than the original value you paid for the raw land.

Like any investment type, land investing has its own pitfalls and specific knowledge that you'll need to understand. But like commercial investing, this is a property type that fewer small and mighty investors pay attention to. For that reason, it can be another low-competition opportunity if you're interested.

HOW TO IDENTIFY YOUR IDEAL RENTAL PROPERTY

As you work on becoming a small and mighty real estate investor, it's a good exercise to describe your ideal property. This includes the topic we just covered of picking the type of property you'd like to focus on, whether it's single-family houses, small multifamily, or something else. But it also includes describing what you're looking for in the property itself.

In this last section of the chapter, I'll explain my criteria for an ideal rental property. In real life there are no perfect properties. But the exercise of describing and *writing down* your ideal property gives you a goal to aim for. By knowing what you're looking for, you'll be more likely to find something close to your ideal!

Keep in mind that it's okay if your criteria are different than mine. The specific criteria will depend on which property type you choose, the unique circumstances of your local market, and your personal preferences. Here's a list of criteria that make an ideal rental property for me.

Lot

- **Lot size:** Small lots are more efficient and reduce lawn maintenance costs for you (with apartments) or for your tenant (with houses). I will cheat with this rule, however, if I have attractive zoning that allows me to redevelop the property into more units in the future. In this case, a larger lot is better to get more units and a higher value.
- **Lot grade:** In rainy areas like mine, water running toward a building's foundation is a big long-term maintenance problem. I prefer a lot that sits above the grade of the road and the neighboring properties, if possible. This allows water to naturally run away from the building without man-made drainage systems that require ongoing maintenance.
- **Flood plains:** I don't want to worry that my house will flood every time we have heavy rain. Even if flood insurance is available, I avoid flood plains.
- **Trees:** Plants and trees are beautiful, and they add to the character and value of your real estate. But ideally, large trees would not be next to the building itself. Falling limbs and leaves add to maintenance, and during windstorms, trees can fall on your house and cause damage. All this ongoing maintenance is very expensive.

- **Fenced yard (for houses):** Many of your best tenants have pets, so if you choose to allow pets, a fenced backyard is a major plus.
- **Amenities (apartments):** I prefer simple, no-frills apartments with as few amenities as possible to reduce management and maintenance costs. I want my location and the building itself to be the amenity that attracts people to rent my units.

Building

- **Size of units:** As with lot size, I prefer the house or the apartment units to be as small as possible while still being attractive for my tenants. This reduces the cost of maintenance, turnover costs, and capital expenses. It also maximizes your rent per square foot, which usually translates to a higher return on investment. The best apartment units that I own are between 300 and 500 square feet. The best houses that I own are about 1,500 square feet (about half the area of a tennis court).
- **Bedrooms/baths:** My best small apartment units are studios or one-bedrooms with one bathroom. My best houses have three bedrooms and two baths. Bathrooms cost money to repair and replace, so you want as few as possible while still making it an attractive place to live. The ideal number of bedrooms depends on your target audience of tenants.
- **Design:** My ideal rental design is virtually a rectangular box. This creates simple, low-maintenance roof lines and exterior joints. The roof also has a good pitch to let water flow off. Flat roofs are not ideal for long-term maintenance in areas with a lot of rain or snow.
- **Layout:** I avoid rental units with strange, impractical layouts that can't be easily fixed. For example, I owned a house once where you had to walk through one bedroom to get to another. That's not ideal for attracting tenants or for selling.
- **Low-maintenance materials:** To reduce the long-term maintenance costs of a property, the types of materials matter.
  - *Exterior:* My ideal exterior of a rental property has brick or other masonry siding, metal or vinyl trim, and metal or vinyl windows. Unlike wood, these materials need very little ongoing maintenance or painting.

- *Interior:* My ideal interior of a rental property has hardwood or tile floors that avoid the cost of ongoing replacement with carpet. A durable brand of luxury vinyl plank is also acceptable. Other surface materials, like countertops, appliances, and walls, are made with standard and durable materials as well.

- **Garage:** A single-family house ideally has a two-car garage. Long-time real estate investor and educator David Tilney likes garages and other storage spaces for his rental houses. He says this creates what's called "mousetrap houses"; his tenants stay a long time because it's difficult to move and find other rentals where they can put all their stuff!

EXERCISE
Ideal Property Worksheet

Like the last chapter, the goal of this chapter is to help you gain clarity with your own ideal properties. To help you continue this process, I've got an **Ideal Property Worksheet** you can download for free in the book resources at **www.biggerpockets. com/smallandmightybonus**.

The worksheet will ask you questions and give you a chance to apply the concepts in the chapter. By the end of the exercise, you'll have your own criteria for your ideal property type and rental property. Once you've finished this exercise, you can move on to the next chapter where you'll learn how to run the numbers and analyze a rental property.

CHAPTER 12
HOW TO ANALYZE RENTAL PROPERTIES LIKE A PRO (PART 1)

As a small and mighty investor, your goal should be to buy *good* deals. This means buying deals that make you a lot of money. When you stack those moneymaking deals together into a small and mighty portfolio, they help you achieve financial independence. It's that simple.

But to buy those good deals, you need to learn how to identify them. That's why the previous two chapters covered the right locations and the right properties. But even with the right property in the right location, not everything is a good deal. The final piece of a good deal puzzle is the numbers. In this chapter you'll learn how to run the numbers and analyze an investment property like a pro.

Thankfully, as a small and mighty real estate investor, you don't need to have a degree in advanced mathematics to analyze deals. The best investment pros I know use simple math formulas that anyone can learn. Computer spreadsheets are also a helpful tool, but deal analysis is more than just crunching numbers.

Analyzing investment properties starts with truly understanding *how* you make money in real estate. You need to understand the primary sources of profits from your investment properties. When you get these business basics, you can then identify and buy the deals that will make you the most money.

HOW TO MAKE BIG PROFITS WITH INVESTMENT PROPERTIES

You can think about a good real estate deal as a rocket ship on its way to outer space. And a bad real estate deal is a rocket ship that crashes and burns. To escape earth's gravity, a good real estate deal needs powerful engines that drive it up and away from the ground. The two primary "engines" or drivers of real estate profits are:

1. Rental income
2. Equity growth

Most of your profits (aka returns) will originate from these two drivers. This means if you want a good return on your investment, you need to look for deals that maximize these return drivers. Now I'll explain each return driver in more detail so that you can understand and look for them.

Rental Income – Return Driver No. 1

Rental income is the regular money that you generate by renting your property. Typically, this comes in the form of rental payments, but it can also include other tenant-paid fees, such as pet fees, late fees, and cleaning fees.

But, of course, as a property owner you don't get to keep all this income. You have expenses to pay, like property taxes, insurance, maintenance, management fees. And if you use debt to buy the property, you also have mortgage payments.

The most important type of income is what you get to keep after paying all these expenses. This leftover income is called your *net income* or *cash flow*. Cash flow is the foundational source of return for a rental property. If it were an engine on a rocket ship, it would be the steady engine you could depend on. For that reason, many of the formulas in this chapter will be focused on measuring it.

But cash flow isn't the only driver of your real estate profits. To send your real estate rocket into orbit, you need a second type of engine called equity growth.

Equity Growth – Return Driver No. 2

The second return driver, equity growth, can often be the biggest source of profits for your real estate deal. It's the engine that can send you deep into the outer space of profitability. But you must understand how to harness equity in order to create the best real estate deals.

Equity is a financial term for what you own. In the stock world, equity refers to shares that you own in a company. But you can also own equity in a piece of real estate. With properties, equity means the difference between the value of the property (your asset) and the balance of your debt (your liability). A chart of the relationship between your assets, liabilities, and equity is called a balance sheet. Here's a simple example.

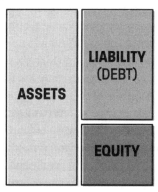

In a balance sheet, the assets on the left always equal the liabilities plus the equity. So as a long-term investor, your goal is to have the value of your ownership (aka equity) grow by increasing the value of your properties (assets) and decreasing the balance of your debts (liabilities). In real estate investing, you can do that with four different profit-building techniques:

- **Price discount:** When you buy real estate below its *current* value, you build in a price discount and a profit from the beginning.
- **Forced appreciation (aka value-add):** Some properties have potential to be improved so that you force the value higher. For example, remodeling a fixer-upper in a good neighborhood often increases its value.
- **Passive appreciation:** In the right locations, the value of a property will passively increase over time. The dynamics of supply and demand that we discussed in the chapter on location help to build wealth while you sleep.
- **Principal paydown:** A typical mortgage payment includes two portions: interest and debt (aka principal) reduction. When you first borrow money, most of your payment will be interest to the lender. But over time, the portion of your payment that reduces your debt will get larger and larger. By simply making your normal payment, you reduce your debt balance. Then you can also use cash flow or other savings to pay extra principal and reduce the debt balance even more. I teach how to do that in the final chapters of the book when I talk about how to win the real estate game.

In the formula sections of this chapter and the next, I'll teach you how to measure and estimate both the equity growth and income return drivers. This will help you confidently analyze deals and only pick the ones with the best potential for profits. I'll also share examples of each formula with real-life situations so that you learn how to apply them in your investing.

Income and equity growth are the return drivers that you can control to make money in real estate. That's why I recommend basing your deal analysis decisions only on them. But you should also know that there's a third potential source of profits for real estate deals. It's called tax savings. I'll explain the basics of this bonus return driver before moving on to formulas for deal analysis.

Tax Savings: Bonus Return Driver

Real estate investing has many tax benefits that allow you to save money on your income taxes. But I call tax savings a "bonus" return driver because you shouldn't count on it. In the unpredictable world of politics, tax laws can easily change. A beneficial tax law today can be gone tomorrow. Your good deal should always stand alone and make sense even without tax benefits. Look at tax savings as the icing on an already good real estate deal cake!

This is a topic that has much more depth and complexity, so I recommend studying it further. I also recommend that you have an excellent accountant on your team to advise you on tax-saving strategies. But here's a summary of some of the key tax benefits within real estate investing:

- Depreciation shelters income and saves money on taxes.
- Rental income avoids the 15.3 percent FICA/self-employment tax.
- Appreciation is not taxed until you sell.
- Capital gains (aka the profits when you sell) are taxed at lower rates than ordinary income.
- Live-in flips produce tax-free profits.
- 1031 tax-free exchanges can defer taxes indefinitely when you sell.
- Installment sales (aka owner financing) defer capital gains taxes.
- Borrowing is tax-free.
- Short-term rentals can use losses to offset active (job) income.
- Self-directed retirement accounts can invest in real estate tax-free.
- Dying with real estate saves your heirs on taxes with a stepped-up basis.[35]

Remember, these tax benefits are based on current tax laws in 2023. They could change in the future! So take advantage of them while they're available, but continue asking your accountant for updates in case the tax laws change.

---

[35] The "basis" is essentially what an investment cost you. When you sell a property, you are taxed on the difference (aka profit or capital gain) between your cost basis and the net sales price. It gets more complicated when you include factors like depreciation. But to understand the basics of the benefit of stepped-up basis, just remember that when someone inherits your property, their basis resets to the current market value. This means they could sell it immediately, earn no profit, and thus pay no taxes. If you had done the same thing, it could have resulted in a large tax bill. This represents a huge tax savings for heirs of investments.

In review, you make money in real estate primarily from the income and the equity growth of properties. Then tax savings create a sweet bonus. Now it's time to learn how to measure and analyze the return drivers of an investment property. Using a group of core formulas, I'll teach you how to determine if an investment property is a good deal.

BACK-OF-THE-ENVELOPE ANALYSIS, LIKE BUFFETT

When I analyze a real estate deal, whether I'm spending $50,000 or $5 million, I begin with an informal process called a "back-of-the-envelope analysis." Although I like to use spreadsheets before I buy a property, I start my analysis with a piece of paper, a pen, and my brain. On this paper I write down the main facts and formulas of the property to analyze whether it's a good deal or not.

You may be surprised that any investor who spends that much money on an investment would use such an informal approach. But back-of-the-envelope analysis is common with experienced investors. Even billionaire investor Warren Buffett, who buys businesses for billions of dollars, says "if you need to use a computer or a calculator to make the calculation, you shouldn't buy it."[36]

Buffett isn't saying that you should never use a calculator. What he means is that a good deal doesn't require fancy math to know it's a good deal. Even with approximate, rough calculations, the deal should jump off the page at you. If the deal looks good at this stage, you then move forward. If it doesn't, you can make an offer at a lower price that does work, or you can move on to something else.

The back-of-the-envelope process is basically a time-saver. It's a way to get to the heart of the matter quickly. Therefore, it's one of your most important skills as a small and mighty real estate investor.

My specific back-of-the-envelope process involves creating a "financial snapshot." I got this term from an excellent real estate book called *The Real Estate Game* by William J. Poorvu. A financial snapshot is a collection of formulas that together give you a picture of the deal's overall financial potential. One formula alone wouldn't tell you enough, but

---

36 "Buffett and Munger: Stay Away From Complex Math, Theories," *Wall Street Journal*, May 2, 2009, https://blogs.wsj.com/marketbeat/2009/05/02/buffett-and-munger-stay-away-from-complex-math-theories/?reflink=desktopwebshare_permalink.

multiple formulas allow you to analyze the deal from different angles to get a complete picture.

FORMULAS TO ANALYZE INCOME QUICKLY AND CONFIDENTLY

My suggested financial snapshot begins with a series of formulas that analyze income. I'll explain these formulas one by one, beginning with the gross rent multiplier.

Gross Rent Multiplier (GRM)

The gross rent multiplier (GRM) is a formula you can use to quickly compare the income potential of one property to another property. You can also use it to compare one real estate market to another. It's similar to the price-to-earnings ratio (PE ratio) in the stock market. The formula is just the ratio of the total price of a property to its gross yearly rent.

$$\text{Gross rent multiplier (GRM)} = \text{Property price} \div \text{Gross annual income}$$

Gross rent means the total rent you expect to collect from a property, before taking out any expenses. For an individual property, this number is easy to estimate using free tools like the Zillow Rent Estimate Calculator[37] or the BiggerPockets Real Estate Rent Estimator.[38] For an entire market, you can use free online tools like Zillow or Redfin to learn the median price and median rent for that location.

Let's look at a real-life example. Imagine that you're analyzing a duplex property with an asking price of $300,000 and a yearly gross rent of $24,000. With your pen and paper, you'd estimate the GRM as $300,000 ÷ $24,000 = 12.5.

By itself, that number doesn't mean much. But let's compare that to a nearby four-unit building for sale. Other than the number of units, let's assume that these two buildings are exactly the same. The four-unit has a price of $500,000 and a yearly gross rent of $48,000. The GRM is $500,000 ÷ $48,000 = 10.42.

---

37 https://www.zillow.com/rental-manager/price-my-rental/.

38 https://www.biggerpockets.com/insights/property-searches/new.

A lower GRM property produces more income per dollar of purchase price than a higher GRM property. In this case with the two properties being similar in every other way, the four-unit building with the lower GRM seems to be the better deal. If their expenses are similar, it will produce more income for every dollar of purchase price than the two-unit building.

Investors also use the GRM as a comparison tool between different markets. A high GRM market produces less income relative to the price than a low GRM market. This doesn't necessarily mean one market is a better investment than the other. As you learned in an earlier chapter, you must evaluate the location fundamentals along with the numbers. Some of the lowest GRM markets are low for a reason and don't make good long-term investments. And some of the higher GRM markets could be good investment locations because their income is more stable and their growth potential is higher.

The One Percent Rule

The one percent rule is a general principle or rule of thumb applied to analyze the income potential of a property. It's similar to the GRM, but it uses the monthly gross rent instead of the yearly rent. Because real estate investors usually think in terms of monthly rent, the one percent rule can be a more practical tool.

For a property to meet the one percent rule, its monthly rent should be at least one percent of the total purchase price. With properties that need repairs, I also add the estimated repair cost to the total purchase price. Here's the formula:

THE 1% RULE

MONTHLY GROSS RENT $\geq$ 1% of total purchase price

For example, let's say you're analyzing a property with an asking price of $250,000. You estimate the property needs $25,000 of repairs, so the total "price" would be $275,000. To meet the one percent rule, the rent should be at least $2,750 per month or one percent of $275,000. If the actual rent is lower, say $1,750, then you could make a lower offer of $175,000 or look for other properties that do meet the rule.

The one percent rule can be useful in some cases, but it does have a couple of major limitations.

1. **Gross rent isn't as useful as net rent:** Like the GRM, the one percent rule only uses the *gross rent*. But with actual rental properties, you'll have expenses like management, maintenance, taxes, and insurance. The leftover, or net rent, is a more important number. A property with high expenses that meets the one percent rule could be a worse deal than a property with low expenses that doesn't meet the one percent rule.

2. **Doesn't account for growth:** The one percent rule focuses on one return driver—income. It ignores the other core return driver—equity growth. It's possible to have a $500,000 property that doesn't meet the one percent rule that grows to $1 million in ten years. If you only use the one percent rule, you could miss deals like that.

For these reasons, you should only use the one percent rule as a starting point. It's a tool to quickly prescreen deals early in the process. But it's not a final analysis. The other formulas we'll cover in this chapter will help you with that.

I also know some of you are saying to yourself, "The one percent rule will *never* work in my market." Especially in high-priced locations, that's true. In these markets, income is not as strong, so you must make money by increasing your equity in other ways. I'll talk about those ways extensively in the next chapter.

Net Operating Income (NOI)

If you care about income as a return driver, net operating income (NOI) is the most important formula you can learn in real estate. NOI is what's left over when you subtract the operating expenses of a property from its gross rent. Operating expenses are the essential expenses necessary to run your rental property, like taxes, insurance, maintenance, and management. The primary expense you do *not* include in NOI is your mortgage expense. I'll explain why later.

Here's the formula for net operating income:

Gross Rent
– Vacancy Reserve
– Management Fees
– Property Taxes
– Landlord Insurance
– Maintenance/Repairs
– Utilities
– Licenses/Fees
– Capital Expenses
_____
= Net Operating Income (NOI)

Depending on the investor, you may see different expenses included in the NOI formula. For example, not all investors include capital expenses (CapEx), which are the large repair expenses to replace or improve things like a roof, heating and air, or a driveway. You may not have a particular CapEx for many years, but when analyzing a deal, I like to account for this cost on an annual basis.

NOI is so important because it tells you how much income your property actually produces. Once you know the NOI, you can then figure out other important analysis formulas, like the unleveraged yield and the cash flow. We'll cover those next.

Unleveraged Yield

In real estate, every investor uses debt differently. This makes apples-to-apples comparisons of one deal to another difficult. But the unleveraged yield formula helps to solve the problem. It analyzes how much income a property produces (aka the yield) while assuming there is no debt (aka leverage) on the property. By temporarily removing debt from the equation, unleveraged yield allows you to make analysis decisions without distortion from debt.

Here's the formula:

Unleveraged Yield (%) = Annual NOI ÷ Total Cost

Here's an example. Let's say you're analyzing a duplex apartment that you could purchase for $175,000 plus $25,000 in repairs and closing costs for a total cost of $200,000. The duplex also rents for $2,000 per month, which, as a review, means it meets the one percent rule. Its operating expenses are $900 per month, so its net operating income is $1,100 per month ($2,000 – $900) or $13,200 per year ($1,100 × 12). The unleveraged yield would be $13,200 ÷ $200,000 = 6.6%.

Is 6.6% a good unleveraged yield? Ultimately, that answer depends on several things. First, it depends on your investment goals. I'll share some of my personal goals below, but you'll have to decide what's "good enough" for yourself. Second, it depends on the other potential return drivers like rent and price growth. If you expect very little growth, for example, you'll probably want a higher unleveraged yield to compensate. Third, it depends on your cost of capital, which means the cost for you to get a mortgage or to raise money from investors. The higher your cost of capital, the higher you'll need the unleveraged yield to be to cover the cost.

My goal for unleveraged yield, for example, changes depending on the type of property I purchase. For a duplex in a solid B-class location in my market, I would currently consider a 7% unleveraged yield a good deal. Although it's not guaranteed, I'm confident that over the long run a duplex in my location will grow at about 3% per year or more. If that happens, I would be satisfied with my duplex's total return of 10%, especially before using any debt.

But even without growth, my B location deal would still produce a 7% yield just from the rental income. If, for example, the cost of my capital from a mortgage or a private investor is 6%, I know that I can at least have a minimal profit. The property earns this profit because of a 1% difference or "spread" between my unleveraged yield and the cost of my capital (7% – 6% = 1%).

In the case of a C-class location, my goal for unleveraged yield would be different. I would need a 9% or 10% unleveraged yield because I'm less confident that price growth will be as strong. I'm also anticipating that my cost of capital could be higher on C-class properties, so I want a higher yield to give me a cushion.

Deals in A-class locations are less common for me, but I would typically accept a lower unleveraged yield than 7% because I expect the growth rate to be higher. We've bought some properties in A-class locations with 5% and 6% unleveraged yields, and we have been very happy with the purchases as the income and prices grew at above average rates. The income in these locations has also been extremely stable because we always have tenants who want to live there. In A-class regional markets like Manhattan in New York or San Diego in California, investors will buy properties at even lower yields in the 3% or 4% range.

You can also use unleveraged yield as a tool to compare risk. In theory, a higher yield means an investment is riskier. A lower yield means an investment is less risky. It's the same principle that gives you a lower yield for low-risk assets like U.S. treasury bonds than for riskier assets like stocks or real estate. For example, here's a comparison of three different asset types and their respective yields at the same point in time:

- 3.82 percent: ten-year U.S. treasury bond interest yield (as of 07/01/2022)[39]
- 4.70 percent: Multifamily real estate cap rates (as of 07/2022)[40]
- 4.91 percent: S&P 500 stock index earnings yield (as of 07/01/22)[41]

Because real estate and stocks are perceived as riskier, investors require a spread or risk premium above the return of the low-risk U.S. treasury bond. This same principle applies when you compare all asset classes, property types, and even individual properties. The more risk you take, the higher yield you should expect. Keep this principle in mind when you're analyzing your deals.

Cash Flow (aka Net Income After Financing)

With all the formulas so far, we've ignored mortgage financing. But most real estate investors *do* use debt to buy real estate. Therefore, you likely also need to use a formula called net income after financing. It's known more simply as cash flow.

---

39 Data for current ten-year U.S. treasury bond yield was collected from https://www.multpl.com/10-year-treasury-rate/table/by-month as of 07/01/2022.

40 A cap rate has practically the same definition as unleveraged yield. Although there are technical differences in how they are used, in this context of comparing assets they can be used interchangeably. Source of cap rate data: "Multifamily Economic and Market Commentary," fanniemae.com, July 2022, https://www.fanniemae.com/media/44136/display.

41 An earnings yield for a stock or index of stocks is the ratio of earnings to price. It's the inverse of a price-to-earnings ratio (aka PE ratio). The earnings yield data for the S&P 500 index was collected from https://www.multpl.com/s-p-500-earnings-yield on 07/01/2022.

Here's the basic formula:

$$\underset{\text{(after financing costs)}}{\textbf{Net Income}} = \underset{\textbf{Income}}{\textbf{Net Operating}} - \underset{\textbf{Costs}}{\textbf{Financing}}$$

This formula tells you how much cash flow you can expect to put in the bank each month. This cash flow is a real, tangible benefit of real estate investing. You can use it to buy more properties, to pay off debt, or to spend personally. For this reason, I recommend making cash flow one of your top goals when analyzing a rental property.

You can pick a cash-flow goal, like $200 or $300 per month. Then you would only buy a potential deal if it could produce that cash flow. If it doesn't, you wouldn't buy the deal.

Let's look at an example. Assume you're analyzing the same duplex apartment as in the unleveraged yield example. The purchase price is $175,000, plus you have $25,000 in repairs and closing costs for a total cost of $200,000. Let's assume your down payment is 20% of the purchase price or $35,000 (20% × $175,000). This means your loan amount is $140,000 ($175,000 − $35,000). Assuming you could get a 6% loan with interest-only payments, your monthly payment would be $700 per month.

With rent of $2,000 per month and operating expenses of $900 per month, the net operating income is $1,100 per month ($2,000 − $900). The cash flow is $1,100 − $700 = $400 per month. If your cash-flow goal is $300 per month, this deal would pass the test.

But don't become so focused on the cash flow formula when analyzing properties that you miss the big picture. Some properties are like fool's gold, the mineral that glitters but has very little value. Some of the lowest-priced properties in your town are probably the oldest properties in bad locations. But once you buy them, the cash flow often disappears from constant repairs, tenant collection issues, and frequent turnover.

Ultimately your goal is to grow your wealth and reach financial independence. Cash flow is only one of the real estate levers that helps you get there. Use cash flow in combination with other formulas so that you get a complete picture. Also always use cash flow with the next formula, cash-on-cash return.

Cash-on-Cash Return (CoC)

After calculating cash flow, I also like to use a second formula called cash-on-cash return (CoC). While cash flow is a raw amount of money, CoC is a return on investment. It tells you how much cash flow you get back in one year as a percentage of your up-front cash investment. Here's the formula:

$$\text{Cash on Cash Return (ConC)} = \frac{\text{Net Income}}{\text{(after financing costs)}} \div \frac{\text{Down Payment}}{\text{(or total cash invested)}}$$

Let's calculate the cash-on-cash return using the same example of the duplex we analyzed for cash flow. Remember that it makes $400 per month, which is the same as $4,800 per year ($400 × 12). Also remember that you had a $35,000 down payment plus $25,000 of repairs and closing costs for a total of $60,000 in up-front cash.

The CoC return is just $4,800 ÷ $60,000 = 8%. This means you get back 8% of your up-front cash investment in the first year. Viewed another way, it will take 12.5 years to get your initial cash investment back using cash flow. I got the number of years by calculating the reverse formula, or $60,000 upfront investment ÷ $4,800 NOI per year = 12.5 years.

CoC return is less helpful if you have a very small down payment. For example, if your up-front cash was $5,000 and you earned $1,200 per year of cash flow, you'd have a 24% CoC return. Not bad, right?! Or if you invested none of your own money (I've done this), the return is infinite—even with a minuscule positive cash flow.

But those high cash-on-cash returns are misleading. They're only possible with extreme leverage. And high leverage also comes with high risk of loss. I began my real estate career this way, so I know it's useful to do low or no-money-down deals. But eventually if you're successful, you should have more cash to invest in your deals.

That's when CoC becomes more useful. Using the formula becomes a type of discipline to help you compare your cash return to other potential investments like bank CDs, bonds, stock dividends, and annuities. With the extra risk and hassle of leveraged real estate, you usually want a higher CoC return than the equivalent cash returns of more passive investments.

But like all the formulas, remember to look at the entire picture. If you're buying a property with potential for huge equity growth, for example, you might be okay with a small or even a negative CoC return for a short period of time. These formulas work best when they're used in combination with one another.

THE VALUE OF INCOME STABILITY

Before we leave the subject of income, I want to mention one other factor that I've alluded to in the previous sections. Many of these formulas measure the *amount* of income. But an intangible yet important factor is the *stability* of that income.

Stability is the likelihood that you'll actually receive the income you project on paper. For example, a Class A location with extremely high demand from renters will be more stable than a Class D location that has crime and other issues. The cash flow on paper could be higher in a Class D location, but the real cash flow from month to month could vary a lot. The cash flow could drop whenever you have issues collecting your rent, finding qualified tenants, or paying large maintenance expenses. The question of stability can also apply to short-term rentals, which can have extremely seasonal rental patterns. A ski resort rental, for example, may have high rents during ski season and lower during the off season.

That doesn't mean investments in short-term rentals or in C or D locations are bad investments. It just means you need to be ready for more extreme ups and downs of cash flow. Investors who don't want to deal with those ups and downs are usually willing to accept a lower amount of cash flow with more stable strategies like long-term rentals or in better locations. They're paying more for the certainty of the income stream. And in many cases, they're also counting on more growth.

When analyzing your own deals, you'll have to figure out what balance you want to strike between the amount of income and its stability. My business partner and I began our careers buying in Class C and Class D locations because we wanted the cash flow to pay our bills. It worked well for us, and we found ways to smooth out the ups and downs using cash reserves and our own hustle. But we've gradually moved to more stable income properties over time as our base of wealth increased and our desire to spend time on investments has decreased. I also have many students who have some short-term rentals for cash flow and other long-term rentals for stability and growth. And as they mature into the Ender phase, they often hire managers or phase out of their short-term rentals.

PRACTICE ANALYZING THE INCOME OF INVESTMENT PROPERTIES

The only way to get good at something is to practice it. This is why you're a better driver now than you were as a 16-year-old. For this same reason, I want to pause here and recommend that you practice using the income formulas we've just covered.

It doesn't matter whether you analyze a property you're trying to buy or a random property on Zillow. The point is to use the formulas we've just covered on real properties in your market. This will take these concepts from theory into practical reality.

To help you in this task, I've included a Deal Analysis Cheat Sheet at www.biggerpockets.com/smallandmightybonus. The cheat sheet has a list of all the back-of-the-envelope formulas I've covered in this chapter. Use these formulas to analyze several deals in your market.

And let me give a warning. You may be shocked and a little depressed when you see how poorly some of these properties perform with these income formulas. Don't worry. Most properties listed on the market are not good deals for you. In future chapters, we'll go in depth about how to find good deals that do make financial sense.

Once you've practiced the formulas in this chapter, let's move on to the next chapter to learn how to analyze equity growth, the second core return driver.

CHAPTER 13
HOW TO ANALYZE RENTAL PROPERTIES LIKE A PRO (PART 2)

I n 2004 my business partner and I were in our second full year as real estate investors. I was 24 years old and just trying to pay the bills, and my business partner was in a similar situation. As a result, we focused almost exclusively on cash flow with investment properties. We knew we wanted to build wealth, but first we wanted to pay the bills!

During this time, we received a call from a seller who had inherited a single-family house in my investing area of Clemson, South Carolina. It was a simple one-story brick house on a big lot. The best part was the location; it was an easy walk to the university campus, to the football stadium, and to the nearby lake. And as I learned later, very few houses in this neighborhood ever sell because people hold on to them. Looking back, this location and property fit our long-term rental buy box *perfectly!*

I negotiated a purchase price of $95,000, but the property needed work. We estimated a cost of about $25,000 to $30,000 for repairs, which would put our total cost at about $130,000 with holding and closing costs added in. We also estimated an after-repair value of $145,000 to $155,000, and a rental value of about $1,000 per month.

When we analyzed this property's income potential as a rental, it wasn't very exciting for us as young investors focused on cash flow. And we didn't have much cash to put as a down payment. As a result, we decided to resell this house quickly when someone offered to buy it for $110,000 in its as-is condition. A week after we bought the property, we resold it and made about $15,000. That buyer did the repair work and has kept it ever since.

Almost nineteen years later, this property is worth at least $375,000 to $400,000. That's a 5.5 to 6.5 percent passive growth rate from our estimated total investment in 2004. The rental rate is now about $2,000 per month, nearly double the original rental rate. Today, this location is even more popular and more exclusive than it was, and it will likely only get better.

FORMULAS TO ANALYZE EQUITY GROWTH

We made a profit from this 2004 deal, which is never something to complain about! And we generated cash flow to pay our bills and financially survive. But we failed to analyze the real value of this property—its equity growth potential. And that taught me to evaluate income *and* equity growth potential on every property going forward. That second type of analysis is what I'll share with you in this chapter.

To begin, let's review the basics of how to calculate equity. Remember that equity is the difference between the property's market value and the mortgage balance. Here's the formula:

$$\text{Equity} = \underset{\text{(after repairs if applicable)}}{\text{Value}} - \text{Mortgage Balance}$$

Figuring out your mortgage balance is easy. For the present balance, you'll just use the amount you're borrowing to buy the property. For a future mortgage balance, you can use any free online amortization calculator to create an amortization schedule. The amortization schedule will tell you your mortgage balance at any date in the future.[42]

---

42 The free amortization calculator I like can be found at https://coachcarson.com/amortization.

Estimating property value requires a few more steps. There are two primary ways to estimate property value. The first is called comparative market analysis, which is used for most smaller residential properties (one to four units). The second is called an income approach to value, which is used for most commercial properties, including medium to large multi-unit apartments.

Comparative Market Analysis

A comparative market analysis (CMA) uses the sales prices of other similar, nearby properties to estimate your property's value. These similar properties are also called comparables or "comps." I recommend having a good real estate agent on your team to create CMAs for you. That's one reason they are a key member of your team.

But I also recommend you practice CMA analysis on your own. With real estate data available for free online, anyone can do it. And it's a valuable skill that you'll need as a long-term small and mighty investor. You can read my blog on BiggerPockets (www.biggerpockets.com/blog/estimate-arv) to help build this skill.

Income Approach to Value

To estimate value using the income or capitalization approach, I also recommend using the help of a real estate agent. With this approach, however, you'll likely need a commercial agent who specializes in investment properties. But I also recommend you learn on your own to calculate value with the income approach. Here's the formula:

$$\text{Estimated Value} = \frac{\text{Net Operating Income (NOI)}}{\text{Capitalization Rate (Cap Rate)}}$$

You've already learned how to calculate the NOI. But to figure out the value, you'll also need to know the cap rate, which is very similar to the unleveraged yield I explained in the previous chapter. The formula is actually exactly the same (NOI ÷ Price), but cap rates are used in a slightly different way.

You figure out the cap rate of your specific location by evaluating the NOI and price for *other* nearby investment properties. Like the CMA process, you want to use comparable properties that are as similar as possible. Then you use the cap rates you discover to estimate the value of *your* property.

For example, let's say a nearby five-unit property sold for $500,000. The property is very similar to a six-unit property you're analyzing. You estimate that the NOI of the five-unit is $35,000 per year. Therefore, the cap rate for the property is $35,000 ÷ $500,000 = .07 = 7 percent.

Now you can estimate the value of your six-unit property using the income approach. Assume that its NOI is $42,000 per year. So, the estimated value is $42,000 ÷ .07 = $600,000.

The toughest part about the income approach to value is figuring out the market cap rates to use in the formula. If you have a hard time determining them on your own, just ask for help. Commercial agents, appraisers, and online services can be a great source for this data.

With a little practice, estimating value and figuring out your mortgage balance will become second nature. It's a skill that will allow you to calculate the equity of a property at any time. And once you have the skill, you can analyze how to *grow your equity* using the four techniques that follow.

Equity Growth No. 1: Price Discount
As a small and mighty real estate investor who is willing to work hard, you can buy properties at a discount to their current value. This can happen for many reasons, but in short, not all sellers are willing to be patient and go through the process of selling a property for a top price. You can think of these as motivated sellers.

I'll explain how to find motivated sellers in a later chapter on finding good deals. For now, just know that it's possible to get discounts of 10 to 30 percent or more from motivated sellers. But to get those discounts, you'll need to actively hunt for deals and make strong offers that solve the seller's problem quickly and easily. Waiting for deals to drop in your lap using Zillow or other online marketplaces isn't enough.

Let's look at an example of how buying at a discount instantly builds your equity. Assume you buy a property at a 10 percent discount from its full value. If the full value is $200,000, you pay a price of $180,000. Your 20 percent down payment is $36,000, which means you borrow $144,000.

Your equity is the difference between the full value of $200,000 and your loan of $144,000. $200,000 – $144,000 = $56,000. Your cash out of pocket was only $36,000, but you have instant equity of $56,000. Simply by negotiating a lower price, you've built $20,000 of equity growth and new wealth!

When you analyze potential deals, make a goal to buy the deal at some sort of discount. In the beginning of your career or in hot markets, that discount may be small at 5 to 10 percent of the total value. But over time as your deal finding and negotiating skills improve, shoot for discounts of 20 to 30 percent or more. Buying with price discounts will build profits and a margin of safety into every deal.

Equity Growth No. 2: Forced Appreciation

Some of the best deals in real estate happen when you change something about a property. This could be *physically* changing a property, like a cosmetic remodel or adding an extra bedroom. It could be *operationally* changing a property, like raising the rents or decreasing the expenses. Or it could be *legally* changing a property, like converting an apartment building into condos that you can sell individually.

These entrepreneurial changes are also known as forced appreciation or adding value. By forcing appreciation, you may spend $25,000 to turn a property valued at $200,000 into a property valued at $300,000. The $75,000 difference is equity growth that builds your wealth!

My business partner and I have used forced appreciation to build a large amount of our wealth. But it took time for us to get good at it. And there are many ways to force appreciation. If you also want to use this technique, I recommend you begin by specializing in one type of property change.

For example, get good at finding two-bedroom houses that are big enough to convert space into a third bedroom. Or study the zoning and land regulations of your town so that you can identify lots that have the potential to be divided into two or more smaller lots. Or get good at property management so that you can buy mismanaged properties to fill vacancies, raise rents, and decrease expenses.

The common theme with these techniques is specialized skill. You must learn and practice a very specific skill of real estate so that you can add value. And the best way to learn a skill is by doing it.

Look for other people in your market doing the thing you want to learn. Find a way to add value to them in exchange for the opportunity to learn. That may mean working for them, volunteering for them, or even loaning them money. You can also sometimes pay another local investor consulting fees to teach you what they know.

To measure forced appreciation, you must get good at estimating values before and after. This is again where your residential or commercial real estate agent can be a big help. You must also learn to estimate the cost of forcing the appreciation to make sure it's profitable.

To estimate remodel costs, for example, I highly recommend *The Book on Estimating Rehab Costs* by J Scott. Grab a copy from the Bigger Pockets bookstore at www.biggerpockets.com/store so that you can get the bonus of J's cost estimating spreadsheets and paperwork. With other techniques, like property management turnarounds, you may not have repair expenses, but you will have other costs such as vacancies, holding costs, and negative cash flow. Learning these techniques will come in the field by doing it and by asking other investors. Start small so you can learn as you go.

Equity Growth No. 3: Passive Appreciation

Real estate in high-demand locations tends to have resale and rent prices that go up over time. This happens because of the economics of supply and demand. As the local population grows, the demand for housing grows. At the same time, the supply of new housing doesn't always keep up in popular locations because of a lack of development land. This combination leads to rising housing prices.

Prices also rise because of the overall background inflation of the economy. As the U.S. Federal Reserve increases the supply of money (dollars) over time, money is worth less and less. This monetary inflation means that everything in society tends to cost more over time. This includes rising costs for materials and labor to build new houses, which indirectly raises the prices of existing housing.

A good investing goal is to buy properties whose growth matches or exceeds the long-term inflation rate of the economy. Although the yearly inflation rate rises and falls, the average U.S. rate between 1913 and 2022 has been 3.27 percent according to the Federal Reserve Bank of Minneapolis.[43]

Investments that I've owned for almost twenty years in Clemson,

---

43 Historical data pulled from "Consumer Price Index - 1913 -," Federal Reserve Bank of Minneapolis, last accessed November 26, 2022, https://www.minneapolisfed.org/about-us/monetary-policy/inflation-calculator/consumer-price-index-1913-.

South Carolina, for example, have passively appreciated near the average inflation rate of 3.27 percent. In other markets like the San Francisco Bay Area of California, I know investors who have averaged 5 to 7 percent appreciation over time. By following the lessons from the previous chapter on picking real estate locations, you can increase the odds that your properties will also passively appreciate.

Equity Growth No. 4: Principal Paydown

Most loans are known as amortizing loans, which means they have fixed payments that include both principal and interest. Over time, the accumulation of monthly principal payments reduces the loan balance to zero. In most cases, the loan is fully paid off in fifteen, twenty, or thirty years. Of course, you can also make early principal payments to pay it off faster.

As a real estate investor, amortizing loans are a great way to grow your equity. Your tenant basically builds wealth for you by making their rent payment each month. This equity growth starts small at first, but it grows and snowballs over time. If you're like me, you'll start to enjoy the end of the year when you measure and celebrate all the wealth you've built passively paying down debt over the prior twelve months!

This is a relatively easy equity building technique to measure and estimate. When you analyze a potential deal, simply use an amortization calculator and create an amortization schedule or spreadsheet. On this schedule, you can estimate how much principal you will pay down each year.

HOW TO PUT BACK-OF-THE-ENVELOPE ANALYSIS INTO PRACTICE

When I teach back-of-the-envelope analysis to students, they sometimes tell me, "Chad, this is going to require one big envelope!" And there's some truth to that. When you first start, there do seem to be a lot of different formulas. To help you avoid getting overwhelmed, be sure to use the Deal Analysis Cheat Sheet at www.biggerpockets.com/smalland mightybonus. Use the cheat sheet as you practice analyzing deals on your own. But I've also got a few suggestions below to help you put these analysis formulas into practice.

First, you don't have to use all the formulas at once. I usually focus on income first, and then I later get into equity analysis. I usually start with GRM and the one percent rule very quickly on the front end of deal analysis. Especially with the one percent rule, I do the math in my head in real time. Rarely does a deal meet the one percent rule right away. But using my knowledge of the market, I'll ask myself whether I could change something, like remodeling the property or adding an extra rental unit, to increase the income and meet the one percent rule or better.

Second, I make goals with a couple of the other income formulas, typically unleveraged yield and cash flow. I then test the deal against those goals. To save time, I use short cuts to make the calculations even easier. For example, to calculate the NOI, I may assume that a rental property will have 50 percent operating expenses (this is sometimes called the 50 percent rule and does *not* include mortgage expenses). For a $1,200 per month rental, I would assume $600 of operating expenses and $600 of NOI per month. That's an NOI of $7,200 per year ($600 × 12).

Why the 50 percent rule? Because it's easy to calculate half of something in your head. It also takes less time than figuring out the actual operating expenses one by one (although I *always* figure those out before committing to buy a property). The 50 percent rule is also a little more conservative than normal. My actual rental deals have operating expenses of about 45 percent on average, and my best properties have an even lower percentage.

With this rough NOI, I can easily do quick-and-dirty math for unleveraged yield, cash flow, and cash-on-cash return. If the income for a deal looks good using this rough math and if it's in my desired location, I jump on it quickly to get it under contract. The best deals rarely last long.

If the analysis does not initially meet my income goals, but it's in a location I like, I'll start digging more. I go through each of the four equity growth scenarios to analyze the deal's potential. Some of the best deals don't initially look good with income formulas, but I find hidden value below the surface.

For example, perhaps I can get a big price discount. Maybe I see opportunities to change something and force the value up. Sometimes it's clear that I could negotiate low-interest seller financing, which would give me more principal paydown or cash flow. And occasionally, I'll find a property that's in a rare location that I believe will appreciate well. The initial numbers aren't great, but I'm willing to take a chance because limited supply and increasing demand will make it much better over time.

With all this back-of-the-envelope analysis, the main point is that I don't waste a lot of time. I use my brain and energy to think about the core profit drivers of the deal. I use my creativity to think about how this deal could be better than it currently is. I don't waste a lot of precious time or energy calculating decimal points or adjusting spreadsheets.

After this step, which could take me from five to twenty-five minutes, I know if a deal has potential or if it doesn't. For the deals that have potential, I'll usually schedule a time to see them in person (or have my agent see them for me). I use this visit to evaluate the property and location in more detail, to verify assumptions with my numbers, and to gather information for an offer to purchase. That's when spreadsheets and a more detailed analysis come into play.

SPREADSHEETS—HOW AND WHEN TO USE THEM

A spreadsheet is a wonderful analysis tool. It organizes information into a format that's easy to visualize. And it allows you to calculate multiple equations at once, like the NOI, cash flow, cash-on-cash return, loan amortization, unleveraged yield, and more. A spreadsheet doesn't change how you analyze a deal, but it makes the process more efficient.

I use a spreadsheet to build my confidence that a property is worth investing in. I also use it to remember the details of analysis that I could forget, like each of the expenses included in my net operating income formula. Just by filling out the information in a good analysis spreadsheet, you'll be forced to double-check all the information and assumptions of a deal.

Spreadsheets also provide one final and very important benefit. They allow you to calculate more complicated formulas like internal rate of return (IRR). IRR brings everything I've covered in this chapter together into one formula. That's why it's my favorite formula for real estate deal analysis, and it's the one I use before I make an offer to buy a property. To close out this chapter, I'll briefly explain what it is, how I use it, and how to get a free IRR spreadsheet.

INTERNAL RATE OF RETURN (IRR)

Internal rate of return is an annual rate of return that considers the time value of money. An unleveraged yield and a cash-on-cash return, for example, just measure a deal's return over one year. But an internal rate of return measures returns over a longer period, like ten or twenty years. It then tells you the annualized (yearly) return within that period.

The IRR also gives you a more accurate view of the profitability of your investment. Unleveraged yield and cash-on-cash return, for example, only measure income returns. But an IRR includes potential profits from rental income *and* equity growth. Depending on the deal, this equity growth could be most of your profits, so you definitely want to measure it!

Once you've calculated the IRR, you can then use it to make a decision, like offering to buy a property. You can compare the IRR of this deal with other investment opportunities, like stocks, bonds, or another property. You can then decide whether the return you expect from this property is worth the trouble and risk. If it is, you can decide to move forward. If it's not, you can decide to negotiate for a better price or move on.

I've made a twenty-minute YouTube video called "How to Calculate Internal Rate of Return (IRR) for Real Estate Investors."[44] Watch this free video if you want a more in-depth review of how it works. But for now, all you need is a spreadsheet to calculate IRR. It's just too complicated to do with paper and pen (at least for me!). For that reason, I've included an IRR spreadsheet that you get for free at www.biggerpockets.com/smallandmightybonus. Use that spreadsheet to practice the IRR formula on your deals.

PRACTICING DEAL ANALYSIS MAKES PERFECT

The key to getting better at deal analysis is practice. If you want to internalize the lessons in this chapter (and in this entire book!), I challenge you to practice analyzing five real deals in the next week. Don't worry about whether they're actually good deals. Just find any property for sale, and practice using the income and equity growth formulas. Then try to put it all together by using the IRR spreadsheet. Like learning to ride

---

44 Watch on YouTube at https://youtu.be/HJnnpXoR6y0.

a bike, this will build your confidence and skill as a small and mighty real estate investor!

Now let's continue to the next chapter where you'll learn the important skill of how to find these good deals.

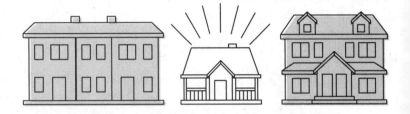

CHAPTER 14
HOW TO FIND GOOD DEALS

As you've learned in the last three chapters, a good real estate deal is a combination of the right location, the right property, and the right numbers. If you buy these good deals consistently, you will build wealth and eventually achieve financial independence. But you can't buy good deals until you find them, which is what you'll learn to do in this chapter.

When I was a brand-new real estate investor at 23 years old, I decided to begin my career by mastering the skill of deal finding. It was the best decision I could have made. At first, the deal finding skill allowed me to make a full-time living wholesaling and flipping houses. Then it eventually allowed me to find rental properties that now support my financial independence with regular monthly cash flow.

Deal finding is extremely rewarding, but it's also the most challenging part of real estate investing. It's difficult because good deals won't just fall in your lap. Most properties for sale won't meet your investing criteria. If you do a quick search on Zillow, good deals won't be highlighted on the first page for you.

Instead, good deals are hidden beneath the surface, waiting for you to discover them. Finding them is like a treasure hunt where you dig, search, and investigate to find hidden gold. But luckily, you can learn from experienced treasure hunters like me and follow in my footsteps. And in my experience, the best real estate treasure hunters follow three key principles:

1. **Create a buy box:** Clearly define the locations and types of properties you will hunt for
2. **Find motivated sellers:** Search for motivated sellers instead of just the average seller
3. **Work the deal funnel:** Use marketing to generate leads instead of waiting for deals to fall in your lap

Let me explain each of these three principles in more detail.

CREATE A BUY BOX

There are thousands of potential properties in your local real estate market, and most of those properties will not be good deals for you. As with GPS guided directions, you need a method to guide your search so that you can focus on the right properties. One of the best methods to accomplish this focus is called a "buy box." This is a short, written statement that describes a good deal for you. It outlines your investing criteria and defines what kind of property you want to buy.

Any property outside your buy box, you ignore. This frees up your attention and mental energy to focus only on the smaller number of properties inside your buy box. These buy box properties are the ones that you'll ultimately try to buy.

Your buy box also helps you stay disciplined as an investor. You will constantly be tempted by new shiny real estate strategies. You will also get FOMO (fear of missing out) listening to success stories from other local real estate investors. But sticking to your buy box will keep you grounded and focused so that you avoid distraction. You'll also avoid big mistakes because you'll stick to properties you know and understand.

Feel free to adapt your personal buy box to whatever works for you. But I suggest you include a few different categories that closely follow what I've taught in the last few chapters of the book about good deals.

Target Location

Identify the target area you would like to hunt for deals. This is usually defined by neighborhoods, zip codes, census tracts, city blocks, or city limits. Keep your target location small at first so that you can get to know it well. You can always expand it later.

Class A, B, C, D

Choose one or more real estate classes (A, B, C, D) that best match your investing strategy and goals.

Types of Properties

List the general property types you'll consider, such as single-family house, duplex, triplex, fourplex, townhome.

Property Characteristics

Identify any basic property criteria that you're looking for in a good deal. This could be things like square footage, bedrooms and baths, age of property, or lot size.

Financial Analysis Criteria

Include the formulas and analysis goals you will use to decide if a deal meets your criteria. For example, this can include the one percent rule, unleveraged yield, cash flow, cash-on-cash return, and equity growth criteria like price discount. Sticking to your financial analysis criteria is very difficult. You will be tempted to cheat and lose discipline when your emotions take over. But having your criteria in writing can ground you and help you maintain your discipline to do only those deals that match your criteria.

A buy box description should be one page or less. Don't get too fancy or complicated with it. Write it on an online document that you can share with your team members—for instance, your real estate agent, property manager, or lender. I've included a sample buy box description at www.biggerpockets.com/smallandmightybonus.

And as you get this important deal finding tool ready, also consider the second deal finding principle—searching for motivated sellers.

FIND MOTIVATED SELLERS

Technically, any property that fits in your buy box is a good deal. But who will actually sell you those good deals? In my experience over the past twenty years, the answer has usually been a motivated seller. So if you want to become an excellent deal finder, you also need to learn how to identify and find motivated sellers.

A motivated seller is a homeowner with a frustrating problem to solve. This problem may or may not be related to real estate, but it usually has some sort of urgency. Instead of patiently going through the process of selling their property for top dollar, they're willing to forgo maximum financial benefit in exchange for solving their problem.

Motivation does not mean desperation. Someone in dire financial straits and about to lose their house to foreclosure could certainly be motivated. But I've also bought properties from seasoned investors who were motivated because they didn't have the time or patience to deal with a particular property. I've also bought properties from multibillion-dollar banks who were motivated to get a property off their books by the end of the month.

This list isn't comprehensive, but here are some examples of situations of motivated sellers that I've worked with to buy their property:

- Accidental landlords
- Burned-out landlords
- Bad property management
- Years of deferred maintenance
- Expired listing with real estate agent
- Loss of a job
- Pre-foreclosures (behind on mortgage payments)
- Foreclosure auction (bidding at the foreclosure sale)
- Post-foreclosure (aka REO or bank-owned)
- Financing balloon payment due
- Estates/probates/inherited properties
- Divorce
- Bankruptcy
- Behind on property taxes
- Income tax lien (state or federal)
- Moving to another state
- Need cash to buy another house

- Water damage to property
- Fire damage to property
- Code violations with local municipality
- Vacant house

Life situations happen. Property problems happen. Finding real estate deals is only partly about the buy box and the actual property. By learning to solve the problems of the human beings who own real estate, you can find and buy as many deals as you want. The next chapter on negotiations will focus on this subject in more detail.

Having a buy box and being on the lookout for motivated sellers will put you ahead of 90 percent of other investors. But there's one more principle that I learned as a new investor that's allowed me to buy hundreds of good deals since then. It's all about understanding the real estate deal funnel.

THE REAL ESTATE DEAL FUNNEL

The best small and mighty real estate investors don't wait for acquisitions opportunities to fall out of the sky. They create their own opportunities by building *marketing systems*. Marketing systems consistently generate leads that can eventually turn into deals.

Marketing systems are basically the top of what's called a real estate deal funnel. Here are a few definitions that will help you better understand what a deal funnel is:

- **Lead:** Potential, unscreened purchase opportunities
- **Viewing:** A promising lead you visit or evaluate in more depth
- **Offer:** A promising viewing where you make an offer to purchase the property
- **Deal:** An accepted offer that you actually purchase

Marketing systems generate a larger number of leads at the top or wider part of the funnel. You then prescreen or filter the leads, which results in fewer viewings. I'll teach you how to prescreen leads in the next chapter. Another round of filtering and negotiation happens between viewings and offers. By the time you reach the bottom of the funnel, you'll have a much smaller number of deals compared to the leads at the top.

100 LEADS
20 VIEWINGS
10 OFFERS
1 DEAL

You can also look at the deal funnel from the perspective of you, the small and mighty investor. Here are the steps you must take to go from a lead to an actual deal. These are also the steps we will use as a guide in the next few chapters on negotiating, making offers, performing due diligence, and closing the purchase.

1. **Lead generation**
2. **Collect and prescreen leads**
3. **Gather information about the seller and the property**
4. **Make offer**
5. **Follow up (if needed)**
6. **Put property under contract**
7. **Due diligence and close the purchase**

The deal funnel is useful to teach you the steps of acquiring a property. But it's also useful to identify problems with your deal finding in real time. For example, I use it regularly to help students figure out why they're not buying more deals.

WHY YOU'RE NOT BUYING GOOD DEALS (IT'S A NUMBERS GAME)

When investors tell me they can't find good deals, I can predict their problem 99 percent of the time. They're usually not generating enough leads at the top of the funnel. When I ask them how many leads they're generating, they usually show me five or ten listings on Zillow or the MLS (multiple listing service). And of course, this means they're also not making enough offers.

These investors tell me that a "competitive market" is the reason they can't find deals. But their lack of marketing is the real problem. Generating five to ten leads and expecting to consistently buy good deals won't work because acquiring good deals is a numbers game.

This means that you must generate a lot of leads at the top of the funnel to find good opportunities at the bottom. In the previous image of the deal funnel, I said you needed 100 leads to buy 1 deal. I can't tell you whether this will be accurate for you. It's possible you may need to generate 400 leads, or you may be able to get by with 25. Your actual number will depend on the competitiveness of the market, your ability to generate well-targeted leads, and your skills as a negotiator. At my best, I would convert about 1 out of 4 offers I made. And I typically needed 40 or 50 leads to make that many offers.

But no matter the actual number, the deal funnel principle will remain the same. You need to get good at generating a large number of leads to buy good deals. And you'll also have to get good at prescreening, negotiating, making offers, and following up. In the next chapters, I'll teach you how to do all of those so that you can convert more leads into deals. But in the rest of this chapter, I want to teach you how to use marketing systems to fill the top of your deal funnel with leads. If you do that well, you'll never run out of good deals.

THREE LOW-COST MARKETING SYSTEMS TO FIND GOOD DEALS

Many real estate investors don't have marketing systems. They just search for properties randomly online and perhaps talk to real estate agents. There's nothing wrong with those steps, but they're only a start. A marketing system is a deliberate process that you can repeat over and over. It's something that you can tweak and improve upon continuously within your business.

There are literally dozens of real estate marketing systems you could choose from. And some of them cost a lot of money and time to implement. But with you small and mighty investors, I want to begin by teaching three low-cost marketing systems that have resulted in the most success for me and my students over the years. We'll start with something called the MLS.

Multiple Listing Service (MLS)

The multiple listing service (MLS) is an online database where real estate brokers share information about properties for sale. There are hundreds of regional MLS databases around the country run by local organizations. Real estate brokers use the databases to cooperate with one another to get their clients' properties sold. As an investor, you can also work with a real estate broker (or an agent who works under the broker) to send you leads from the MLS in your area.

You may hear some investors complain about the MLS and say that you can't find good deals there. Their justification is usually that there is too much competition. It's true that you'll often have to compete with many buyers on MLS properties, and in hot sellers' markets you'll find fewer deals than in buyers' markets. But it's also true that 86 percent of all home sellers use an agent to sell their property.[45] This means most properties available to buy will be on the MLS!

As a small and mighty real estate investor, you *can* buy good deals on the MLS. Mark Ferguson, an investor, house flipper, and blogger at investfourmore.com, has purchased dozens of rentals and more than two hundred flip properties. Most of his deals came from the MLS. I bought my first property off the MLS, and I've bought many others off the MLS since then.

Other than the sheer number of properties on the MLS, here are a few other benefits that will help you as a small and mighty investor:

- **Easy automation:** Your agent can set up an automated search based on your buy box so that you can get email notifications with any new properties for sale.
- **Free to you as a buyer:** You normally won't pay a fee or commission until you buy a property. And even then, it's normally paid by the seller as part of the purchase price as a fee split between the listing and buyer's broker.

---

45 "Quick Real Estate Statistics," National Association of Realtors, last accessed November 29, 2022, https://www.nar.realtor/research-and-statistics/quick-real-estate-statistics.

- **Wealth of data for research:** The MLS has the richest, most helpful data about the real estate market. It includes information about properties for sale, but also sold properties. You can use this data to study your market.

Because the MLS is free for you to use and so valuable, every small and mighty investor should choose it as one of their first marketing systems. But to successfully generate leads with the MLS system, I recommend that you follow these steps:

1. **Work with an investor-friendly agent:** This was one of the key team members I recommended in the chapter on team building. An agent who understands investment properties can not only send you MLS leads, but they can also help you refine your target market and negotiate deals.

2. **Use your buy box criteria to set up an automated search:** Your agent can use the basic property characteristics and price range criteria from your buy box to set up an automated MLS search. You want all *new listings* and *price changes* to be sent to your email inbox every day. I recommend that you *don't* get too restrictive with this at first. Err on the side of being too broad with your filter so that you can manually sift and sort through the opportunities. Even if you pass on most leads at first, reviewing them will help you improve your market knowledge.

3. **Be prepared to act fast:** Good deals don't last long on the MLS. Have your money ready (we'll cover that in a future chapter). Have your purchase contract ready (your agent can help with that). And be ready to visit a property at the drop of a hat, analyze it, and make an offer in hours (not days).

4. **Make offers:** You can't buy properties without making offers. So, make them as often as possible. I'll discuss more offer strategies for MLS properties in a future chapter on negotiations and making offers.

5. **Follow-up:** In my experience, good deals from the MLS come from being the first offer or the last offer. We already discussed acting fast, but you also need to be organized and persistent. Use some sort of spreadsheet or follow-up system to track your offers, and schedule reminders for your agent to follow up with the listing

agent. Many times, a seller will change their mind as time and circumstances change. There's usually a lot *less* competition on the follow-up than on new listings.

If you're serious about buying more investment properties, it's time to get started setting up your MLS marketing system. If you haven't already worked on your buy box description , do that now. Then work on finding an agent who can begin sending you MLS leads.

I also want to mention a variation of the MLS strategy in which you contact listing agents directly. You can search for MLS properties for free on Realtor.com or other free websites, and then you can reach out to the listing agent to tell them you are interested but don't have an agent. You're not necessarily looking for the agent to represent you, as that creates a conflict of interest or dual agency situation. But it does sometimes grab the attention of the listing agent who can earn the whole 5 percent or 6 percent commission. Or it gives them some room to reduce their fee to get a deal done if you and the seller can't meet on price.

Driving for Dollars

After the MLS, Driving for Dollars is the second marketing system I always recommend to small and mighty investors. It's my favorite way to consistently find good deals that other buyers don't know about. And like the MLS, it's one you can start for little or no money.

Driving for Dollars involves driving (or walking) in your target neighborhoods, and you (or people you hire to drive for you) look for potential deals while in the neighborhood. You then reach out directly to the owners of the properties to ask whether they would like to sell. There are several major benefits to this marketing system:

- **Very little competition:** This strategy requires more effort than searching for properties online or receiving leads from the MLS. Therefore, fewer people do it. Also, most properties you find aren't even listed for sale, so you avoid a lot of competition.
- **Motivated sellers:** You'll be looking for vacant, run-down, for sale by owner, and for rent by owner properties. Property owners in these situations aren't all going to be motivated, but these indicators increase the likelihood of motivation compared to a cold list of all property owners. It's basically a lead generation filter.

- **Start immediately:** You can begin Driving for Dollars today, right after reading this. It's one of the fastest, most direct ways to start finding deals.
- **Low cost:** If you drive, you'll need to pay for gas. But you can walk or bike for free to find deals while also getting exercise! If you live a long distance from your target market, you may need to pay people on the ground to Drive for Dollars for you. But you can also use technology tools like Google Street View to virtually drive for dollars.
- **Learn target market:** Not only can you find deals, but you'll also learn an enormous amount about your market while observing it firsthand.
- **Potential referral sources:** While out looking for deals, I often meet neighbors, Realtors, repair contractors, mail carriers, delivery people, and other investors. These people can become referral sources for future deals if you stay in touch and let them know what you're looking for.

All these benefits make Driving for Dollars an effective marketing system. If you're ready to give it a try, here are my recommended steps to get started.

1. **Pick neighborhoods to drive:** Use your buy box criteria to pick neighborhoods to drive or walk in.
2. **Block time:** Find times that fit into your schedule and block them off. Then make a routine of visiting neighborhoods at the same time each week.
3. **Find properties:** Drive or walk your neighborhoods and look for one of several different types of properties.
   - **Vacant properties:** It's obvious no one is living there. I look for signs such as no window blinds, empty garage, tall grass, mail or newspapers piled up in driveway, or personal items set by the road (like after an eviction or move).
   - **Run-down properties:** Even if occupied, the property clearly needs repairs or has major deferred maintenance.
   - **For sale by owners:** The owner has a For Sale by Owner sign in the yard.

- **For rent by owners:** The owner has a For Rent sign in the yard. I ignore property manager signs and include only signs that look like they represent for rent by owner.

4. **Track properties:** You may find dozens of properties during a good session, so you want to record and track your properties somehow. You can use pen and paper, which is how I tracked them originally. But today there are also paid phone apps, like DealMachine, which specialize in making Driving for Dollars easier and more efficient.

5. **Find owner's contact information:** Before you can reach out to the owner to let them know you're interested in buying their property, you need to get their contact information. If you use a paid app like DealMachine, you can often find the owner's phone numbers right away using their built-in skip trace service. If not, you can talk to neighbors. They often know the owner's story and phone number. And especially if the property is vacant, they usually want to get it fixed up. I also leave notes on the door of the house itself asking for a call back from the owner.

6. **Call property owners (if possible):** If you have a phone number, simply call the owner. It's the fastest and most direct way to get in touch. Let them know you're interested in buying their property and find out whether they're interested in selling. I'll have more details on talking to sellers in the next chapter on negotiations.

7. **Mail campaign:** If you can't reach an owner by phone, send them letters or postcards. In most states, you can search for a property owner's mailing address on the public tax records. Or in nondisclosure states, you'll need to use an app like DealMachine or other direct mail services to find it. I like sending personalized mail that references the actual property. This will increase your response rate. And don't just send one letter. Most responses come after three or four tries. If you're not willing to send multiples, it's not worth sending them at all. You can do the printing and mailing of letters yourself if you're on a tight budget, or you can use a deal-finding app such as those I referenced before to automatically and easily send mail for you.

8. **Make an offer:** In a future chapter, I'll teach more about how to make offers. But for now, just know that if the property seems like

a good deal, act fast and make an offer as soon as possible. And like you did with the MLS, follow up if the seller doesn't initially accept your offer. If a listing is still active, I usually follow up every week or two. Or if it's under contract, I'll follow up around the estimated date of closing to make sure it closed.

I mentioned briefly that if you live outside your target market, you can pay others to drive for you. Both long-distance investors and busy local investors can use this variation of the Driving for Dollars strategy. In the past, I built a small team of "bird dogs" who drove neighborhoods for me. I paid them $5 to $10 per lead, which had to include pictures of the house and other basic information.

Yes, paying for bird dogs costs extra money. But if you had more money than time, wouldn't you like to pay $1,000 for one hundred leads on potential deals? If one of those leads could become a deal that builds *hundreds of thousands* of dollars in wealth, wouldn't that be worth it? It was for me.

But whether you drive yourself or pay someone else, Driving for Dollars is a process that is a little more involved than simply receiving MLS leads. The effort required, however, is also your biggest opportunity. By doing what others won't, you'll be able to get deals that others can't. This is the essence of the deal-finding treasure hunt!

Networking for Referrals

MLS and Driving for Dollars are marketing systems to quickly get leads coming in. But I also recommend one other broader marketing system—networking for referrals. When I built this marketing system for myself, it took a little longer to get results. But over time, it brought me more deals and better deals than any other source. These leads also cost me little or nothing, and I was often the only person to know about them.

By networking for referrals, I mean letting everyone in your world know that you are buying investment properties and then asking them for referrals. I'll explain how to go about this networking using a few different methods.

- **Friends and Family:** Let your family, friends, colleagues at work, fellow church members, exercise buddies, or anyone else know the type of properties you're looking for. Also let them know that referrals will be very helpful for you.

- **Email PS:** I use an automated PS message on all my emails. They all end with something like "PS—I am always on the lookout for houses and apartment buildings in the greater Clemson area. Do you know of a property that needs some TLC? Or know a landlord who doesn't want to be? Or did someone inherit a house they don't want? Call, text, or email me anytime. Any leads would be a big help. Thank you!" You'll be surprised how many leads you get with an army of referral sources looking for you!

- **Social Media:** Consider telling real estate stories on social media. Your friends and followers love to see behind the scenes, so you can share stories about your property searches, learning, and the actual properties you buy. Be sure to give a "call to action" occasionally, when you ask people to send you referrals for properties in your area.

- **Real Estate Investor Meetups:** Other investors aren't always your competition. They can also send you leads! Attend local educational and networking meetings, and let other investors know about your buy box. Most people just tell everyone "I want a good deal." Be the weird one who is very specific and says "I want brick duplexes on the east side of town in the ##### zip code." You'll stand out and people will remember to send you the leads that they can't handle or want to resell. You can find meetups in the BiggerPockets forums, in Facebook Groups, and by searching for real estate investor associations in your town.

- **Wholesaler Lists:** Wholesalers are in the business of finding good deals and selling them to other investors for a profit. Search for local wholesalers in your town and get on their email list so that you'll receive their latest deals. But also take this a step further. One of my successful students, Sean McKay in Charlotte, North Carolina, mentioned that he gets many deals by building relationships with wholesalers. He takes them out to lunch, stays in touch, and lets them know what he's looking for. As a result, the wholesalers often think of him first. Not all deals from wholesalers are good deals, so screen them like you would any other. And you may also have to use a non-bank source of financing to close your deal with wholesalers. I'll share ideas on that in a future chapter on financing.

- **Commercial Agents:** I have bought some of my best deals from commercial real estate agents. I told them what I was looking for (say, smaller residential investment properties), and they sent me leads when they came across opportunities. They were often looking to list larger or different types of properties, so they were happy to get a referral fee from me on these smaller deals that weren't ideal for them.

- **Local Professionals:** CPAs, attorneys, financial planners, insurance agents, and other trusted local professionals get to know a lot of clients. Sometimes their clients fit the description of a motivated seller and they need to sell an investment property that fits your buy box. Get to know these professionals and let them know what you do. Then follow up occasionally to remind them of your service buying properties.

There are many other creative ways to generate referrals. Let your imagination flow! But whatever you do, know that it may take some time before you harvest the fruits of your efforts. Just be patient. In a world where everyone wants instant gratification, your small and mighty real estate investment business will benefit from a persistent and patient strategy like this one.

OTHER LEAD GENERATION TECHNIQUES TO GROW INTO

I shared the most detail on the three marketing systems in the previous section. Those are great places to start if you're on a budget or if you're looking for a smaller volume of deals. But if you want to increase the volume of deals or just try other strategies, there are plenty of other marketing systems available. I'll briefly describe a few, and you can do more homework on each if it looks interesting.

Car Signs

For years I had vinyl or magnetic signs on my vehicle that said "I Buy Houses" along with my phone number. I have bought at least ten properties that have made me hundreds of thousands of dollars now. The hundreds of dollars these signs cost was probably the best investment I ever made!

Vinyl Yard Signs

Early in my career, I also used vinyl yard signs that said "I Buy Houses." I'd put them in the yard of my houses that were being remodeled. I also put them on telephone poles and busy intersections. I learned the hard way that this is illegal in most towns and results in a fine. So make sure you know the local laws before putting out signs. But if it is possible, they are very effective at generating leads for a low cost!

Direct Mail

I've bought many properties by sending letters to a variety of different lists of property owners. These lists include absentee owners (don't live in the property), pre-foreclosures (the foreclosure court case has begun), tax liens (owe property taxes), owners with equity (owned for over ten years), multifamily owners, expired listings (from your MLS agent), and more.

Direct mail is a big subject that's beyond the scope of this book. But in short, I like my mailers to be personal. The messaging is personal, it comes in a personal-looking envelope, and it has my personal contact information. I find this increases my response rate compared to a more corporate, impersonal approach.

Websites and Advertising

We're in the internet age, so buying properties using a website can make a lot of sense. You essentially have a billboard that tells people how you can help and gives them a chance to get in touch with you. The motivated sellers will then contact you.

The trick is getting people to find your website. This involves paid advertising (usually on Google and Facebook) or getting your site to organically rank in Google search (known as search engine optimization or SEO). These online strategies cost more money and require expertise, but they can pay off big if you implement them well.

As I said in the beginning of the chapter, I made learning this subject of deal finding my top priority as a new investor. And it paid off big time in the form of hundreds of good deals over the past twenty years. If you want to learn even more about generating leads to buy properties, I recommend *Finding and Funding Great Deals* by fellow BiggerPockets author Anson Young. It will help you build your deal finding muscles even more.

TURNKEY COMPANIES

Before we move on from lead generation, I want to talk about one other opportunity to find deals. Turnkey investing is an approach to real estate investing in which you buy properties that have already been remodeled and have tenants in place. This allows you to avoid the hassle and risk of fixing up and renting properties yourself. An entire industry of turnkey companies has emerged to buy, fix up, and sell these turnkey properties to rental investors.

I include turnkey companies in this chapter because this may be a viable deal finding strategy for some small and mighty real estate investors. Especially if you have very little time to find deals or if you're a long-distance investor, turnkey investing can be attractive. The companies themselves are also easy to find on BiggerPockets or by Googling "turnkey rental providers." But there are some challenges and cautions to consider before you buy turnkey.

First, it's less likely that you will buy properties that have upfront equity building opportunities. The turnkey companies are in the business to make a profit, so they likely won't sell to you at a discount. And they've already forced the appreciation by remodeling it. Since you're paying a retail price, you'll need to ensure the cash flow and the other equity building drivers (principal paydown, passive appreciation) combine to still meet your financial criteria.

Second, turnkey companies have a built-in conflict of interest. They are selling the property to you for a profit while also making the case to you why it's a good deal. That doesn't mean they're bad people, but it does mean you need to do your own homework. Verify your own price and rental assumptions with independent team members. Hire your own inspectors. And run your own numbers. Basically, follow everything I teach you in this book as if you were buying it from any other source.

Third, as in any industry, there are good actors and bad actors among turnkey companies. The good actors will serve you well and give you an excellent experience. But bad actors can cause you to lose a lot of money. In the worst case, I've heard of people buying vacant lots who thought they were buying remodeled, rented houses. In other bad cases, I've heard of people buying properties with shoddy remodeling work and with other details not completed as promised.

Here's the key takeaway. Before you buy from a turnkey company or use them to manage your property, do thorough due diligence on the company itself. Meet the owners and founders. Talk to existing customers. Inspect their business systems and team members. Discuss their plans for future growth. If you see any red flags, move on. There are plenty of other options to buy good deals.

ONE-HUNDRED-LEAD CHALLENGE

You've now got a crash course in finding good deals. If you're already buying properties, hopefully you've learned some new techniques to try. And if you're brand-new, I hope you'll be able to use one or more of the marketing systems to begin generating leads as soon as possible.

While learning is fantastic, as someone who goes by the name "Coach Carson," the coach in me won't let you leave this chapter without a challenge to take action. Specifically, I want to challenge you to generate one hundred leads in the next four weeks.

In all my years of teaching and coaching others, I have seen that the successful students were always the ones who took action. They didn't simply read books or listen to podcasts. They practiced what they learned as quickly as possible!

I'd love for you to be one of those successful students right now. And here's how you can do it.

Using one or more of the marketing systems from this chapter, generate a hundred leads that could eventually turn into a deal. A lead could be an active MLS listing from your real estate agent. A lead could also be vacant property that you find from Driving for Dollars.

I know from experience that generating a hundred leads will give you other positive results. In the best case, you might find a deal to buy. But without a doubt, you'll also learn, get excited, and build momentum. And you'll also have the opportunity to negotiate for good deals, which is the topic of the next chapter.

CHAPTER 15
HOW TO SOLVE THE NEGOTIATION PUZZLE

The previous chapter was all about using marketing systems to generate leads from people who want to sell their house. But remember that is only the first step of the real estate deal funnel. Once a lead comes in, you have many more steps before it becomes a deal that you buy:

1. **Lead generation**
2. **Collect and prescreen leads**
3. **Gather information about the seller and the property**
4. **Make an offer**
5. **Follow up (if needed)**
6. **Put property under contract**
7. **Exercise due diligence and close the purchase**

In this chapter, we'll cover Step No. 2—Collecting and prescreening leads, and Step No. 3—Gathering information about the seller and the property. By mastering these steps, you'll know what to do with leads so that you can prepare to make offers to buy deals.

While the deal funnel presented this way seems very logical and organized, don't forget that *people* are at the center of everything. To make
progress in this funnel and to buy good real estate investments, you
must get a *yes* from these real people. In other words, you must solve
the negotiation puzzle.

THE VALUE OF NEGOTIATION SKILLS

Negotiation means different things to different people. As I see it,
negotiation is just a form of communication. It's a process that you use
to make agreements with people. And it's nothing new, because you
negotiate daily with family, coworkers, and friends, and in other smaller
interactions.

But in regular life, you may negotiate without consciously thinking
about it. In this chapter, however, I want to get you thinking about how
your negotiation skills can help you acquire better real estate investments. **Improving your ability to negotiate can literally create thousands of dollars more profit on your next deal.** For this reason, the
lessons you learn in this chapter can pay for the cost of this book many
times over. They can also become some of the most valuable skills of
your entire investment business.

WHAT IT MEANS TO WIN A NEGOTIATION

Most people think of negotiating as a battle. You put on your emotional
armor, and you prepare to outlast the other person. It's a bargaining
wrestling match back and forth until the strongest wins. In this style of
negotiation, one or both negotiators leave the ring with their emotions
and egos bruised.

Maybe there are some investors and entrepreneurs who succeed with
this approach. I've especially noticed it as a tactic with corporate-style
"it's just business" negotiators. But that's not the approach you'll learn
here. As a small and mighty real estate investor, we often live and work
in the towns where we negotiate. We may bump into the people we
negotiate with at the grocery store, and we want to be able to look them
in the eye without feeling awkward or guilty.

In short, we aren't willing to sacrifice people in the process of doing business. Instead, here's a better goal for a real estate negotiation:

> Buy a good deal while maintaining or improving my relationship with the other party.

This goal assumes I must buy a good deal because that's why I'm in business. But it also assumes I'm focused on serving the other person. Their goals, needs, and feelings are just as important as mine. But to accomplish this balancing act between my needs and theirs, I must play a completely different negotiation game. Instead of battling or playing tug-of-war, I have to solve a puzzle.

THE NEGOTIATION PUZZLE

Think back to the last time you worked on a puzzle. You open the box, dump the pieces on the table, and start with a pile of puzzle pieces. Some pieces are right side up, and others are upside down. The pieces are all disorganized, and they don't look anything like the picture on the cover of the box.

The beginning of a negotiation is a lot like this process of starting a puzzle. You'd like to make a deal, but there's no clear path on how to get there. Most of the essential information needed to solve the negotiation puzzle is still disorganized or unknown.

You Have Two Ears and One Mouth

Your first job as a solver of negotiation puzzles is to simply turn over the puzzle pieces. This means you listen and learn. And I want to emphasize the word *listen*. You have two ears and one mouth. That means you should listen at least twice as much as you speak!

As you listen, you'll learn about the other person and turn over more pieces. That's when the puzzle starts to make sense. You can begin to see the outline of a finished puzzle as you put the essential pieces together.

As with a real puzzle, negotiating in this way requires collaboration. Both you and the seller (or their agent) have to be willing to play the game and work together. More than anything, it requires trust because turning over puzzle pieces and sharing information can make you feel vulnerable.

My Old-School Lesson in Listening

When I was still a real estate rookie, I got a call from a woman named Eileen. She had received my letter in the mail, and she and her husband, Ed, had a house to sell. They were both retired Methodist ministers, and this house had been their home until they moved and rented it out.

Eileen was in her late sixties, and she was one of the sweetest and wisest people I've ever met. She's one of those types of people who have a twinkle in their eye. And when I talked to her on the phone, she pretty much took control of the conversation.

Eileen told me that she knew I was an investor, and she knew I had to make money. She also told me that a real estate agent had told her never to talk to someone like me. But she liked my personal letter, and she liked what she saw when she looked me up on Google. She wanted to meet, talk, and have us get to know one another. In short, we were going to *listen* to what each other had to say.

Human Beings Are Storytellers

We did meet, complete with folding chairs and a table that Ed and Eileen brought for the living room of their vacant house. And we did listen to one another. I learned stories about Ed and Eileen's family. I learned the precious memories that were formed in that house. Ed even shed a tear during one particularly moving story about his daughter.

And I learned about Ed and Eileen's journey from owning this house to buying a modest but wonderful retirement house on a little lake. The rent from this house was going to help them finish paying the mortgage on their retirement house. They had never made a lot of money as ministers, but this house was going to help them enjoy peaceful years at the lake, watching sunsets together on the porch.

But bad renters had ruined that plan. Not only did they stop paying rent, but they also trashed the house. Ed and Eileen were devastated to see how badly they treated their home. They weren't cut out to be landlords. After paying to repair the damage, they vowed not to rent the house again.

You Never Know Where Listening Will Take You

About that time, Ed and Eileen got my letter. I'll fast-forward the story to tell you that I bought their house. They also listened to me as I presented an alternative solution to simply selling the house through a real estate agent.

I offered to pay them a similar *net* price to what they would receive after paying commissions and costs. In Chapter 16, I'll explain more about how to make this type of offer. And they agreed to finance most of the purchase with seller carry-back financing. I bought a wonderful brick rental house with positive cash flow, and they got a passive income stream from a trustworthy person who would handle everything.

The final part of the story is that I continued the friendship I formed with Ed and Eileen. I would sometimes visit them for conversations on the porch overlooking the lake. It was my opportunity to hand deliver a report to update them on their investment with me. We became so close, in fact, that my wife and I asked Eileen to be the minister at our wedding a couple of years later. You never know where a negotiation will lead when you listen!

Not Every Negotiation Goes Smoothly

Ed and Eileen taught me the power and the joy of listening. It's truly a negotiation technique, because it's the key to turning over all the essential puzzle pieces. But it's also just being a normal, curious human being. Listening and telling stories is how we get to know people and build relationships.

But with that said, I want to acknowledge up front that real-life negotiations don't always end up as smooth and wonderful as my conversations with Ed and Eileen. I've had many other situations where the seller cut the conversation short and held their cards close to their chest. This especially happens with MLS leads using real estate agents.

The best real estate agents I've hired in the past do use the listening and puzzle solving approach I've described here. But many others are more transactional and even combative during negotiations. You or your agent can always ask the listing agent for more information about the seller, like what else they might want in addition to price. Perhaps they need to rent the house back or close by a certain day.

But if an agent or the seller chooses to play a less collaborative type of game, you just have to go with it. Ask questions and do your best with the information you can gather. But just know every negotiation will be different.

This reality is one reason I love generating off-market (non-MLS) leads to buy properties. Although I've bought plenty of deals from the MLS, most of my best deals have come by negotiating directly with the seller. These sellers and I have been able to put together some beautiful puzzles, some of which neither one of us expected to see in the beginning.

After my experience with Ed and Eileen, I became hooked on the powerful art of negotiation. I wanted to learn as much as I could about how to solve more puzzles as a real estate investor. And as I studied more, I learned that one of the best negotiation puzzle solvers of all time wrote down his advice thousands of years ago. It was the philosopher Aristotle in ancient Greece.

ARISTOTLE'S ART OF PERSUASION

Back in the fourth century BCE, Aristotle wrote a book called *The Art of Rhetoric*. Although the title sounds dry, it contains some of the best lessons about human communication ever written. The work is also known as *The Art of Persuasion* because it gives practical lessons about how to persuade others to your way of thinking.

Aristotle's approach to persuasion is a lot like our metaphor of the puzzle pieces. He defined rhetoric (or negotiation) as the art of "observing … the means of persuasion."[46] In other words, you have to discover the pieces of the puzzle that may persuade this particular person in this particular situation.

In my negotiation with Ed and Eileen, the puzzle pieces were a series of stories. Those stories communicated their emotional attachment to the home. They told me why this home mattered to them. And they told me about their journey to the present day.

But the stories also gave me the key to solving their situation. Once I learned the key pieces, I could organize them into a request for something. In my case with Ed and Eileen, that request was an offer to buy their property in a certain way.

---

46 Aristotle, *Rhetoric*. Translated by W. Rhys Roberts. The Internet Classics Archive by Daniel C. Stevenson, Web Atomics. World Wide Web presentation is copyright (C) 1994-2000, Daniel C. Stevenson, Web Atomics, http://classics.mit.edu/Aristotle/rhetoric.1.i.html.

In every negotiation—and this applied to my negotiation with Ed and Eileen—there are three unique but related ways to persuade someone. Aristotle called these the three means of persuasion.

1. **Ethos/Character:** The first method focuses on you, the person looking to buy the property. Most of all it relates to your character and credibility with the other person.
2. **Pathos/Emotion:** The second method focuses on the other person in the negotiation. It's about impacting the seller's emotions and how they feel.
3. **Logos/Reason:** The third method focuses on the offer or request itself. To be persuasive, the offer must be reasonable and solve the other person's problem.

To improve your skills as a negotiator, Aristotle said you must get better at each of these methods of persuasion. And as a small and mighty real estate investor, you must learn how to specifically apply these methods to the process of buying properties. To help you do that, I'll share some tips and stories for each of the three methods.

1. ETHOS—HOW TO IMPROVE YOUR CREDIBILITY

Credibility is about earning people's trust. Eileen began our negotiation by looking me up on Google. People used to judge a book by its cover, but now they judge you by a Google search! Fair or not, this is how people begin learning whether they can trust you.

Be Authentically Yourself

Beyond keeping your internet reputation clean, the quickest way to build trust is to simply be yourself. People will quickly recognize you as authentic (or fake) through your words, body language, and other non-verbal communication. When I talked to Ed and Eileen, I was a rookie real estate investor. I acknowledged that, and they were okay with it. If I had tried to fake being a big shot, they would have seen through me.

Tell Your Story

The second way to build your credibility is to tell your story. With Ed and Eileen, I told them about my upbringing outside of Atlanta, Georgia, and why I moved to South Carolina to go to school at Clemson University. I also told them briefly about my career journey—deciding not to pursue professional football or medical school and instead becoming a full-time entrepreneur.

These opening stories had nothing to do with their real estate, but they made me a real person. They also allowed me to share something I had in common with Ed and Eileen. I explained that I grew up attending a Methodist church, which was the same denomination that they had been ministers in.

That may seem like a lucky coincidence. But in my experience, there's *always* something we have in common with another person. It's our job as negotiators to discover it by listening to their stories. And when we do, it builds credibility and brings you closer to the other person.

Let Other People Tell Your Story

For years, I've also used a third way of building credibility with property owners. Whenever I visit a seller's property, which we'll talk about more in the next chapter, I bring a physical packet of reference letters and testimonials. When I first arrived at Ed and Eileen's house, I handed them these letters to review. While I walked around to inspect the house, they read *other people* telling them that I'm trustworthy. This is much more effective than me telling them myself.

When I was a beginner, my letters came from college professors, my football coach, my banker, my attorney, and other people locally who could vouch for my character. But over time as I bought more properties from sellers, I also collected testimonials and happy pictures at closings with the sellers. In fact, here's my picture with Ed and Eileen when I was 25 years old!

These photos and testimonials share the positive experience that the sellers had working with me. They provide a sort of social proof of my credibility that I couldn't create on my own.

2. PATHOS—HOW TO TOUCH THE EMOTIONS

Aristotle taught that people make different decisions when they experience positive emotions (happiness, relaxation, laughter) than when they experience negative emotions (anger, fear, anxiety). Therefore, as a negotiator you can harness the emotions of the other party to help with persuasion. There are a couple of different ways to do that when buying properties.

Empathetic Listening

The first way is to listen empathetically. In *The 7 Habits of Highly Effective People*, author Stephen R. Covey says that "[w]hen you listen with empathy to another person, you give that person psychological air. And after that vital need is met, you can focus on influencing or problem solving."[47]

During my first conversation with Ed and Eileen, I empathetically and actively listened. When they began telling the stories about renting their house, I showed that I was engaged and asked follow-up questions. Then I stopped talking to cue that I wanted them to go deeper and tell

---

47 Stephen R. Covey, *The 7 Habits of Highly Effective People* (New York: Simon & Schuster, 2004), p. 253.

me more. When you listen in this way, it communicates that the other person is important to you.

Empathetic listening also means to listen with the goal of understanding. In his book *Never Split the Difference*, former FBI hostage negotiator Chris Voss says your goal should be to hear a "That's right!" from the other person you're negotiating with. When you hear that, it means you've listened carefully and then reflected back to that person both the feeling and the facts of their situation.

When I heard the story about Ed and Eileen's bad tenants, that was an important moment. It was the underlying emotion of that situation that led to the decision to sell the house. I assumed after hearing the story that they would never rent again, but I asked them if that was true. And I got an emphatic "that's right" and both of them nodding their heads.

Use Metaphors and Stories to Connect to Emotions

A second way to affect emotions is by using stories, analogies, and metaphors. We humans understand other people and the world around us primarily through stories. And most of all, stories connect us to our emotions.

I already mentioned that I regularly tell a story about myself to build credibility. But I also like to use other stories or metaphors during the negotiation. For example, after positive negotiation experiences with Ed and Eileen and others, I started telling the "solve a puzzle" metaphor to other sellers. I used it to diffuse the initial tension and to explain to the seller why I wanted to ask questions and learn as much as possible about them.

When a seller first meets you, they're understandably skeptical. They're asking themselves the question "How does this person fit into the story of my life?" And based on popular myths, they may be imagining negative stories, like investors are greedy and just want to take advantage of them. The emotion of *that* story connects them to tension, fear, and a need to protect themselves.

But the "puzzle solver" metaphor connects to a different place. If they believe it, it makes them feel more relaxed and open. You've transformed the story of how you fit into their lives from a battle to a fun, cooperative game.

Use Stories to Explain Complicated or Technical Offers

I also use stories to help the seller understand a very technical offer in a human way. For example, if I ask a seller to finance the property to me, I could use technical real estate jargon like monthly installments, promissory notes, and a mortgage as collateral. But if they don't understand that jargon, which is likely, they'll feel nervous, guarded, and less likely to say yes.

Instead, I could translate that jargon into a story. I might tell them that after a fast and seamless closing on the date of their choice, they'll start getting automatic payments from me on the first of every month. Instead of being the landlord, they'll be like the bank. They'll never have to deal with any property headaches again because I'll make them my headaches.

And in a worst-case scenario, like if I get hit by a bus, I hope they'll shed a tear or two and attend my funeral. But after that's over, they'll still have the real estate if my heirs don't follow through. They can take back the property, keep my down payment and all the improvements I've made to the property, and resell it again.

Empathetic listening and stories are the key to pathos or emotion, which is the key to unlock persuasion. But in the end, pathos isn't enough. You also have to appeal to their logic, or logos.

3. LOGOS—HOW TO CREATE REASONABLE SOLUTIONS

Logos is an appeal to reason. If you've succeeded with ethos and pathos, you'll ultimately have an opportunity to offer a reasonable solution to the other person's situation. The "truth" of the negotiation is whether you can satisfy the other person's needs or not.

In the vocabulary of real estate, logos is making an offer to the seller. In the next chapter on making and presenting offers, we'll dig into this subject in much greater detail. But I want to point out now that a large percentage of my negotiations with sellers *don't* lead to a yes. Getting a yes from one out of four sellers I make an offer to would be successful. This means that three out of four people I negotiate with perceive other solutions to be the more reasonable choice for them. And that's okay!

I've learned that the most effective negotiating strategy is to just let go of the result. Do your best to listen, learn, and offer solutions to someone's situation. Build credibility and appeal to their emotions and to their reason. And then let them make their own decision.

If you follow this process, you'll purchase *plenty* of good deals. You'll own properties like the one I bought from Ed and Eileen, which earn profits, build wealth, and generate cash flow. But whether you buy their property or not, you'll maintain or build relationships with the people on the other side of the negotiation. And that's always a win!

In the rest of this chapter, I want to return to the concept of the deal funnel and focus on some practical methods to handle seller leads as they come in from your marketing systems.

STEP NO. 2: COLLECT & PRESCREEN LEADS

If you do a good job of applying what you learned in the last chapter, you'll have leads coming in from your marketing systems. Some of them will be listed properties on the MLS. Others will be individual property owners who contact you from Driving for Dollars, referrals, or some other marketing system. In all these cases, you want to create an organized system to collect and make the most of these leads so that you can have more successful negotiations.

Lead Collection System

For years, I wrote down every lead in a simple spreadsheet that identified the seller's (or agent's) name, contact info, source of lead (aka marketing system), and additional notes. I've included a copy of the spreadsheet at www.biggerpockets.com/smallandmightybonus. The spreadsheet kept me organized and avoided chaos as more leads came in.

The spreadsheet also allowed me to learn from my marketing efforts. I tracked the progress of each lead all the way to a deal so that I could estimate my conversion rates from one step to another. I also used the results to track my return on investment for each marketing system by seeing which system led to deals.

With technology now, you can replace my spreadsheet with a CRM (customer relationship management) app or other project management software. But I recommend you keep things as simple as possible, especially early on. Find success doing the basics before you optimize and spend time and money on technology.

The Process to Prescreen Leads and Find Potential Deals

After collecting the lead, you begin communicating with the seller (or their agent). This is also the step where you want to prescreen the lead to determine if it has the potential for a good deal. Here's how that prescreening process works:

1. **Connect with Seller and Learn:** Remember the lessons about negotiation. Use your first communication with the seller to build credibility, listen, and explain the basic benefits of your service. You want to learn as much as you can about the other person, their reason for selling, and the basics of the property itself.

2. **Decide—Hot or Cold:** This step of negotiation is about prescreening. Not every lead is a deal. Remember from the chapters on deal analysis that you want deals that produce income, grow equity, or do both. In this step, you gather information to help you determine if this lead has potential to meet your analysis goals or not.

3. **Take Action:** There are two possible actions, depending on whether the lead is hot or cold.
   - **Hot:** If a lead is hot, move to the next step of the negotiation. This usually means you or your agent will visit the property to gather more information and to continue the negotiation with the seller.
   - **Cold:** If the lead is cold, politely move on. Don't spend more time on it.

Connecting with Sellers (Or Their Agents)

This first step of connecting with and learning from the seller will vary depending on the type of lead. MLS leads are much more impersonal and transactional. You don't typically get to know the seller or communicate with them because there are agents in-between. But if your agent can ask and learn anything about the seller, it always helps. You can also do a quick search of the public records to see who the seller is and how long they've owned the property.

A lead directly from the seller, however, is different. You have the opportunity to directly connect with and learn from them. This is one of the most valuable opportunities of the entire negotiation.

If your lead is directly from the seller, take the opportunity to get on the phone and have a real conversation. I prefer a phone conversation because it's much easier to build a human-to-human connection with the seller than texting back and forth. A phone conversation also allows you to better use all three means of persuasion—ethos, pathos, and logos—while you also try to determine if this is a hot or cold lead.

How to Decide Hot vs. Cold Leads

If you do a good job generating leads, you'll get more than you can handle. So you have to do this second step and quickly determine whether it's worth a further investment of your time and energy. To do that, I like to classify leads as hot or cold. It's an informal process that uses these three criteria:

1. **Buy Box:** How well does this lead meet your criteria for location, property type, and property characteristics?
2. **Motivation:** How strong are the signs of seller motivation?
   - For example, if an MLS seller has repeatedly dropped their price or if it's been on the market for a long time, this could mean a motivated seller.
   - If you talk directly to the seller, is there a nonfinancial motivation for selling? To draw out this information on the phone, I like to borrow a phrase from Jack Miller, a real estate teacher I learned from early in my career. I ask the seller: "Now, why would you sell a nice house/property like that?" Be silent after the question and just let them talk. You'll learn valuable details about their motivation for selling.
3. **Equity:** Does the property obviously have equity building opportunities, such as an already low price, forced appreciation potential, or a rare location? And, if possible, can you find out whether the property owner has equity (aka a gap between their debt balance and the property value)? You can sometimes guess this by a quick search in the public records to see their mortgage age and/or their length of ownership. Or you can simply ask them over the phone. I'll sometimes say, "If I were to buy the property from you, would I be paying off a mortgage or do you already own it free and clear?" Not everyone will answer the question, but it can be helpful if they do.

3 of 3 = Hot: If a deal has all three criteria for a hot lead, I try to make an appointment to see the property that day or as soon as possible. The best deals will always move fast. This is what all your hard work has led to, so reshuffle your schedule and make it happen!

2 of 3 = Warm: If a deal has two of the three criteria, it's on the border of hot and cold. Unless I'm just overwhelmed with hot leads (which does happen!), I'll probably still make an appointment to view the property. For example, a property may meet my buy box and have good opportunities to build equity. But the seller may be unmotivated. Motivation is nice, but it's not a requirement if the deal looks good otherwise.

0 of 3; 1 of 3 = Cold: If a deal has zero or one of the three criteria, it's a cold lead. For example, the property may fit my buy box for location and property type, but the seller is extremely unmotivated, asking for more than the property is worth, and there are no opportunities to force the value higher. I'll thank the seller for calling but tell them it doesn't seem to fit my criteria right now. With a cold MLS lead, I'll just ignore it and wait to see if they drop the price in the future.

If your screening results are anything like mine, it's possible that you have three cold leads for every one warm or hot lead. For those remaining 25 percent of leads that are warm or hot, it's time to move to the next step of the negotiation. With both MLS leads and direct-to-seller leads, this normally means viewing the property to gather more information about the seller and the property.

STEP NO. 3: GATHER INFORMATION ABOUT THE SELLER AND THE PROPERTY

Each deal that you negotiate will be a little different. But in most cases, you or your agent will want to view the property in person so that you can gather more information. Like Step No. 2, you will want to focus on gathering information about both the seller and the property.

Face-to-Face Negotiation with Sellers

Meeting face-to-face with a seller is the best approach if you want to follow Aristotle's advice of using all available means of persuasion. In-person meetings allow both you and the seller to get to know each other better. We communicate not only with our words, but also with our tone, voice inflections, body language, and other nonverbal forms of communication.

I prefer to meet the seller at the property, especially if it's their residence or if they inherited the property. Their home is a rich environment of pictures and other clues about their personality, values, and life. Their home is also an opportunity to take conversational off-ramps.

Take Conversational Off-Ramps

As you talk with the seller, use a mindset that I learned from a real estate teacher of mine named Greg Pinneo. Imagine that the conversation is an interstate highway that takes you toward your goal, a real estate deal. You'll be tempted to stay on the four-lane highway, which is the conversation about the property. But don't be afraid to take off-ramps, which are opportunities to talk about the seller.

For example, if the seller's toddler granddaughter walks into the room, shift the conversation to her. It may seem like a detour, but this conversational off-ramp can be valuable. First, it's the authentic, human thing to do. It builds credibility and warms up the conversation beyond the robotic focus on real estate. Second, off-ramps can often turn over valuable puzzle pieces in the negotiation. Later, when you make an offer, you can wrap the technical aspects of the deal with their personal story to show how relevant and helpful it is.

Your in-person meeting with the seller could be thirty minutes or three hours. I've had both! If the deal has potential, the longer meetings are not a waste of time. You'll be turning over a lot of puzzle pieces, building credibility, and giving yourself time to think about an eventual offer to buy the property.

Find a Seller Negotiation Approach That Works for You

My hands-on, meet-at-the-seller's-house approach isn't the only right way to go about it. John Schaub, for example, asks sellers to come to his office and bring all their house paperwork with them. If they do that, it shows him they are motivated. I've also negotiated good deals over the phone and over email. It's harder to handcraft a deal that way, but it's still possible.

You'll have to find an approach to negotiating with sellers that works for you. But no matter how you approach it, you'll need to either make an offer or decide that the property doesn't meet your criteria. I'll talk more about making offers in the next chapter. But to first decide whether the property is worth making an offer on, you need to gather more information about the property itself through an in-person property viewing.

In-Person Property Viewing

In addition to talking with the seller, you will want to spend time investigating the property and the neighborhood around it. If you're long distance and can't be at the property yourself, have your agent or a trusted person on the ground record a detailed video that can be shared with you later. Although this investigation isn't as thorough as an actual inspection or appraisal of the property, you still want to be thorough enough to make a confident offer.

Here's a list of things my real estate agent or I try to verify while at the property during this initial viewing:

Red flag problems to avoid

- **Neighborhood:** Walk the neighborhood at different times of day. Any issues with crime? Is the property too far from amenities?
- **Nuisances:** Noise? Bad smells? High-voltage power lines in backyard, etc.?
- **Street and Sidewalks:** Is the property on a busy street? Are there sidewalks or other easy places to walk?
- **Neighbors:** Are there issues with the neighbors that would make your property difficult to rent or sell? For example, loud or vicious dogs?
- **Water:** Is the lot in a flood plain? Does the building sit "below grade" where water runs toward the house and could create moisture problems?
- **Trees:** Are there large trees next to the building? Any at risk of falling?
- **Other:** Old buried oil tanks (look for valves and meters), environmental issues (like backyard auto shop waste dumped on ground).

Property Value

- **Property Characteristics:** Verify the primary factors that affect value, such as number of bedrooms and baths, square footage (rough estimate), amenities, and layout. Look for strange layouts or other problems that could hurt the value.

- **Comps:** Ride by comparable, recently sold properties. Make notes about similarities and differences that make them worse or better than subject property.
- **CMA:** Use comparable property information to perform a Comparative Market Analysis (CMA). You can also ask your real estate agent to perform one for you. If the property needs to be repaired or if you plan to force the appreciation somehow, do a CMA before and after those improvements.

Repair estimate

- **Repair list:** Make a list of any obvious repairs needed. Keep in mind both necessary repairs for safety and code requirements and other cosmetic repairs for optimal leasing (like replacing functional but ugly carpet with luxury vinyl plank floors). Use your property manager and contractor team members to help. At this stage during an initial viewing, it doesn't always make sense to do a thorough inspection. But they can give you approximate values that allow you to make an offer contingent upon further inspection.
- **Use the video:** The video you take during your walk-through can be uploaded and shared with your contractors, property manager, or investor friends to help you with this step.
- **Improve this skill over time:** Estimating repairs and their cost is both an art and a science. As you build this skill over time, it will make you a better investor. My favorite recommendation and the system I use can be found in *The Book on Estimating Rehab Costs* by J Scott. Look for it in the BiggerPockets bookstore.

PRACTICE MAKES PERFECT

Just as you learned the skill of lead generation in the previous chapter, you'll get better at the skills of this chapter—seller negotiations, prescreening leads, and viewing properties—with practice. If you are brand-new to negotiations, you will likely feel awkward at first. So was I as a new investor! But like when you learned to ride a bike, your initial awkwardness will eventually turn into confidence as you practice over and over.

The best way to build that confidence is to do it. You need to practice talking to sellers and looking at properties. Remember, I was a rookie when I first talked to Ed and Eileen. I made plenty of mistakes, but I learned a lot in the process (and still got the deal!).

You will also want to practice prescreening leads in your location. And you need to visit properties so that you see firsthand what it's like. This is one reason I love the Driving for Dollars marketing system. It gives you the opportunity to find properties and practice as soon as today if you're ambitious.

You can also use MLS leads as any easy first step to practice. If you have the right real estate agent, they should have some experience negotiating and viewing properties. You can lean on their experience and borrow their confidence at first. But eventually don't be afraid to guide the process. You're the one buying the property and investing your money, so ultimately, it's your responsibility.

Once you've had some success prescreening leads, talking to sellers, and viewing properties, it will be time to make an offer. And that's the topic of the next chapter.

CHAPTER 16

HOW TO CONFIDENTLY MAKE OFFERS THAT GET ACCEPTED

I n December 2003 I made the very first offer to buy a property on my own. I was 23 years old, and my real estate agent, Toni, sent us a promising property. It was a vacant house in our target market, and it was owned by a bank. They had recently foreclosed on the property, and the asking price was below the full value potential of the house.

In my previous twelve months in the role of bird dog, I found twelve properties that I helped another investor to buy. But this was different. It was my deal. For better or worse, my business partner and I would have to finance, fix up, pay expenses, and be responsible for everything.

We visited the property to do our inspection, estimate the repairs, and guess the resale value of the house. We used that information to run the numbers and to determine our maximum allowable offer (MAO). Then we told our agent a number slightly below our MAO, and she prepared the contract paperwork for an offer. Signing that paperwork was both exciting and terrifying.

But the real excitement (and terror!) began when they eventually accepted our offer. After a day of back-and-forth negotiations, we were officially in the real estate investing business. As with every property I've bought since then, it all began with an offer.

In this chapter I'll help you master the process of making an offer. We'll cover making offers on properties listed by real estate agents, and we'll cover making offers directly to sellers. I'll also share tips to increase the likelihood that your offers will be accepted. When the chapter is over, you'll be ready to confidently make more offers on your own.

REVIEW: THE DEAL FUNNEL

In previous chapters, we began the deal funnel by learning how to generate leads (Step No. 1), collect and prescreen these leads (Step No. 2), and then gather information about the seller and the property to help with our negotiation (Step No. 3). In this chapter, we've arrived at Steps No. 4, No. 5, and No. 6 where you make an offer, follow up when needed, and put the property under contract.

We'll begin with the basics of how to make an offer.

STEP NO. 4: MAKE AN OFFER

An offer is the natural next step of your negotiation with the seller. It's basically a written request to buy their property. After receiving the offer, they can say either yes or no. But your approach to an offer will be different depending on whether you offer through an agent or whether you offer directly to the seller.

Offering Through an Agent

When you make an offer to buy a property listed by a real estate agent, the offer will usually be in contract form. Most agents use a purchase contract template created by their local association of fellow agents. Your signature on this contract means you promise to buy the property at the price and on the terms included in the contract.

If the seller likes your offer as is, they can sign the contract to make it a mutual agreement. If they like part of it but not others, they can send a counteroffer on an edited contract. And if they don't like the offer at all, they can ignore it until the offer expires (a date stated in the contract), or they can send a message of rejection.

Offer Directly to the Seller

When you make an offer to buy a property directly from the seller, you can also use a contract to make an offer. But I've found that it works better to start with a simple one-page explanation called a Memorandum of Offer. This document usually includes the price, closing date, and any contingencies, like the example below.

Memorandum of Offer

Offers to Purchase: 123 Normal Street, Greenville, SC

All of these offers include the following:
- As-is purchase. You do not have to do any repairs or improvements.
- Close on a date of your choice.

1) $160,000 = Price
- $20,000 = Down Payment
- $140,000 = Seller Financing note
  - Payment = $700/mo
  - Interest Rate = 4%
  - All principal due in 25 years

2) $140,000 = Price
- All cash at closing
- Flexible closing date

_____   _____

Seller   Date

_____   _____

Seller   Date

_____   _____

Buyer   Date

Most sellers aren't familiar or comfortable with contracts, so this memorandum is less intimidating and makes for better discussion. If the seller accepts the basics of my offer, I can then put the offer into contract form. If they don't accept my offer, that's often where the real negotiation begins!

When the Real Negotiation Begins

If you're sitting face-to-face with the seller when you make your offer (my preference), you will learn a lot in the moment right after your offer. Go back into active listening mode. Observe their verbal and nonverbal communication. If they reject your offer, ask them questions. Instead of accepting their simple "no," see if they will tell you what they will do instead.

In this stage of the negotiation, you'll often learn the true motivations and priorities of the seller. You might hear a statement like "I can't accept your offer because I won't be able to [whatever their goal is]." Don't take the rejection personally. See this as an opportunity to continue turning over important puzzle pieces in the seller's situation.

For example, let's say a seller told you, "I can't accept your offer because I won't be able to buy the next property I've been looking at." You should then start asking questions about that other property. What's it like? How much does it cost? Do they plan to finance it or pay all cash? These open-ended questions turn over more puzzle pieces that were originally hidden.

Eventually you can end that line of questions with a theoretical question, "So from what I understand, the main financial goal of selling this house is being able to purchase this other house or one like it?" You want to get a head nod and a "that's right" from the seller.

You may or may not be able to solve that problem. But you can try thinking creatively and put yourself in their shoes. For example, perhaps you know someone who has a house like that at a much lower price!

You can also reframe your offer so that it's focused on that goal. If you have room to come up on your price, you can make a counteroffer. You can then help the seller connect the dots between your new offer and how it can solve their problem.

This is also the stage of the negotiation where you must address objections. And the biggest objection is usually about price.

COMPARING YOUR OFFER TO THE NET SALES PRICE

Because price is such a big issue, I like to help the seller contrast my offer price with their other options. Very often they begin by comparing my offer to their perceived full value of the property. But they usually aren't comparing apples with apples.

For example, they may be comparing my offer to an automatically generated market value on Zillow. Or they may compare my price to an overly optimistic price from a real estate agent. But the most important number isn't those potential market prices. What really matters is what they'll get to keep in the end. This important number is called the *net* sales price or the price after all expenses.

Before I even make an offer directly to a seller, I go through the exercise of showing the seller their potential net sales price through a traditional sale. I deduct commissions, closing costs, holding costs, and repairs. This final net price is often 10 percent to 30 percent less than the market price, depending on the number of repairs. Here's an example.

NET SALES PRICE

Market value	$250,000
Real estate agent commission – 6%	- $15,000
Seller closing costs – 2%	- $5,000
Holding costs (taxes, insurance, utilities) – 2%	- $5,000
Repairs to make ready for sale	- $50,000
= Net Price After Expenses	**$175,000**

My cash offer is still usually less than this net price. I need to make a profit, after all, and I tell them that up front. But if my offer is $150,000, the difference between my price and the $175,000 *net* sales price is only $25,000. This is much closer than the $100,000 difference between $250,000 and $150,000! This allows the seller to decide whether the cost of my services (aka my profit margin) is worth the other benefits like an as-is, cash, flexible sale.

This net value exercise also sets up another of my favorite strategies, making multiple offers.

MAKING MULTIPLE OFFERS

When I am making offers directly to sellers, I like to include multiple options for the seller to choose from. For example, one offer may be all cash with a quick close at my lowest price. A second offer may be requesting attractive seller-financing terms at my highest price. And a third offer may be a medium price with less attractive seller-financing terms, for example, with a larger down payment and a shorter length of financing.

In the chapter on financing, I'll share more details about how seller financing works. But for now, the point is the negotiating benefit that multiple offers give you. Normally a seller has one offer, and their choice is to say yes or no. But now they have a choice among three options. And they can compare each of those options to the net price I have already given them. Their response to these three options can turn over even more puzzle pieces and lead to a productive discussion about their true priorities.

Case Study of Making Multiple Offers

I once bought a property from a gentleman in his eighties. It was a rental house that needed a lot of work, and he was tired of dealing with it. Sitting in his living room, I presented three offers to him. He took out his pen and quickly crossed out the two lower-priced offers. Then he crossed out the down payment of the highest price offer and put a question mark next to my owner-financing proposal. But he circled the price and said, "That'll work."

He initially rejected almost everything on my offer sheet, but we had a place to start. And this led to discussions about his priorities and how an adapted offer might solve those priorities. In the end, I bought the property with seller financing, a small down payment, zero percent interest, and payments that started off very small and gradually increased over a two-year period. That gave me time to spend money fixing up the house and getting it rented.

In the end, he no longer had to deal with the property, and he got his desired price. I got terms that allowed me to make money with positive cash flow, an aggressively amortizing loan, and a well-located property that would passively appreciate over time. Making multiple offers increased my chances of getting to that end goal.

Many Sellers Get Stuck on Price

It's very common to find sellers who are stuck on price like my seller was in this example. If you can figure out a way to make money on a property while still paying their price, you'll increase the number of offers you get accepted. The secret to making this work is getting excellent seller-financing terms.

This does not mean you should overpay for a property. When I've done this, I still pay at or a little below full price. It's just a reminder that you don't have to get a bargain price when you buy excellent real estate with great terms. If creative offers like seller financing or lease options allow you to have positive cash flow, quickly build equity through amortization, and safely hold on while a good property appreciates, you should use that to your advantage in negotiations!

Now let's look at even more ways to increase the likelihood that your offer will be accepted.

TEN TIPS TO GET MORE OF YOUR OFFERS ACCEPTED

Up to this point, you've done lot of work to generate leads, prescreen those leads, and evaluate the property to ensure it meets your criteria. Now you want to do everything you can to increase your chances that your offer will be accepted. Here are ten tips to help you do that.

1. Be the Only Offer

When you are the only buyer making an offer on a property, you increase the chances of the offer being accepted. The seller is more likely to consider your offer, negotiate, and counteroffer if there aren't other obvious options. Although this can happen occasionally on MLS properties, generating off-market leads through other marketing systems will give you the best opportunity to make offers with little or no competition.

2. Be the First Offer

Especially on the MLS, you need to make offers *fast*. Many sellers simply accept the first offer that meets their needs. So if you see a good deal come in from your MLS leads, jump on it right away. As soon as possible, go view the property (or have your agent view it) and make your offer. If you even wait hours to make an offer, you will probably miss out. Other buyers will already beat you to the deal.

With most MLS properties, the seller has already picked an opening "offer" with their list price. So it makes sense to be the first offer. But when you negotiate directly with sellers, don't be too quick to make your offer during negotiations. Let the seller make the first offer by naming a price. Most of the time, this price will be higher than what you're willing to pay. But occasionally, their price will be *lower* than you would have paid. Letting them be first can pay off.

3. Remove the Financing Contingency

Make strong offers if you want to increase your acceptance rate. One way to make a stronger offer is to remove your financing contingency. You shouldn't do this if you are unsure about your ability to get financing. But if you have cash, a HELOC (home equity line of credit), or a reliable private lender, removing your financing contingency can increase your acceptance rate on offers.

4. Buy in As-Is Condition

Some of your best property purchases will need repairs and cleanup. If you offer to buy the property in its as-is condition, the seller will know they don't have to deal with the hassle or risk of handling those repairs. That can increase the likelihood that your offer is accepted.

Even with an as-is offer, you can still get an inspection to understand exactly what kind of cost and risk you're taking on. You can do your own inspection, but I normally pay for a professional inspection from an inspector or a general contractor. If you have an inspection contingency, you would still be able to get out of the contract or renegotiate if you found a major unexpected problem.

5. Remove the Inspection Contingency

I recommend that most investors, especially new ones, use a well-drafted inspection contingency to protect yourself. But as you gain experience and confidence, strategically removing an inspection contingency can increase your chances of getting an offer accepted. This removes one more layer of uncertainty for the seller, and it increases the strength of your offer.

I bought an MLS property one time that had multiple offers on the very first day. It was a four-unit rental property in my target market that had repair and tenant problems. But it was listed at a low price of $140,000. After $20,000 to $30,000 of repairs, I knew this property would be worth $200,000 or more and rent for $2,400 per month.

The listing came on the MLS at 8:00 a.m. I saw the listing on my computer at 8:30 a.m., and I made an appointment to meet my handyman at the property at 9:15 a.m. We spent forty-five minutes crawling in every part of the property so that we could estimate the repair costs. I then made an offer at 10:30 a.m.

My offer was $135,000, no financing contingency, no inspection contingency, and close the sale in seven days. My offer was about as certain and fast as it could possibly be. As a result, I got a call from the listing agent to see if I could come up to $139,000 with the same terms. He had received at least five offers, some of them over list price, but he and the seller knew my offer was for real. That's why I got the call, and that's why we own the property today.

6. Increase Your Earnest Money Deposit

An earnest money deposit shows the buyer's good faith and intention to purchase the property. I normally make a $500 or $1,000 earnest money deposit on listed properties. If you have extra money in the bank and find yourself in a competitive situation, consider increasing your earnest money deposit. This shows the seller you have more financial resources, and it can make your offer appear stronger.

In most cases, the only risk is that it will be tied up for a period without interest. And for most investor purchases, this is only two to four weeks. Plus, if you have an inspection contingency, you should be able to get your money back.

There is, however, a risk that your earnest money could get tied up in mediation or court arbitration should you have a conflict with the seller. So you never want to make more of a deposit than you're willing to lose. Keep that risk in mind before raising your deposit amount.

7. Be Flexible on Timing

In my story of the four-unit offer, did you notice that the *timing* of my offer increased the strength of my offer? Because I could close so fast, the seller knew they could get their cash quickly and move on from this property. In many cases, speed is worth money to the seller. In other cases, patience and flexibility are worth more than speed. One time I made an offer directly to the seller that gave them a window of three months to sell me the property. All they had to do was give me seven days' notice and I would close. I made this offer because I knew the seller was moving across the country and needed to buy a new house.

Because they knew their house would be sold, they could go shopping for a new property with my money before they moved. My offer was less than they could have made listing on the open market, but my offer solved their problem. Presenting the flexibility of my offer as a potential solution is what got me the deal.

8. Solve the Seller's Emotional Problem

I bought another house directly from a seller by purchasing the house and then letting them lease the house back for three months. First, this gave them the money they needed to fund a down payment on their new house, which was under construction. But second, this gave them time to enjoy their final Christmas at home. This house had been the place for many family memories over a twenty-year period. One final Christmas in their home gave them a chance for emotional closure.

I've bought many properties from people who inherited the house from a relative. In most cases, there was a *lot* of personal stuff in the house. In my offer, I included a statement that they could leave whatever they didn't want, and we would handle it. In addition to the practical cost savings, this would give them enormous emotional relief because giving away or getting rid of stuff while thinking of their loved one could be very difficult.

Some problems to solve are practical and financial. Other problems are emotional. If you can *listen* for these emotional negotiation puzzle pieces, you can creatively find ways to solve them and get more offers accepted.

9. Tell a Story

In the last chapter, I mentioned that stories are a key tool in your negotiation toolbox. In the language of Aristotle, they build your credibility (ethos) and they help touch the emotions of your audience (pathos).

Because stories are so powerful, be sure to include your story as a part of your offer.

One way to do this is a cover letter. I've had many students include a letter that tells their story as part of their offer on an MLS property. For example, when these small and mighty real estate investors were buying a house hack, they told the seller about their situation. They let them know a little about who they were, and they told them how this property would positively affect their life and the life of their kids (if applicable).

People become emotionally attached to their properties. Knowing the story of the person who will live there makes a difference. If there are two relatively equal offers, your story can push you over the edge. Even if this doesn't work in every case, it's worth making it a part of your practice.

10. Make a Net Offer

This strategy is related to the net sales price I covered earlier. But it's got a slightly different angle. A net offer means that, as the buyer, you offer to pay for all the closing costs. For the seller, it means that your price is what they will actually walk away with at closing.

With an offer directly to a seller, you can then compare this net *offer* to the net *market sales price* I discussed earlier. It will help the seller understand their options, and it will help them visualize what this sale will look like for them financially. This can increase the likelihood your offer will be accepted.

If the property is listed, the seller typically already has an agreement to pay the listing agent a commission out of the purchase price. In that case, the "net offer" will be the net price before commissions. Their real estate agent will typically explain that to them.

Keep Your Offer Techniques Ready

You won't necessarily use all ten of these techniques on every deal. But treat them like tools in a toolbox and have them ready to use whenever you can. And even if none of these techniques work and your offer is rejected, the deal isn't over yet! As I've learned, many of the best deals are made by following up months or even years after the initial offer.

STEP NO. 5: FORTUNE IS IN THE FOLLOW-UP

Your first offer through an agent or directly to a seller will likely be rejected. But there is an old axiom in sales that "the fortune is in the follow-up." Follow-up is the key to converting many of these rejections into deals. It's also Step No. 5 of the deal funnel.

You never know when or if a seller will be ready to accept your offer. The timing of the offer in their life has a lot to do with whether they will accept it. I once bought a property five years after the original offer! The seller wasn't ready originally, but eventually things changed.

Stay Organized with Follow-Up

To follow up on dozens of offers at a time, you must be organized. I originally used a physical system called a "tickler file" to help me follow up. The system had twelve file folders labeled with each month of the year. Then it had thirty-one file folders labeled 1 to 31 for each day of the month. You can google "tickler file folder system" to see examples of this.

If it was January and I wanted to follow up on an offer in March, I would write the follow-up date on the top of a piece of paper and put it in the March folder. At the beginning of March, I'd pull out all the March papers and follow up with each one. I would use the 31 daily folders in the same way if I wanted to follow up later in the same month.

Today you can use the old-school tickler file or simply use an online equivalent. I've seen people adapt freemium project management software like Asana or Trello to manage the entire deal funnel. These are very flexible digital tools if you want to systematize your follow-up or entire deal funnel.

Using this type of system with discipline over time has bought me dozens of deals that would have never come about otherwise. Over the long run, this means I've made hundreds of thousands or perhaps millions of dollars as a result! If you want to convert more leads and offers to deals, I recommend you implement a follow-up system too.

With persistence and a little luck, you'll eventually get a yes from a seller. That's when you need to be familiar with how to negotiate and execute a real estate purchase contract.

STEP NO. 6: SIGN A PURCHASE CONTRACT

This step of the deal funnel is to put the property under contract. Once a seller accepts your offer, you want to get this done as soon as possible. If a real estate agent is involved, they can prepare the paperwork and send it to you and the seller for approval and signatures. Or if you're buying directly from the seller, you or your attorney can fill out a contract.

It's beyond the scope of this book to give you an in-depth explanation of contracts or real estate transactions. Every state has slightly different laws in this area. That's one reason that you should have a good, local real estate attorney on your team. When you're a new investor or new to a market, I recommend that you make an appointment with your attorney to review the purchase contract used by local real estate agents so that you can understand it and be ready to use it. You can also ask the attorney for an investor-friendly contract to use on your own.

I also recommend that you take a class to learn the basics of contracts. Every state requires real estate agents to take this type of class. Even if you don't want to become an agent, these classes are an excellent way to learn how to fill out a contract and to learn how real estate works in your area.

ALWAYS BE WILLING TO WALK AWAY

I want to end this chapter with a reminder to keep your offers in perspective. It's easy to let yourself get carried away by emotions during a negotiation. The negotiation process is exciting, and being so close to a good deal can be tantalizing.

But to be a successful negotiator, you must find a way to detach yourself emotionally from the final result. As much as you want to do a deal, the cold, unemotional, numbers-driven part of your brain must have the final word. Be willing to walk away if the deal doesn't meet your objective criteria.

Billionaire entrepreneur Richard Branson likes to say, "Opportunities are like buses—there's always another one coming."[48] When you believe there are more opportunities out there, you won't try to force the one right in front of you. It also helps to *actually* have more opportunities

---

[48] Richard Branson (Twitter: @RichardBranson), "Opportunities are like buses—there's always another one coming," November 1, 2012, 11:13 a.m.

coming in by generating plenty of leads as you learned in an earlier chapter!

Warren Buffett, one of the most successful investors of all time, compares buying investments to hitting a baseball. In baseball, batters have a sweet spot or their favorite pitch that they can hit the best. As an investor, you also have a sweet spot, and you've already defined it with your buy box.

But investing has one important difference from hitting baseballs. There are no called strikes if you don't swing! This means you can look at hundreds of leads and make as many offers as you need to get a good deal. You don't have to "swing" and buy the property, even if you feel internal or external pressure to do it.

Buffett says that "the trick in investing is just to sit there and watch pitch after pitch go by and wait for the one right in your sweet spot. And if people are yelling, 'Swing, you bum!' ignore them."[49]

If you make enough offers, you'll get good deals. It simply requires patience, persistence, and practice. And when your offer is accepted and you put your property under contract, you'll want to know the details of how to perform due diligence and close the purchase. That's what we'll cover in the next chapter.

49 Kathleen Elkins, "Warren Buffett Simplifies Investing with a Baseball Analogy," CNBC, last accessed December 12, 2022, https://www.cnbc.com/2017/02/02/warren-buffett-simplifies-investing-with-a-baseball-analogy.html.

CHAPTER 17
DUE DILIGENCE AND CLOSING

I've bought hundreds of properties during my twenty years as an investor, and I've made my share of mistakes. Some of these mistakes were small, and some were large, painful, and expensive. In most cases, my large mistakes could have been prevented by a better due diligence process and a more thorough checklist when I closed (bought) the property. That's why this topic is Step No. 7 of the deal funnel.

In this chapter, I want to give you a framework I use to avoid the biggest mistakes before buying a property. Using this process, I can't guarantee that you'll never make a mistake. As an entrepreneur and investor, you must take some risks to make money and that means mistakes will happen. But if you can eliminate the biggest red flags and potential problems, you can live with and learn from the smaller mistakes.

In the last chapter, we ended with Step No. 6 of the deal funnel, putting a property under contract. And a key part of most contracts is a due diligence clause. That's where we'll start in this chapter.

THE DUE DILIGENCE PROCESS

There are different types of due diligence clauses in a contract. Some are general, some are related to financing, and others are related to specific problems like termites, radon inspections, or a clean title. A due diligence clause lets you get out of the contract if you discover something unsatisfactory during the due diligence period.

On a small residential property purchase, I typically use one general due diligence clause that gives me ten to fourteen days to investigate a variety of due diligence items that I'll cover in this chapter. Then I also have a contingency clause for a clean title that lasts all the way up to the closing date. I recommend that you work with your local attorney to understand and then draft due diligence clauses that you can use to suit your needs and meet your local laws.

But no matter what type of due diligence clauses you use, the common goal is always the same. Due diligence increases your confidence. Your goal is to arrive at closing with more certainty that you're getting the deal you thought you were. And due diligence helps you do that in two ways:

1. Verifies assumptions
2. Discovers big, expensive problems

You had a lot of assumptions when you made your offer. The due diligence period allows you to evaluate and verify those assumptions. For example, you may have assumed that the repair costs would be $15,000 when you ran your numbers. But if you now discover that the repairs will cost $30,000, the entire deal has changed.

Investing requires projecting into the future, and the future is always uncertain. So, you will always be surprised by some future problems. But due diligence gives you time to identify *current* problems that may be hidden below the surface. Your job is to eliminate the most expensive of those problems.

In the rest of the chapter, I'll go through a list of items that make up my due diligence checklist. Feel free to add more to your own checklist, but this will give you a good idea of what to evaluate before you make a purchase.

Review Red Flag Checklist (Again)

Back in Chapter 15, I told you about a red flag checklist I use when visiting a property for the first time. During a due diligence inspection period, I revisit this checklist. And specifically, I like to physically walk the property and take my time to carefully look for any red flags or problems. If you live a long distance from the property, you will need to decide to do this step yourself or to entrust this walk-through to someone else. But someone you trust needs to do it!

Here's the checklist again:

- **Neighborhood:** Walk the neighborhood at different times of day, especially during an evening on the weekend (when people are off work). Any issues with crime? Is the property too far from amenities?
- **Nuisances:** Noise? Bad smells? High-voltage power lines in the backyard?
- **Street & Sidewalks:** Is the property on a busy street? Are there sidewalks or other easy places to walk?
- **Neighbors:** Are there issues with the neighbors that would make your property difficult to rent or sell (for example, loud or vicious dogs)?
- **Water:** Is the lot in a flood plain? Does the building sit "below grade" where runoff water could create moisture problems?
- **Trees:** Are there large trees next to the building? Any risk of trees falling?
- **Other:** Old buried oil tanks (look for valves and meters), environmental issues (like backyard auto shop waste dumped on grounds)?

I also like to have other people I trust look at the property. Sometimes my wife, my business partner, my property manager, my real estate agent, my handyman, or my contractor will pick up on things that I missed. I don't want to have the weight of big mistakes fall just on my eyes and ears.

Verify Value

The value of the property is one of the most important variables of the entire real estate deal. Your financial analysis and offer usually depend on it. And if the property needs repairs, you want to know the value in its as-is condition and in its after-repair condition. This lets you know if you'll make money remodeling the property.

During the due diligence process, I like to ask my real estate agent to prepare a comparative market analysis (CMA) if they haven't done it already. Or if they did the analysis several months before (like if I've been following up on this property for a while), I ask them to update their valuation. Then I use this updated value to recalculate my financial analysis to ensure my offer is still a good deal.

Verify Repair Costs

Perhaps the most critical piece of due diligence is verifying repair costs. During my initial evaluation of the property, I did my best to create a thorough list of repairs. I also tried to estimate the cost of these repairs so that I could make an offer.

But at this stage, I want to get more accurate on the repair list and on those estimates. I do this first by creating a more detailed list of repairs. And then I get help from my contractors to create a more accurate budget for repairs.

Here are some more specific ways I put all this together:

- **Ask for a list of CapEx repairs:** Ideally, I've already asked the seller for a list of the major capital expenses they've repaired and when they repaired them. But if I haven't, I ask for it at this point. For example, I want to know whether they have made any repairs to the roof, HVAC system, foundation, driveway, appliances, kitchen or bath remodels, etc. This knowledge will help me estimate the remaining life on all those items. If the item clearly needs to be replaced, I add it to my repair list.

- **Ask property manager for cosmetic recommendations:** Your property manager knows what types of property conditions potential tenants will like or not like. That's why I ask for their opinion on cosmetic repairs and other issues that may affect rentability. I consider their recommendations and often add them to my repair list. Almost every property will need interior paint and some sort of flooring. Exterior painting and landscaping are also common to improve curb appeal. Beyond that, the improvements will be very market specific. For example, we won't automatically install high-end countertops unless the property manager thinks it will give us additional rent value.

- **Get a professional inspection:** A professional inspector evaluates the property to find both big and small repair problems. Then they organize their findings into a neat report that includes pictures. Whereas I lean on my property manager for cosmetic recommendations, I lean on this report for functional and safety recommendations. I then add items I want to fix to my repair list.

- **Get a termite/moisture inspection:** In rainy and warm areas of the country, like where I live in South Carolina, moisture problems and wood destroying insects can be a major problem. I hire my own termite/moisture inspector to evaluate the property to look for active moisture problems and previous damage from insects.
- **Verify flood zones:** Using federal flood maps online or your local tax assessor maps, verify whether your property is in a flood zone. Being in a flood zone may not only add risks of future damage, but it may also make it difficult to get regular insurance on the property.
- **Get specialty inspections (as needed):** Sometimes you will need to bring in specialty inspectors for specific problems that you find or are worried about. Some examples of those are inspections for sewer line problems (from a plumber), foundation issues (from an engineer), radon (from a radon inspector), mold, asbestos, lead paint, or buried tanks (from an environmental inspector). Not every property needs all these inspections, but particularly with older buildings, these problems can create massive extra costs. You want to be extra careful in those situations.
- **Create a scope of work:** This is a list of the repairs that I'm planning to make for the property, organized by types of repairs.
- **Get quotes from contractors:** Using the scope of work as a guide, I get quotes from my contractors on major expenses. In most cases, I like to get a formal, written quote. But if I'm in a hurry, I may give them details over the phone and get an approximate quote that I won't hold them to. Having one or two contractors you work with repeatedly for each trade (heating and air-conditioning, electrical, plumbing, etc.) helps in these situations. When they know you'll bring them more business (or your property manager will), it's easier to get their assistance.
- **Create a repair budget:** This is the scope of work translated into a list of itemized costs, with a total repair budget at the bottom of the list.

- **BONUS TIP:** If you buy *The Book on Estimating Rehab Costs* by J Scott from the BiggerPockets bookstore, you'll get the estimating spreadsheet that I use in this process. With each deal you do, you can update this spreadsheet so that you eventually have a comprehensive list of repair costs in your area.

In a best-case scenario, you did a good job estimating repairs during your pre-offer evaluation of the property. But it's not uncommon to find that your repair budget is higher than your estimate. In that case, you must decide whether to renegotiate, continue as is, or walk away from the deal. I'll talk about that decision and how to renegotiate, if needed, later in the chapter.

Verify Rent Amount

Like property value, the amount of rent you can expect to receive is a critical factor in your analysis of an investment. If you haven't already done it, ask your property manager to give you a written estimate of the rent for the property. If you don't use a property manager, do your own evaluation.

But don't just rely on algorithms from online tools to tell you what the rent is. Instead, use these tools to show you *comparable properties.* At a minimum, drive by those properties to evaluate if they're better or worse than your property. But if possible, getting inside would be even better if you can set an appointment or visit an open house. Reality and online pictures can be very different! Using this process, you can make a low-end and high-end guess about what your property will rent for.

Perform Tenant/Lease Due Diligence (if applicable)

If the property is being sold with renters in place, you want to do extra due diligence on those current tenants and their lease paperwork. You'll get most of the data you need from the seller or their property manager. Here are the things I ask for:

- **Rent roll report:** A report that lists the name of each current tenant, their current rent amount, the start and end date of their lease, and any delinquent payments they owe. If the owner doesn't have a rent roll report, which is common on good deals because they're not managing it well, you need to create your own summary of the report. Here's a sample of what a rent roll looks like.

Unit	BD/BA	Tenant	Status	Market Rent	Rent	Deposit	Lease From	Lease To	Past Due
		Clemson, SC 29631							
1 - 1	--/--		Current	280.00	810.00	810.00	08/10/2021	07/25/2022	0.00
1 - 2	--/--		Current	280.00	0.00	0.00	08/10/2021	07/25/2022	0.00
1 - 3	--/--		Current	280.00	0.00	0.00	08/10/2021	07/25/2022	0.00
2 - 1	--/--		Current	280.00	810.00	810.00	08/10/2021	07/25/2023	280.00
2 - 2	--/--		Current	280.00	0.00	0.00	08/10/2021	07/25/2022	0.00
2 - 3	--/--		Current	280.00	0.00	0.00	08/10/2021	07/25/2022	0.00
3 - 1	--/--		Current	280.00	270.00	270.00	08/10/2021	07/25/2022	0.00
3 - 2	--/--		Current	280.00	270.00	270.00	08/10/2021	07/25/2022	0.00
3 - 3	--/--		Current	280.00	270.00	270.00	08/10/2021	07/25/2022	-2,160.00
4 - 1	--/--		Current	280.00	810.00	810.00	08/10/2021	07/25/2023	280.00
4 - 2	--/--		Current	280.00	0.00	0.00	08/10/2021	07/25/2023	0.00
4 - 3	--/--		Current	280.00	0.00	0.00	08/10/2021	07/25/2023	0.00
12 Units			100.0% Occupied	3,360.00	3,240.00	3,240.00			-1,630.00
Total 12 Units			100.0% Occupied	3,360.00	3,240.00	3,240.00			-1,630.00

- **Security deposits:** If not already in the rent roll report, ask for a list of the security deposits being held on behalf of the tenants. These will need to be transferred to you or your property manager at closing so that you can return them to the tenants when they move out or you can use them to pay for tenant damage. Also ask for initial move-in inspection reports, if available.
- **Leases and tenant paperwork:** In most cases, you will be bound to any existing lease contracts when you buy the property. You want to carefully review any current leases, addendums, and contract extensions to understand your obligations and when the lease expires. If possible, you also want to get the initial application from the tenant so that you get background information on them.
- **Delinquency reports:** If tenants are currently behind, ask for notes or reports on the timeline of communications and actions related to the delinquency. Again, mismanaged properties likely won't have this. But try to piece together the situation as best you can. Also don't be afraid to talk directly to the tenant to get their side of the story and to understand the type of tenant you'll be inheriting.

The major problems that would concern me are extremely long-term leases (like multiple years) at sub-market rents. And if you're in a state with tenant-friendly laws, I would also be on the lookout for potential tenant problems. An upset tenant who knows the local laws could delay your plans for many months, even if they're not paying rent. Be on the lookout for those types of red flags.

Verify Operating Expenses

We've already verified the rent, but we also need to verify our operating expenses. This will let us know if our estimate of the net operating income of the property is accurate. To gather this information, you can begin by talking to the seller.

If the seller is a landlord, ask for a copy of their prior year tax returns for the property and a profit and loss statement. Sellers won't always be willing to share this, and in other cases they won't always be accurate. But if you can get the information, it will provide a helpful historical summary of the property's operations.

I also like to ask sellers for their recent utility bills. On some multi-unit properties, the owner pays the water, heating, or electric bill, so this will help you understand your costs. And in other cases, knowing the electrical, water, and gas bills will help you understand your tenant's costs. If they are too high, the tenant may have a hard time paying your rent.

Even if the seller is willing to share information, I still like to do my own verification. Here are a couple of the important items you want to check:

- **Property tax bills:** Look at the historical tax bills to understand the trends. And then estimate the tax bill *after* you buy the property. If you're paying a price above the current tax value, chances are the taxable value will reset to your new price. This could dramatically increase your tax bill. You also must be careful of homeowner tax exemptions or reductions. If you're buying from a longtime resident, they may have a much lower tax bill than you will have as an investor. If you're unsure, call or visit the local taxing authority to get help estimating your bill.
- **Insurance estimate:** If you haven't already done it, contact your insurance agent to get a quote for a landlord insurance policy. This type of policy pays for replacement of the property in case of fire or water damage, and it also has a liability insurance component. If you're doing a major remodel first, also get a quote from a builder's risk policy that will cover you during the vacant construction

period. And if you decide to invest in a flood plain, earthquake fault zone, or other disaster-prone area for some crazy reason, get quotes for those insurance policies as well.

Once you have an updated understanding of your rent and your operating expenses, you can rerun your numbers. Make sure you're still happy with the financial analysis of the deal. If you're not, you'll need to either renegotiate or walk away, assuming you're still within a due diligence period.

Make an Itemized List of Personal Property

A property purchase often includes items that are not permanently attached to the property. These personal property items include appliances and furniture. But you might also find that the seller wants to take (or leave) other items that are not quite so fixed.

We've had sellers dig up plants and trees from the yard. Others have removed dishwashers, which I thought were part of the property. And in one case, we had someone leave a boat in the backyard that was so big it could have been an oceangoing vessel! This boat was in such disrepair that it cost us a lot of money to have it cut up, scrapped, and removed.

The bottom line is that you want to create a list of personal property and other items that will either stay or go. If the item is an essential part of the house, estimate the costs of replacing it. But in many other cases, you can figure out how to get the items hauled off.

Consider a Survey

A survey is a process in which a professional surveyor physically marks the corners, boundaries, and easements of your property. The surveyor also creates a plat map that gets recorded in the public records. Without surveys, separation of property between owners wouldn't be possible.

It's not a bad idea to have a property resurveyed if you can't find an existing survey done in the past few years. Even on a simple subdivision lot, it's useful to find all the property corners and property line to make sure the neighbor's garage, fence, or shed aren't over your line. And on an older or larger property, there's no question that I would hire a surveyor.

A survey can give you peace of mind that you know exactly what you're buying. And it can also alert you to any other issues affecting your property, like unusual easements. Most easements are fine, such as buried utilities on the edge of your property. But other easements could be a problem, like a 110-year-old invisible railway bed still owned by a railway company that crosses your property. I've dealt with that one before!

Verify Zoning and Local Regulations

Zoning laws and other regulations can sometimes have a negative effect on your investment. So you also want to perform due diligence in this category. Here are a few things I look at:

- **Zoning laws:** Local zoning divides properties into districts with different allowed property types, densities, and uses. For example, you can't build a commercial or multifamily property in a single-family zone. Or in the case of my small university town of Clemson, South Carolina, you can't rent a single-family house to more than two unrelated tenants. You want to find out your property's current zoning and understand what's allowed and not allowed.

- **Density allowances:** Based on your zoning, you can find opportunities for future redevelopment based on density allowances. For example, a large single-family house lot could be subdivided into two smaller lots. Or one duplex lot could be used to build a larger multifamily property in the future. This is valuable information to know.

- **Grandfathering rules:** If your property does not conform to the current zoning, you need to carefully read the "grandfather" rules. In my city, for example, I own a duplex in a single-family zoned neighborhood. I'm allowed to continue renting the duplex, but if it burns down or sits vacant for more than a few months, I can lose my ability to use it as a duplex and potentially lose a lot of money in the process.

- **Historic and architectural review districts:** Local governments can create historic and architectural review districts that limit what a property owner can do to their property without going through a process to gain permission. This isn't always a bad thing, but you want to know about it up front. Being in one of these districts could delay your timing, increase your cost of repairs, and limit what repairs you can do.

- **Rental licensing:** Find out if your local government requires a rental license for long-term or short-term rentals. Especially with short-term rentals, many governments are limiting or even eliminating short-term rentals. And even when allowed, you may be required to get a license. In my city, for example, all rental owners of single-family houses and other small rentals must perform an annual inspection and pay for a license.

Check for Remodel Permits

Before you buy a property, research any past remodel permits that have been pulled for that property. Most local governments will have an online or physical database where you can search by your property address. If your property has additions or other major remodels, you want to make sure they did that work with a permit. If not, you may be responsible for fixing their work after the fact, or in the worst case, even tearing part of the property down if it wasn't done properly.

Review HOA and Neighborhood CC&Rs

If your property is in a subdivision or condo development, there's a good chance it has an HOA or a condo owners' association. These are entities made up of property owners who pay for common area maintenance and enforce rules outlined in the neighborhood's CC&Rs (covenants, conditions, and restrictions). If you violate these rules, the HOA may be able to fine you, suspend your rights to use common areas, or even file a lawsuit.

You may be okay with many of the HOA rules, such as requirements to cut grass and pick up trash in the yard. The typical intention of the rules is to preserve and enhance property values. But other rules could interfere with your investment, say, a prohibition of certain types of rentals or of rentals altogether. Clearly you want to know these rules before you buy a property.

In addition to researching the rules, you also want to investigate the finances of the HOA or condo association. First, what are the dues? You need to include these in your financial analysis of the property. But second, is the HOA or condo association funded well enough to handle future common area expenses?

I have a friend who bought a condo, and within one year, the association required a one-time assessment to replace the building's roof.

This was more than $4,000 per condo unit, and it wasn't something he expected. You may have to dig, but you can find these kinds of problems in the meeting minutes and budget documents of the association.

Title Search and Title Insurance

Ownership (aka title) to real estate is transferred from one owner to another through a special contract called a deed. These deeds are recorded in the local public records to create a permanent "chain" or history of title. Having a public chain of title makes it easier to verify that someone owns a property.

In some states an attorney must perform a real title transfer, while in others a title company can do the same thing. But whichever you hire, they will first investigate the chain of title for your property. They normally go back thirty to fifty years to make sure there are no breaks or problems with the chain. If they find something, they'll alert you and work with the seller to correct it, if possible.

Most contracts have contingencies for a good and marketable title. This means if your attorney or title company finds a title problem, you don't have to buy the property. But there's always a chance that the attorney or title company missed a problem. In that case, a title insurance policy can help you cover the cost of fixing those problems.

I always hire a professional to perform title searches. They are a key member of my team. And I also always buy title insurance as an owner and for my lenders. In twenty years of investing, I've had only one situation where I needed to call the title company about a problem. But it gives me peace of mind when investing and borrowing large sums of money.

HOW TO MAKE A GO/NO-GO DECISION AFTER DUE DILIGENCE

If you're new to real estate, this long list of due diligence items may seem intimidating. There are a lot of things that could go wrong! On the other hand, investors just like you successfully buy properties every day. So be confident that you can handle this with the right process.

Using this type of checklist process is sort of like an airplane pilot's pre-departure checklist. It will help you ensure everything goes smoothly. But inevitably, you will find problems during your due diligence process. That's when you need to make a "go/no-go" decision about whether to move forward with your purchase.

Almost any problem is fixable with enough money and enough time. But if the problem is big enough, complicated enough, or expensive enough, most investors will probably want to pass and look for an easier deal. Here are some problems that might fit into that category:

- Major foundation issues
- Extensive water damage
- Extensive mold infestation
- Bad title or can't get title insurance
- Major environmental problems (lots of asbestos, leaking oil tanks, etc.)

These problems can be solved, and I know investors who actually look for those situations to buy properties at great prices. But as a new or part-time investor, you'll have to decide if that's a game you want to play.

My Go/No-Go Decision Process

For all the other problems you may find during due diligence, you can apply a go/no-go decision-making process. Here's my own process and list of questions that I use to make a decision:

1. Evaluate the problem:
   - Can I figure out a solution to this problem? (Get help if necessary)
   - If so, how much will it cost?
   - Is this a problem I want to deal with?
   - Can I sleep well at night with it?
2. Reanalyze the financials given this new problem:
   - Do I have enough cash to deal with the problem?
   - Will it affect my financing?
   - Does the deal still meet my cash flow and return-on-investment goals?
   - Does it add risk that I'm not willing to take?
3. Determine a walk-away scenario:
   - What's the bottom-line scenario that will cause me to refuse this deal?

This is basically a process to reanalyze your deal. And in the end, you've got to decide if the current deal you've negotiated will work for you or not. If it doesn't, you'll need to renegotiate or walk away.

HOW TO RENEGOTIATE (OR WALK AWAY)

I've seen some investors who make a habit of putting properties under contract at one price, "finding" problems during due diligence, and then asking the seller to drop their price as a result. It's a sneaky way to beat competition. They originally agree to a higher price, but they ultimately get a lower price by playing on the seller's desires to just get the deal done.

Treating sellers that way will get you a bad reputation among agents and others in the real estate business. Do your best to evaluate properties accurately and build a cushion for problems into your offer process. But even when you do your best, renegotiations will sometimes be necessary.

When that happens, you can renegotiate in a few different ways—preferably in writing:

1. **Price reduction:** Show the seller evidence of the cost of fixing this problem and ask for a price reduction of the same amount.
2. **Repair concession:** The net result to the seller is the same, but instead of a price reduction, ask for a repair concession that's taken from the seller's proceeds at closing. This could be beneficial to you so that your financing covers more of the purchase.
3. **Seller fixes the problem:** You can ask the seller to fix or pay to fix the problem at their expense. For example, if the roof is leaking, ask them to replace it. Be careful to follow up on their work if you choose this solution, and make sure you approve of their choice of contractor.
4. **Seller finances the problem:** If I'm on the fence about solving a problem myself, I may ask the seller to carry back financing for the cost of fixing it at zero percent for a long period of time (ten-plus years). For example, if the problem costs $10,000 to fix, I would prefer to get a price reduction for that amount. But as a Plan B, the seller would agree that $10,000 of the price would not be paid in cash to them at closing. Instead, I would owe them a note for $10,000 that has no payments, no interest, and one single payment in ten years. The present value of that future payment is a lot less

than $10,000, so you're essentially getting them to pay for part of the repair by waiting on their money.

If all else fails and the seller won't agree to your bottom line, be ready to walk away from the deal. Just be sure you're still within your due diligence period and that you understand what your contract says. It can be frustrating to walk away after all your work, but sometimes the best deals are the ones you don't do. There's no reason to force a bad deal.

And don't make a habit of walking away from deals. It should be a little painful when you must do it. Learn from the process so that next time you can find and account for those types of problems up front.

HOW TO PREPARE FOR A SMOOTH CLOSING

If you made it through the due diligence process, you're now on the home stretch. But things can still go wrong before you close and buy the property. Here are a few best practices that I follow so that the closing process goes as smoothly as possible.

1. **Communicate clearly and often:** Clear, frequent communication can avoid or reduce the impact of problems. This of course applies to the property seller and their agent. But it also applies to the closing attorney or title company who will handle your closing.

2. **Take extreme ownership (It's all your job!):** It's tempting to assume that other people will take care of closing details for you. But this is *your* closing, and no one will take it as seriously as you do. I like to take extreme ownership of the closing process and pay attention to every step as my responsibility, even if someone else is handling it.

3. **Prepare for roller coasters:** No matter how much you prepare, there seem to always be some roller-coaster–like ups and downs during the closing process. Just be prepared and be flexible so that you can adjust as needed.

THE PROPERTY ADVENTURE CONTINUES

You've now been through the entire process of buying an investment property. We started with building a team, creating a buy box for your target market and properties, and analyzing the numbers. And we finished with working the deal funnel through lead generation, negotiations, due diligence, and closing.

This has been a detailed section of the book. I put so much emphasis on these tactics because I think buying good deals is the most difficult part of becoming a small and mighty real estate investor. If you can learn and master this skill, the entire business will become much easier.

But there is one other critical piece you must have to consistently buy good real estate deals. That missing piece is the money. In the next part of the book, I'll teach you my approach to getting financing and finding the cash you need for deals.

PART IV
FUNDING YOUR PROPERTIES

CHAPTER 18
HOW TO SAFELY FINANCE YOUR SMALL AND MIGHTY EMPIRE

In Chapter 2, I told the story of how Dave Ramsey went bankrupt as a 28-year-old real estate investor in the 1980s. I first heard that story as a new 23-year-old real estate investor. Dave's story shook me up for days, and it forced me to ask a lot of difficult questions.

How could a successful real estate investor who owned properties worth $4 million and who owed debt of only $3 million suddenly go out of business? How were his lenders able to force him to repay $1.2 million of debt in such a short period of time? And most important, could this also happen to me?

Dave's story and these questions gave me a permanent but healthy fear of the risk of debt. And it forced me to think about how I should use debt in my own real estate investing business. Would I try to eliminate debt altogether? Or would I find a way to safely use it to build my small and mighty real estate empire?

BE CAREFUL WITH POWER TOOLS

Dave Ramsey's response to his situation was to eliminate debt from his business and his life. I respect Dave's decision, and it's worked well for him. If you prefer to follow Dave's example as a real estate investor, that's fine. It will take longer to get started, but plenty of investors have made this work.

In my own case, I found a middle ground with debt that's worked for me. My philosophy with debt is to compare it to a power tool like you would use to build a house. Power tools can help you build a house much easier and faster than you can with your bare hands. Similarly, debt can help you build your small and mighty real estate business much easier and faster than you can by paying cash for everything.

For example, the simplest way to become a millionaire is to buy a million dollars of rental properties and then pay off the debt. You could buy five properties each worth $200,000, put $40,000 down (20 percent), and borrow $160,000 on each house. That's $200,000 total of cash out of your pocket. If the net rent covered the payment of the amortizing mortgage, your $200,000 would eventually turn into at least $1 million as the loans were paid off.

But just as with power tools, you must use debt with extreme care. If you're careless, the tools can hurt you just as much as they can help you. In Chapter 2 in the section "Be the Real Estate Tortoise," I told a story about fellow real estate investors I knew who went out of business, lost millions of dollars, and damaged their reputations because of careless use of debt. They were smart and ambitious people who simply over-extended themselves with debt. Dave Ramsey's story is not an isolated event.

Using debt carefully means understanding the difference between good debt and bad debt. Not all debt is created equal. If you only use good debt, you'll decrease your chances of getting hurt. In the next section, I'll explain what bad debt is. And later in the chapter, I'll share my rules for good debt.

But even with good debt, using debt carefully also means knowing when to put the tool back in the toolbox. Instead of always maxing out leverage, mature investors invest more of their cash in deals as time goes on. And instead of having debt forever, mature investors start paying off debt eventually. Perpetual use of debt is unwise and unnecessary. In the final chapters of the book, I'll talk about how to pay off debt to win the game of the wealth-building journey.

GOOD DEBT VS. BAD DEBT

Robert Kiyosaki, author of *Rich Dad, Poor Dad,* says "There is good debt and bad debt. Good debt makes you rich, and bad debt makes you poor."[50] Good debt is a tool that you use to build wealth. Bad debt takes wealth from you.

By this definition, it's obvious that some debt is bad. Credit card debt, personal loans, and car loans are bad loans because they take your wealth. And even home loans cost you money (unless you house hack!), so I would consider them bad debt that you should eventually pay off.

But within real estate investing, bad debt sometimes looks like good debt. You may think that all rental property debt is good because rentals build wealth. But Dave Ramsey's debt clearly took wealth from him. And there are other situations where debt can hurt you as a real estate investor. To explain what those are, I'll share examples of bad debt for us as real estate investors.

Negative Leverage

Negative leverage is debt that costs more than your property's net operating income. Said another way, the cost of financing is higher than the unleveraged yield, an important formula that measures the overall rate of cash flow of a property. I explained unleveraged yield in more detail in Chapter 12. Positive leverage, on the other hand, has debt that costs less than the property's net operating income and unleveraged yield. Here's the formula:

Positive leverage = Unleveraged yield > Cost of financing

Properties with positive leverage produce positive cash flow, and negative leverage produces negative cash flow. For this definition, I consider the entire payment to be a "cost," even if part of the payment builds

---

50 Robert Kiyosaki, "New Rule of Money #2: Learn How to Use Good Debt vs. Bad Debt," richdad.com, last accessed on 12/14/2022, https://www.richdad.com/good-debt-vs-bad-debt.

equity through principal. Although principal paydown can become real wealth eventually, it doesn't reduce your risk because the payment stays the same.

Here's an example of a property with positive leverage. Let's say you buy a property for $200,000 that has an NOI of $1,250 per month or $15,000 per year. The unleveraged yield would be 7.5 percent ($15,000 ÷ $200,000).

If you put $40,000 down and get a $160,000 loan for thirty years at 6.4 percent interest, your payment would be $1,000 per month or $12,000 per year. The cost of financing is $12,000 ÷ $200,000 = 6 percent. Your unleveraged yield of 7.5 percent is more than your 6 percent cost of financing, so you have positive leverage.

That same deal would have negative leverage with a loan of fifteen years at the same interest rate of 6.4 percent. The payment would be $1,385 per month or $16,620 per year. The cost of financing in this case is $16,620 ÷ $200,000 = 8.31 percent. That's higher than the 7.5 percent unleveraged yield, so this would produce negative leverage and negative cash flow.

Mortgage lenders also look at a variation of positive leverage when deciding to approve you for a loan. Their formula is called a debt service coverage ratio (DSCR). It's the ratio of your net operating income to the mortgage payment. A 1.25 DSCR is the cutoff for many lenders, but even higher ratios like 1.5 or 2.0 will keep you safe and increase your chances of a loan approval.

An example of a 1.25 DSCR is a mortgage payment of $1,000 per month and a net operating income of $1,250 ($1,250 ÷ $1,000 = 1.25). You would also earn $250 per month of cash flow in that situation. A mortgage payment of $625 per month would be an even safer 2.0 DSCR ($1,250 ÷ $625 = 2.0). This higher DSCR situation would produce $625 per month of cash flow.

How do you practically avoid negative leverage and increase your DSCR? First, borrow at lower interest rates. Second, borrow with a longer amortization like thirty years, or even with interest-only payments. These lower-payment loans will be much safer than a fifteen-year mortgage, and you can always pay the loans off faster by making extra payments if you want. Third, put more money down (borrow less) to reduce your payment and create positive leverage.

Balloon Notes

Dave Ramsey's mortgages had a clause that required him to pay a large lump-sum payment. This type of payment is known as a balloon payment or a callable mortgage. Most residential thirty-year mortgages don't have balloon payments. But balloon payments are very common with commercial loans, which is what Dave Ramsey had. I'll talk about commercial loans more in the next chapter, but you typically get them from local banks or the commercial lending department of larger financial institutions.

To give you an example, think of a typical, thirty-year mortgage. Let's say you buy a property for $200,000, put $40,000 down, and borrow $160,000 at 6 percent interest. Your payment would always be $959 per month for thirty years or until you paid it off.

But let's say you have the same type of loan with a balloon payment after five years. In that case, you'd still borrow $160,000 and pay $959 per month. But your sixtieth payment would be $149,846. Talk about a big payment!

You might rightly ask, "How can you afford to make a payment that big if you don't have enough cash saved?!" The answer is normally you'd refinance with a new loan. Or, in a worst case, you'd sell the property.

But what happens if your credit changes or you lose a job so that you no longer qualify? Or what happens if the lending markets freeze up and no banks want to make loans to investors? And what if during that same time, the market crashes and the resale price of your property is less than what you owe on the debt?

All of that can happen and has happened. This is how investors I knew lost money and went out of business during the 2008–2009 financial crisis. It's also why many larger banks and financial institutions went out of business or needed government bailouts during that same time. Borrowing with balloon notes is risky, bad debt.

Does that mean you should never borrow money with balloons? I've certainly had a few situations where the rewards outweighed the risk and I chose to use one. But I also had a solid plan to handle the risks of the balloon payment, and it wasn't a regular practice.

For example, we bought a multiunit apartment property for over $1 million, paid a $500,000 down payment, and borrowed a $500,000 commercial mortgage with a seven-year balloon. We then invested $300,000 into property improvements.

The property had a very strong positive cash flow. We also felt safe that we could refinance or sell the property in seven years because of the low loan balance. And we knew the property had a much higher potential value of $2 million or more after the repairs we performed.

With all that said, my business partner and I never felt comfortable having more than a couple of loans with balloons. We wanted most of our debt to be long-term, safer debt. Our opinion was that a portfolio of balloon notes is asking for financial trouble when the economy gets bad.

Adjustable-Rate Notes

A typical residential mortgage has an interest rate that's fixed and stays the same throughout the duration of the mortgage. But it's also possible to borrow mortgages with adjustable rates. After a certain period, the interest rate "floats" and can change depending on the overall market interest rates.

Adjustable rates are less risky for lenders because they'll be able to make more interest as interest rates rise. Therefore, you can usually get lower interest rates on an adjustable-rate mortgage than on a fixed rate mortgage. If you believe interest rates will stay low, adjustable-rate mortgages could be a way to save money on interest.

To use our same example, let's say the $160,000 mortgage at 6 percent interest begins with a payment of $959 per month. But after five years, the interest rate adjusts to 9 percent. The payment would suddenly jump to $1,256 per month. If you earned a $200 per month positive cash flow before, you would now have a negative cash flow of almost $100 per month!

This is certainly not a positive situation, but I consider adjustable rates less risky than a balloon payment. If you had five properties like this, you'd lose $500 per month or $6,000 per year. While painful, that would be easier to survive than five balloon payments of almost $150,000 each!

Lack of Cash Reserves

Even the best rental property debt on excellent rental properties can become bad debt if you don't have adequate cash reserves. If you own rental properties long enough, you'll have some bad luck. You may experience a longer vacancy without tenants paying, and you'll have to cover the mortgage payment. Or you may have several vacancies at one time, right after you had two different and unexpected $10,000 repair bills.

It's during the unexpected cash crunches that any debt can become a problem. That's why I'm a big advocate of healthy cash reserves as a rental investor. On your first few rentals, I recommend a minimum of $5,000 per property (and adjust that up for inflation) that you set aside in a separate savings account. This will help you pay for unexpected repairs and property expenses when you don't have a tenant. As I've grown, I've switched to a metric like three to six times my total monthly expenses in a cash reserve account. This approach would also be a simpler way to calculate reserves if you own duplex, triplex, fourplex, or other multi-unit property.

Personal Guarantees

Most institutional mortgages will require you to personally guarantee the loan. This means that not only can the lender take your property in a foreclosure to pay back the loan, but if they still lose money, they can also take your other personal assets. This means any bank accounts, stock investments, or other properties you own are at risk.

This is probably the reason Dave Ramsey went bankrupt. If he had not personally guaranteed his debt, he could have just given the properties back to the bank. Yes, he would have lost all his money on those properties. But the lender couldn't have pursued him for any money beyond that. He could have licked his wounds and started over again.

If you can avoid personal guarantees on debt, your borrowing will be much safer. This is normally only possible to negotiate with private loans, seller financing, and other creative financing. I'll talk more about those techniques in the next chapter, but that's one reason I have almost exclusively used those financing sources in my business. If you're borrowing against large commercial properties ($1 million+), you may also find some commercial lenders who'll remove a personal guarantee with a large enough down payment.

COACH CARSON'S SAFE DEBT RULES

You can put all this together into a set of rules for how to safely use debt in real estate investing. Think of these as my guidelines, not as the Ten Commandments. You may choose to knowingly break one or two rules and take a risk if the overall deal is worth it. But don't break too many rules at one time. That's how you can get into trouble.

1. **Own quality properties:** The best properties in the best locations are less risky as collateral for your loans. This is true because they're more in demand. People want to buy them, so you can more easily rent them or sell them quickly and pay off your loans, if needed.

2. **Use positive leverage:** Make sure your cost of financing is less than your property's unleveraged yield. The larger the positive leverage, the safer your debt will be (measure with DSCR [debt service coverage ratio]). Use loans with lower payments (like thirty-year or interest only) to reduce your payment and cost of financing.

3. **Avoid balloons:** Balloons are fun at kids' birthday parties. They're a potential nightmare in real estate investing. Avoid them if possible, and if you must use them, push them off as long as possible. You need to negotiate any longer balloon periods *before* you get a loan, not after. Five years is too short in real estate, but ten years may give you enough time to ride out down market cycles.

4. **Fix your interest and payments:** Borrow with fixed-interest rates and payments. If you use adjustable rate, include an annual and overall cap on how much the interest rate and payment can rise.

5. **Hold healthy cash reserves:** To start, hold at least $5,000 (and adjust for inflation) per property in a separate savings account. As you grow, consider holding three to six months of your operating expenses, including mortgage, taxes, insurance, maintenance, and more, in a cash savings account.

6. **Avoid personal guarantees:** When possible, limit your risk to the property that's collateral for the loan and nothing more. This won't be possible for most traditional loans, but that's okay because you get low, fixed-interest rates and payments. But be very careful combining personal guarantees with balloons or other risky loans.

7. **Only work with friendly lenders:** At best, a lender is like your partner. So find friendly partners who will stick with you when things get rough. Some local commercial lenders with whom you have a relationship can fit this description. But don't forget that individuals retire or change jobs. The safest lenders are the ones who loan their own money, like private lenders or sellers. In a tough situation, they're more likely to work with you to solve the problem together.

HOW SAFE FINANCING HELPED ME SURVIVE THE FINANCIAL CRISIS

Feel free to adapt these rules to whatever makes you feel comfortable. These are just the rules that have worked for me. But I do have practical experience with them because they're the rules that helped me survive the 2008–2009 financial crisis.

In the early chapters, I shared the story of how my business partner and I financially survived the 2008–2009 financial crisis. There's no doubt luck played a role, as it always does. And our hard work and flexibility helped. But our financing probably played the biggest role in our survival.

Our first five years of growth as real estate investors were in 2003 to 2007. This was also the time when we had the highest leverage and took the most risk. The financial crisis hit its peak in 2008 and 2009. That's when the credit markets froze, few banks loaned money to investors, and prices for real estate dropped.

I'd love to say we saw it coming, but the truth is that we didn't. The scope of the crisis blindsided us like it did many other people. But listening to Dave Ramsey's story so early in my career helped save us. Without a healthy fear of debt and without following our own rules, we could have easily gone out of business like many others.

Because I didn't have a steady job, I was not able to get many traditional loans. My only traditional loan was a thirty-year mortgage refinance on my four-unit house hack. I got the loan because it was owner-occupied, I had good credit, and it already had three tenants paying rent to give me enough income to qualify.

Most of the financing my business partner and I used for rentals were private loans, seller financing, and other creative techniques like lease options and buying subject-to the mortgage. We occasionally borrowed commercial loans from a local bank, although we limited our use of them because of the balloon payments. At the time of the crisis, more than 90 percent of the payments we made were to individuals and not to banks.

I'm not saying this is the only way to invest safely. If we could have borrowed twenty 30-year, fixed-interest loans instead of private loans, we might have been better off. But we found a way to check most of the boxes on our safe debt list. And that's why we survived.

With quality properties (for the most part), no balloons, fixed payments, healthy cash reserves, few personal guarantees, and friendly lenders, we were able to ride out the storm. We didn't make much money for a year or two, but we didn't collapse, either. And on the other side of the storm, we were able to buy some of the best deals of our career because we were still in the game and because we had good relationships with our lenders!

These rules about safely using debt are the foundational ideas for financing your small and mighty rental property business. But in the next chapter, we're going to get into the nitty-gritty of different types of financing. I'm going to share a list of the best financing options so that you can choose the best source for yourself.

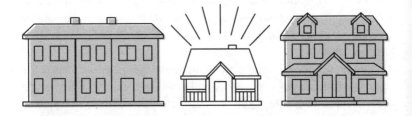

CHAPTER 19
THE BEST TYPES OF FINANCING FOR RENTAL PROPERTIES

This chapter will help you choose the best type of financing for your real estate investing. Look at it as if you're reading a menu in a restaurant. I'll make some recommendations, and then you can pick the financing option or options from the menu that suits you best.

To avoid overwhelming you, I won't give you a menu of every possible method to finance real estate. Instead, I've chosen the ones that I think will help you the most as a small and mighty real estate investor. Your job is to go "all-in" on one or two types of financing. Learn all you can about them so that you'll have the confidence to keep building your small and mighty real estate portfolio.

I'll start here with a basic list of the financing options. I'll continue with some specific recommendations based on your unique real estate strategy. And then the final part of the chapter will have more details on each of the financing options on the list.

Here's the menu:

- **Conforming and Government-Insured Residential Mortgages**
  - FHA Loans
  - VA Loans
  - Conforming Loans
- **Commercial Mortgages**
  - DSCR Loans
  - Portfolio Loans
- **Private and Hard Money Loans**
  - Private Money Loans
  - Hard Money Loans
- **Seller Financing**
  - Seller Carry-Back Financing
  - Subject-to the Mortgage
  - Master Lease Option
- **Cash Purchases**
  - Cash Savings
  - HELOC (Home Equity Line of Credit)

WHICH FINANCING SOURCE IS BEST FOR YOU?

Just like when you pick a real estate investing strategy, it's important to narrow down your financing options. The best small and mighty real estate investors specialize in one or two financing options at a time so that they can get good at them. Then once they've mastered them, they come back to the financing menu to expand their options.

The easiest way to narrow your options is by your chosen real estate strategy. Certain strategies will match up with certain financing options better than others. I'll give you some recommendations, starting with house hacking.

House Hacker

If you are focused on the house-hacking strategy, your best financing option will be one of the owner-occupant type of mortgages. If you have good credit, a reliable source of job income, and cash savings for a down payment, conforming mortgages give you the best financing terms possible. If you have less than perfect credit or you're short on down payment funds, try an FHA or VA loan to get your foot in the door.

If you are buying a fixer-upper house hack, you could try one of the renovation programs for conforming mortgages or FHA mortgages. Or you may want to consider a portfolio lender who can make a short-term construction/renovation loan to homeowners. This second option will be faster and more flexible to fund your purchase and renovation. Then you can refinance with a better long-term conforming mortgage after the property is rented and stabilized.

Rental Investor—Pretty/Turnkey Property

If you are buying a non-owner-occupied rental property that is "pretty," meaning it doesn't need any work and is ready to rent, you have the most financing options available to you. If you have good credit, a reliable source of job income, and cash savings for a 25 percent down payment, a conforming investor mortgage will probably be your first option.

In that case, just focus on getting thirty-year, fixed-interest mortgages until you reach your loan limit of four or ten loans. And if you're investing with a partner or spouse, you may be able to double how many loans you get by borrowing separately. Later, if you leave your W-2 job or if you hit your limit of conforming mortgages, you can graduate to some of the other financing options.

If you don't fit in the qualifying box for conforming loans for whatever reason, DSCR (debt service coverage ratio) loans have become a great second option. The interest rate will be higher than with conforming loans, but they still have a lot of benefits. Most of all, this type of loan has fixed interest and payments for thirty years, which will be tough to find with any other type of investor financing. You can also scale easier by getting multiple loans with fewer headaches.

Seller financing, subject-to, and lease options can also be excellent ways to acquire long-term pretty rentals. In my case as a young entrepreneur, I focused on these strategies for most of my first rentals. It allowed me to avoid strict bank qualifying, use less cash up front, and leverage my strengths, which were communication skills and lots of time available to hunt for deals.

Finally, don't forget about cash purchase options. If you have a HELOC available or if you have enough cash in the bank, that can be a simple way to purchase your rental properties. It will take longer to buy more properties while you replenish your cash savings, but that slow and steady approach can work just fine in the long run. And if you want to scale more, you can always refinance with a long-term mortgage.

Rental Investor—Fixer-Upper Property

You sometimes get the best deals with fixer-upper properties. But to acquire deals that need a lot of work, you'll have to use a different type of financing. You can use the renovation programs with conforming or FHA loans. The benefit is that you only need to borrow money once, and the renovation loan transitions into a long-term loan. But the challenge with these loans is that they're slow to be approved and more rigid in terms of inspections, appraisals, and other processes.

To get the best fixer-upper deals as an investor, you may want to add hard-money lenders, portfolio lenders, private money, HELOCs, or cash purchases to your financing toolbox. You will buy the property and fund your remodel using these short-term funding strategies. Then after the property is fixed up, stabilized, and rented, you can refinance with a conforming or DSCR long-term mortgage. I'll talk about this more with the BRRRR (buy, rehab, rent, refinance, repeat) strategy in the next chapter.

Short-Term and Medium-Term Rentals

The financing you use for short-term or medium-term rentals will depend on how you get into this strategy. For example, if you are doing a traditional house hack, you can use an owner-occupant mortgage. This will allow you to rent out the extra bedrooms or units in your property. The same approach works if you move out of a house, condo, or townhome and then keep it as a short-term or mid-term rental (aka live-in-then-rent strategy). As long as you follow the occupancy rules of your mortgage, this is an excellent way to finance your short-term or medium-term rentals.

But if you are buying a property purely as a short-term or medium-term rental from the start, you will have to use other financing options. First, you can try a conforming investor mortgage if you qualify. The biggest limit with these mortgages may be your debt-to-income ratio. Unless the property already has a history as a short-term rental, the lender likely won't give you credit for the potential rent of the property.

This may limit how many conforming mortgages you can qualify for.

Once you use up these options, you can turn to DSCR loans. These loans use the income from the property and not your personal income to qualify. You still may have problems, however, using the income from a short-term or medium-term rental if it doesn't have a history of renting. You may want to begin with an alternative source like hard money, private money, or seller financing until the property has a rental history. Then you can refinance with a better long-term loan.

One final consideration I really like for short-term and medium-term rentals is the master lease. Instead of buying property, you can simply lease it from other property owners with the right to sublease it to your short-term tenants. For example, if you lease a property for $1,000 per month and net $3,000 per month from your short-term rental, you could make $2,000 per month in cash flow *without owning the property!* If you also have an option to purchase the property, you could then benefit from appreciation and purchase it in the future with a long-term loan.

LIST OF RECOMMENDED FINANCING OPTIONS

I've used a lot of financing terms that you may not be familiar with. And you probably have a lot more questions about how different financing works. So, in the rest of the chapter I'll go into more detail about each of the recommended financing options. But before we get into the list, I want to make a couple of disclaimers.

First, I tried to provide as many details as possible to help you understand which financing is right for you. But keep in mind that this information was based on the early 2023 financing market. Some of the details may have changed by the time you read this. Use this information as a starting point to understand your options, then use your financing team members as a resource to keep you up to date.

Second, this is all based on United States mortgage financing. For those of you investing in other countries, the specifics of this chapter will be less relevant to you. Hopefully, you'll still find the general financing principles and lessons helpful.

1. CONFORMING AND GOVERNMENT-INSURED RESIDENTIAL MORTGAGES

Conforming and government-insured residential mortgages are the typical mortgages used to buy houses and small residential properties. These are your best bet to get the lowest interest mortgages with the best terms. These are your ideal long-term loans for house hacks and regular rental properties.

In most cases, government agencies or quasi-government entities like Fannie Mae and Freddie Mac are involved in the market for this type of mortgage. This means the loans will all have a standardized application and approval process that can sometimes become tedious and slow. But the benefits of these financing options can be worth it in the end.

FHA LOANS

What Are They?

A loan program insured by a government agency called the Federal Housing Administration (FHA). The actual loans are made by banks or other lenders, but the FHA insurance protects these lenders from losses that could result from borrower defaults. The program is designed to help low- to moderate-income families own their home.

Positives:

- Down payment minimum as low as 3.5 percent of purchase price
- Credit score can be as low as 580 and still qualify for normal program
- Credit score can be as low as 500 with a larger 10 percent down payment[51]
- Fixed-interest, thirty-year loans
- One-, two-, three-, and four-unit properties are eligible
- Remodel loans available with 203(k) program
- Streamline refinance program available

---

51 "203(b) Mortgage Insurance Program," Federal Deposit Insurance Corporation, pg. 22, last accessed on 12/15/2022, https://www.fdic.gov/resources/bankers/affordable-mortgage-lending-center/guide/part-1-docs/203b-mortgage-insurance-program.pdf.

- Can keep loan after moving (if you meet minimum occupancy requirements), which means you could keep it as a rental property. But it will be difficult to get another FHA loan.

Negatives:
- Only available for principal residence, not pure investment properties
- Higher closing costs and fees, including a 1.75 percent up-front mortgage insurance premium
- Ongoing mortgage insurance paid monthly that lasts for the entire term of the mortgage unless you put more than 10 percent down[52]
- Application and approval process can be slow and tedious

Who Are They For?
- You must live in the home with this type of loan. It's perfect for any of the house-hacking strategies (traditional, live-in-then-rent, live-in flip) with a one-, two-, three-, or four-unit property
- If you have limited down payment funds or your credit is less than perfect, this may be the first choice for you

Where to Find Them:
- Lenders must be approved by the FHA. Search for lenders at banks, mortgage brokers, credit unions, and other online lenders.
- Ask local real estate agents who work with first-time home buyers for referrals to good FHA-approved lenders.

VA LOANS

What Are They?
A loan program for veterans and active-duty members of the U.S. military services. The program is insured by the Veterans Administration (VA), and like the FHA program, loans are made by banks or other lenders. The VA insures these loans to encourage lending and protect lenders from losses.

---

[52] "Appendix 1.0—Mortgage Insurance Premiums," U.S. Department of Housing and Urban Development, last accessed on 12/15/2022, https://www.hud.gov/sites/documents/15-01MLATCH.PDF.

Positives:

- Down payment as low as zero percent of the purchase price
- No official credit score requirement, although most lenders require a 620 score or higher to qualify
- Fixed-interest, thirty-year loans
- One-, two-, three-, and four-unit properties are eligible (although multi-unit properties may have stricter credit requirements)
- Multiple property purchases are possible
- Can keep loan after moving, which opens possibility of keeping property as a rental

Negatives:

- Only available for principal residence, not pure investment properties
- Higher closing costs and fees, including an up-front funding fee that varies depending on how much you put down
- Application, appraisal, and approval process can be slow and tedious
- Not a good fit for fixer-upper properties. The VA appraisal process has strict requirements to ensure a property is safe, sound, and sanitary.

Who Are They For?

- You must live in the home with this type of loan; it's perfect for any of the house-hacking strategies (traditional, live-in-then-rent, live-in flip) with a one-, two-, three-, or four-unit property
- If you are a veteran or an active member of the military with limited down payment funds, you should strongly consider this loan program

Where to Find Them:

- Lenders must be approved by the VA. Search for lenders at banks, mortgage brokers, credit unions, and other online lenders
- Ask local real estate agents who work with first-time home buyers for referrals to good VA-approved lenders

CONFORMING MORTGAGES

What Are They?

Any loans that meet the terms and requirements of Fannie Mae and Freddie Mac. These are government-sponsored entities (GSEs) who buy most of the conforming mortgages originated by other lenders. For borrowers with good credit and for properties that qualify, conforming loans can give you some of the best interest rates and terms of any mortgages.

Positives:

- Owner occupants *and* non-owner occupants (investors) are eligible
- Fixed-interest, thirty-year and fifteen-year loans
- One-, two-, three-, or four-unit properties are eligible
- Multiple property purchases are possible
- 3 percent to 20 percent down payments (for owner occupants)
- 15 percent to 30 percent down payments (for investors)[53]
- Renovation loans available (through HomeStyle program)

Negatives:

- More strict credit and income requirements than government loans
- Down payments below 20 percent normally require private mortgage insurance
- It is more difficult to get multiple conforming loans, with increasing difficulty above four loans and a maximum amount of ten loans
- Longer, slower closing process compared to private loans

Who Are They For?

- If you have good credit and income, this is usually the most affordable type of loan with the best terms (fixed interest, low payments).
- House-hacking strategies (traditional, live-in-then-rent, live-in flip)

---

53 "Eligibility Matrix," Fannie Mae, last accessed on 12/15/2022, https://singlefamily.fanniemae.com/media/20786/display.

- Rental strategies, especially long-term rentals. Short-term rentals are also possible, but using short-term income to qualify may be more difficult.

Where to Find Them
- Most lenders at banks, mortgage brokers, credit unions, and other online lenders will offer conforming mortgages
- Ask local real estate agents for their favorite mortgage lender who understands and closes a lot of conforming loans

2. COMMERCIAL MORTGAGES

This category of loans is a catchall for any institutional loan targeted to investors that doesn't fit into the conforming or government-insured categories. Some of you will graduate to these types of loans after beginning with the first category. Others may use this category of loans from the start because of its greater flexibility and scalability for investors.

Both DSCR and portfolio loans have their pluses and minuses. I see small and mighty investors using DSCR loans for long-term and short-term rentals with one-, two-, three-, or four-unit properties in good condition. Portfolio loans are more flexible for commercial and multifamily property, as well as fixer-upper properties if you build a relationship with the lender (this is how I financed my first few remodel projects).

DSCR (DEBT SERVICE COVERAGE RATIO) LOANS

What Are They?
DSCR or debt service coverage ratio loans allow investors to qualify with the income from a rental property and not from personal income. These loans are ideal for investors who've hit a loan limit with other programs or self-employed investors. Loan terms are typically fixed for thirty years, although there are also adjustable-rate, interest only, and forty-year loan programs.

Positives:

- No tax returns or personal income requirements
- Fixed-interest, thirty-year loans available
- Five- and seven-year ARM (adjustable-rate mortgages) available at lower rates
- Can use for purchase or refinance (like with BRRRR strategy)
- Can use for long-term or short-term rentals
- One-, two-, three-, or four-unit properties are eligible, including condos and townhouses in many cases
- Can scale to multiple rental properties faster
- Often faster closing times (versus conforming or government-insured loans)
- Available to foreign nationals who want to invest in the U.S.

Negatives:

- Won't be ideal for fixer-upper properties; will need to use a different loan product first and then refinance
- Higher interest rates than conforming or government-insured loans
- Up-front loan fees
- Minimum 20 to 25 percent down payment
- Higher credit score requirements than government-insured loans
- Rentals with lower cash flow may not meet DSCR requirements
- Prepayment penalties for several years after loan are common

Who Are They For?

- Any investor who has hit their borrowing limit with conventional or government-insured loans
- Any investor who doesn't fit the strict application requirements of other loan programs, such as self-employed, retired, or full-time investors

Where to Find Them:

- DSCR lenders usually specialize in these types of loans, so you will need to look beyond the traditional mortgage lenders
- Search online for DSCR and "non-qualified" mortgages. There are many lenders now offering this type of mortgage.

- Network online and at local meetups with other investors and ask around to see which lenders other active investors are using

PORTFOLIO LENDERS

What Are They?

Portfolio lenders are local or commercial banks who keep their loans in-house, in their "portfolio," instead of selling them on the open market. This means that the qualifying process is much less standardized and rigid than with residential mortgages. This flexibility with loan approval means you can often borrow more loans and borrow against different properties (including fixer-uppers and five-plus-unit properties) using portfolio lenders. You can also build relationships with individual loan officers at a bank who can do repeat business with you. Although interest rates are competitive, portfolio lender terms are not usually as attractive as residential mortgages, with balloons or adjustable rates after five or ten years being very common.

Positives:

- Less rigid qualifying process and potentially easier approval
- Flexibility with property types (small residential, larger multifamily, commercial, land, and more)
- Remodel and construction loans are possible
- Faster closings because of less red tape and fewer third-party approvals
- Relationship lenders who could finance deals for many years and help with other business banking needs
- No official loan limit like with conforming loans (although lenders may cut you off after a certain number of loans with their bank)
- Some flexibility and negotiation possible with loan terms
- Lower interest rates than hard money

Negatives:

- Usually require five-to-ten-year balloons and/or adjustable interest rates

- Payments are usually higher with amortization lengths between ten and twenty-five years instead of thirty
- Personal guarantees normally required, even with loans to a limited liability company (LLC)
- Relationships with lenders can change if bank is sold or individual retires (Dave Ramsey's commercial loan difficulties were like this)

Who Are They For?
- Any investor who has outgrown conforming or government-insured loans
- Any investor looking for a lower-interest alternative to hard-money loans (this was how I funded my first few fixer-upper properties)
- Any investor who wants more flexibility with approval and loan terms
- Any investor looking for a relationship lender and banker

Where to Find Them:
- Ask around for commercial loan officers at local banks; I've found smaller and regional banks to be excellent sources of this type of loan
- Network with other veteran investors, builders, and entrepreneurs and ask who they use for commercial loans

3. PRIVATE AND HARD MONEY LOANS

This category of loans branches beyond bank and institutional lenders into loans from private individuals or small lending businesses. Private money has been the No. 1 source of funds for my own deals over the last twenty years as an investor. Unlocking access to these funds was a turning point in my ability to scale and buy properties consistently. And just as important, my payments have been extremely helpful to my private lenders. They have used the interest to grow their retirement accounts and pay for their lifestyle without having to do all the work of real estate investing.

Because I built private money relationships, I never used hard money. But for many investors, hard money can be an excellent source of additional funds that requires less up-front work than private money. They're especially useful on fixer-upper properties for flips or BRRRR method deals when other lenders may not make the loan.

PRIVATE MONEY LOANS

What Are They?
These are loans from individuals or the self-directed retirement accounts of individuals. Because they are loaning their own money, the private lenders have much more flexibility than an institutional lender or bank. The interest rate, terms, and property criteria are all negotiable between the lender and you as the borrower.

Positives:
- Easier or no qualifying to get a loan
- Flexibility, as all the terms of the loan are negotiable
- Fast, simple closings make it easier to negotiate discounted purchases
- Low closing costs and fewer hurdles, such as appraisals
- Fixer-upper properties are fine with many private lenders
- Long-term relationship possible so that you can borrow money for years
- Possible to expand to other lenders with positive referrals

Negatives:
- Learning curve to understand, explain, and negotiate
- Takes time and work to find private lenders
- Interest rates could be higher than bank loans
- Many private lenders want shorter terms, meaning not twenty or thirty years

Who Are They For?
- Investors who need short-term financing for fixer-uppers
- Investors who want easier qualification processes than bank loans

- Investors who want to expand their financing options beyond bank loans

Where to Find Them:
- Tell people you already know that you invest in real estate and pay interest to private lenders; someone who shows interest may be a potential lender
- Network at real estate meetups with other investors; many of them also make private loans or prefer to invest passively instead of actively
- Don't forget about self-directed retirement accounts. Educate friends and other investors about making loans with retirement funds by moving them to a self-directed custodian. Be careful, however, with regulations against self-dealing and making loans to close family members.

HARD MONEY LOANS

What Are They?
Hard money loans are very similar to private money loans, except the lender is in the business of making these loans. Hard money loans, sometimes called bridge loans, usually have shorter terms, from six to twelve months. Hard money lenders focus on the value of the "hard" asset and less on the credit or personal qualifications of the borrower. The loans are most often used for fix-and-flip or BRRRR (buy, rehab, rent, refinance, repeat) type deals where the property's condition wouldn't qualify for a normal bank loan.

Positives:
- Easier qualifying to get a loan
- Fast, simple closings make it easier to negotiate discounted purchases
- Fixer-upper properties are fine
- Easier to find hard money lenders than private money lenders

Negatives:
- Interest rates and fees are usually very high relative to other loan types

- Short terms mean you must have a strong plan to refinance or sell quickly
- Typically, more transactional, less relationship-driven than private money

Who Are They For?
- Investors with fixer-upper properties who need easy, fast loans
- Investors with credit or other qualification issues

Where to Find Them:
- Hard money lenders often advertise and hang out at local real estate networking meetings
- Search for hard money lenders or bridge loans online, on BiggerPockets, and in real estate Facebook groups

4. SELLER FINANCING

Sometimes the best source of financing for real estate investments comes from a seller and not from a third-party lender. I have made seller-financing purchases with $3,000 down payments, very low interest rates (including zero percent in a few cases), and extremely flexible terms (like payments that don't start for three months). All seller-financing terms are negotiable, and there are no loan limits or strict qualifying criteria. Your results with seller financing are limited only by your creativity and ability to explain the benefits.

Most sellers will not be able or willing to finance your purchases, but for certain sellers, it can be a beneficial method to sell their property. As an investor, you need to understand how it works and be willing to ask for it during your negotiations. There are a few different variations of seller financing that I'll explain in this section.

SELLER CARRY-BACK FINANCING

What Is It?
When a property owner sells their property, they can choose to receive some or all of their equity over time. Instead of getting

cash at closing, they can receive installment payments (usually including interest) from the buyer. This delayed purchase is called seller financing. The paperwork is very similar to a normal real estate loan, including a promissory note and a security instrument such as a mortgage or deed of trust.

Positives:
- All terms are negotiable, including interest rate, down payment, monthly payment, and length of financing
- Easy or no qualifying, although most sellers will want to know more about your credibility and ability to perform
- Fast, simple closings
- Potential discount later if seller wants or needs cash
- Non-recourse financing without a personal guarantee is typical

Negatives:
- Learning curve to understand and explain how it works
- Not always easy to negotiate; requires patience and a different strategy
- Many sellers don't have large amounts of equity, which makes seller financing less helpful unless you use a different strategy like subject-to or lease options

Who Is It For?
- Any investor looking for easy qualifying and better terms
- Investors willing to spend more time learning and practicing negotiation

Where to Find It:
- I've found the most seller-financing deals from long-term rental owners who are looking to get out of the management of their properties. You can use Driving for Dollars, direct mail, and other marketing campaigns to find these property owners.
- Pay attention during all your negotiations for opportunities to make an offer that includes seller financing. Be ready to explain the benefits to the seller, which include passive income, secured investment, estate planning (aka not giving lump sums of cash to their heirs), and potential tax benefits from an installment sale.

SUBJECT-TO THE MORTGAGE

What Is It?

This financing technique is a variation of seller financing in which you buy a property (get a deed to the property) and leave an existing mortgage in place. You are buying the property "subject-to" this existing mortgage, and you begin making payments on it each month. You do not qualify to assume the mortgage. Instead, the mortgage stays in the name of the original borrower and property seller.

Positives:

- No qualifying
- No expensive loan fees, appraisals, or other up-front financing costs
- Take advantage of existing low-interest, fixed, thirty-year financing
- Little or no down payment possible
- Help sellers who could hurt their credit or lose a property to foreclosure
- Many subject-to purchases are of newer properties in good condition

Negatives:

- A due-on-sale clause in most mortgages means that the lender could call the entire loan due and payable after your subject-to purchase. This is like a balloon payment that could happen anytime the lender chooses. In practice, many residential mortgage lenders do not call the loan due, which is why the strategy has remained popular among investors.
- You must find very motivated sellers who are willing to sell subject-to. Usually, they are behind on payments or about to be behind on payments.
- Difficult to explain to sellers, insurance agents, closing attorneys, and others involved in the transaction.
- Many investors try to be sneaky and hide their transactions using trusts or other techniques to avoid the due-on-sale clause. This is a mistake and a bad business practice. Do

any transaction, including subject-to purchases, with full transparency to the seller, lender, and everyone involved.
- Learning curve to execute the transaction correctly, including getting a new insurance policy on the property, dealing with existing escrow accounts, and communicating with the mortgage company for the seller.

Who Is This For?
- Can be a helpful strategy for investors looking to use alternative financing strategies without qualifying for bank loans.
- In my opinion, not a strategy for beginners the way it's marketed by some online gurus. It requires extra learning, understanding of paperwork, and financial reserves to execute the strategy well.

Where to Find It:
- Market to owners of properties who are behind on payments or experiencing some sort of financial challenge related to their house.

MASTER LEASE OPTION

What Is It?
This is another variation on seller financing. An option contract is like a purchase and sale agreement, but the difference is that you as the buyer can choose to walk away from the purchase and simply lose your option deposit. The seller, on the other hand, must sell to you at the option price during the agreed-upon window of time. A master lease gives you possession of the property and the right to sublease it to others. The option and master lease can be used separately or at the same time as a master lease option.

Positives:
- No qualifying required
- No expensive loan fees, appraisals, or other up-front financing costs

- Small option deposits of 3 percent or less of the purchase price are possible
- Control the equity and income of the property without actually owning it
- Use as a tool with motivated sellers to avoid the need for third-party financing
- Use as a tool to Airbnb properties for a large cash flow without owning the property
- Use as a tool with money partners who can buy the property using their cash and credit, then master lease option the property back to you for a profit and passive income. This is known as a credit partnership.
- Use your optioned properties as replacement properties for your 1031 tax-free exchanges when you sell other investment properties
- Use your optioned properties as replacement properties for *other* people's 1031 tax-free exchanges, and then master lease option the property back from them after the sale

Negatives:

- Learning curve to understand and explain how it works
- Not always easy to negotiate. Requires patience and a different strategy
- Any money you spend could be at risk since you don't have title, for example, if the property owner goes bankrupt, dies, or changes their mind. You do have a contract that you can "cloud" the title with, but defending your position can be expensive if the owner or the owner's heirs choose not to sell.
- If the owner has an existing mortgage, you must ensure they use your rent to make the mortgage payments. Otherwise, the underlying loan could go into foreclosure.
- Lease options could trigger the due-on-sale clause if the seller has a mortgage and the lender discovers the lease option.

Who Is This For?

- Any investor looking for easy qualifying and better terms
- Investors willing to spend more time learning and practicing negotiation

Where to Find It:
- Use similar strategies to find master lease options as you would with seller financing
- Avoid spending much of your money on fixer-uppers if you only have a lease or option. The best deal candidates are pretty properties or properties with small, inexpensive repair costs.

5. CASH PURCHASES

To pay for an investment property, you don't actually have to get financing on the property! You can pay cash for the deal. Here are a couple of ways to do that.

CASH SAVINGS

What Is It?
You simply save up enough money to pay cash for a property without a loan. For high-priced markets with $500,000 properties, this could be impossible for newer investors. But in lower-priced markets, saving $50,000 to $100,000 for a purchase could be more reasonable. If you don't have enough cash, you could also partner with someone else so that combined you have enough to pay for it. Or you could buy the property using a self-directed retirement account if you have enough retirement savings. This requires moving the retirement money to a custodian who specializes in real estate investments.

Positives:
- Simple
- Low risk because you have no debt
- Positive cash flow from the beginning that you can save for more deals or use to fund your lifestyle
- Easier to negotiate discounted prices with cash purchases

Negatives:
- Could take time to save up enough cash for a purchase

- Slower way to grow your rental business
- No third-party financing approval, which sometimes helps you avoid mistakes. You're on your own.

Who Is It For?
- Conservative investors who like to keep it simple
- Advanced investors who prioritize reduced risk over maximizing growth

Where to Find It:
- In your savings account!
- Search for self-directed retirement account custodians to use that strategy

HELOC (HOME EQUITY LINE OF CREDIT)

What Is It?
A home equity line of credit (HELOC) is a revolving type of loan that lets you borrow against the equity in your principal residence. Once the loan is set up, it works by allowing you to draw the money (write a check) anytime you need it, including when you want to buy an investment property. You will own the investment property without any debt, but the debt on your home will increase by the amount of the check. You'll also have to pay interest on the HELOC loan.

Positives:
- Fast, easy closings because you can write a check
- Unlimited access to as little or as much of the money as you need
- Low closing costs on the investment property purchase
- Interest rates are usually lower than investment property loans
- Pay interest only during the initial "draw" period
- Easier qualifying because it's an owner-occupant loan
- Repeat process indefinitely by refinancing the investment property to repay the HELOC balance back to zero

Negatives:

- This is a home loan, so you could lose your home to foreclosure if you face problems and can't repay the loan
- Many HELOC loans have adjustable interest rates
- After the draw period, which is typically five to ten years, you can no longer draw money and you must repay any balance over a fifteen- to twenty-year period, depending on the lender.
- Lenders can cancel a line of credit during tough economic times, right when you might need it most.
- Can't access all your home equity. Most lenders have a max loan to value (LTV) of 80 percent or 85 percent of the home's value. If you have an existing first mortgage, the difference between the max LTV and your loan will be the maximum you can borrow on a HELOC.

Who Is It For?

- Investors who feel comfortable borrowing against their home equity to accelerate their progress as a real estate investor
- Investors with enough equity to pay for an investment property
- Be careful using a HELOC for down payment funds unless the property has a very strong cash flow that can pay for all HELOC interest costs and if you have a plan to repay the HELOC quickly
- HELOC loans are a great *short-term* financing tool, but I don't recommend them as long-term financing because of their terms and the risk of a lender calling them due in tough economic times

Where to Find It:

- Start by asking the existing bank where you have personal accounts about their HELOC loan programs; ask them to pay your closing costs when possible
- Search online and ask other investors where they got a good deal on HELOC loans

LOCK IN YOUR FINANCING, UNLOCK THE REAL ESTATE BUSINESS

When I first began investing in real estate on my own, I spent months studying, learning, and talking about what I wanted to do. But then one day I realized that to *actually do* real estate investing, I needed to secure the money. It would never work if I couldn't come up with the funds to buy properties.

That's when I got serious about studying a small number of financing options until I could use them to buy a property. I started with two sources: local bank portfolio loans and private money. I built relationships, got preapproved for a mortgage, and then began making offers. Locking in these financing sources made all the difference for me. It literally unlocked the rest of the business for me, and I've never looked back.

That's why this step of your journey is so critical. I provided a menu of financing options in this chapter because there's no *one* right way to finance your real estate. But you do need to choose one or two options to specialize in. Once you're preapproved for a bank loan, have a relationship with a private lender, or have a strategy to acquire seller financing, you can make real progress as a small and mighty real estate investor.

But even after you secure financing, there might still be one other challenge related to funding your deals. And that's when you run out of cash for down payments! I've been there plenty of times with my own real estate investing, but I figured out creative ways to safely continue growing. So, if you don't have personal funds for your next deal, I'll help you solve that in the next chapter.

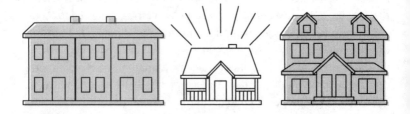

CHAPTER 20
CREATIVE STRATEGIES IF YOU DON'T HAVE ENOUGH CASH

Buying a rental investment property can cost a lot of money. Even in a less-expensive market, a property will cost tens of thousands of dollars. And in most markets, your deals will cost hundreds of thousands or even millions of dollars.

As I showed in the last chapter, you have financing sources available to help you pay 65 to 100 percent of your purchase price. But in almost every case, you will still have to come up with more cash. This extra money covers your down payment, closing costs, and other up-front costs.

I have faced this reality many times in my twenty-year journey as a real estate investor. When I first started, I literally had about $15,000 in the bank, saved up from my first year finding deals for other investors. But I had to use this money as an emergency fund and as the way to pay my bills until I could generate money from our real estate business. I couldn't afford to use it for down payments on real estate.

Later in my journey, I began making money flipping houses. I used this money both to pay my bills and to fund long-term rental investments. But inevitably, I ran out of money after investing it into deals. And as luck would have it, that's exactly when a *great* deal that I couldn't pass up would come along.

Both as a brand-new and a growing investor, I had to find creative ways to help me fund deals without a lot of my own cash. That doesn't mean I tried to always invest with no money down. As I shared in a prior chapter, too much leverage can lead to a lot of problems. And I think having your own cash in deals is a good form of investing discipline over the long run.

But I realize that many of you may be in the same place I was. You need some strategies to make the most of your limited cash so that you can continue making progress with real estate investing. And you also want to do it in a safe way so that you don't slide backward with big financial mistakes.

In this chapter I'll share some of the strategies that worked well for me. Just pick the ones that make the most sense for you, and work on applying them to your next real estate deal. I'll start by helping you figure out how much cash you actually need to do a real estate deal.

HOW MUCH CASH DO YOU NEED TO BUY A RENTAL PROPERTY?

Your down payment isn't the only cash you'll need to buy a rental property. You'll also need cash for several other up-front costs. I'll explain each of these cash needs in more detail so that you'll know exactly how much cash you need on your deals.

Down Payment

A down payment is the portion of the purchase price that's not paid for by your lender. I like to think about it like a bucket that gets filled with enough money to buy the property. With an 80 percent loan, the lender fills up 80 percent of your bucket with their funds. Then you top off the bucket with the other 20 percent using your own cash. That's your down payment.

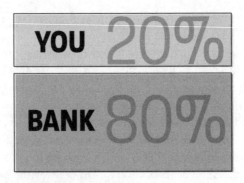

Traditionally, most bank lenders required 20 to 30 percent as a down payment. This is still true today in the universe of commercial and investment mortgages. But with owner-occupied mortgages, lenders have developed programs for smaller down payments, like 5 to 20 percent of the purchase price. When you pay less than 20 percent down, the lender will require you to pay for mortgage insurance. This is paid upfront at closing or monthly in addition to your principal and interest payment.

With an FHA loan, you can pay as little as 3.5 percent down. And the VA loan program allows a zero percent down payment. I've also bought properties with little or no money down using creative financing strategies like private money, lease options, or subject-to.

Closing Costs

Many new investors forget about closing costs, but they can add up to a lot of cash. These are the costs you pay during the actual transaction of purchasing the property. A very rough rule of thumb is that closing costs are between 1 and 4 percent of the purchase price. But with your real deals, you need to move beyond a rule of thumb and get estimates for all these costs from your team members.

Here is a list of some of the common closing costs you'll pay:

- **Financing costs:** These costs are higher with institutional and hard-money lenders and can be lower with private and seller financing. They may include:
  - *Appraisal fee*: pays for a value report for the property
  - *Application fee*: pays for processing of application
  - *Credit report fee*: pays to check your credit

- *Document preparation fee*: pays to prepare your mortgage paperwork
- *Loan origination fee*: up-front lender fee for processing the transaction
- *Points*: up-front interest payment usually charged by hard-money lenders
- *Escrow reserves*: If your mortgage has an escrow to pay taxes and insurance, a lender may require extra funds for a cushion or reserve
- **Title insurance:** A type of insurance paid one time that protects you if a future problem arises that affects your title or legal ownership of the property
  - *Lender's policy*: Protects the lender; required by most lenders
  - *Owner's policy*: Most attorneys and title companies also recommend an owner's policy to protect your equity as the owner
- **Title search fee:** Pays for someone to produce a report of the ownership and title history of this property in the public records
- **Closing/Escrow fee:** Title company or closing attorney fee to handle "escrow," which includes the transaction paperwork, signatures, and transfer of all funds. Some states require attorneys to handle closing while others allow title companies to do it.
- **Transfer tax:** Many states and local governments charge a tax upon the transfer of a piece of real estate from one entity to another. This can be as low as .01 percent to as high as 4 percent of the purchase price.
- **Recording fees:** A charge to record the official paperwork in the public records
- **Property insurance:** Most insurance companies require you to pay for insurance upfront at the time of closing
- **Real estate commissions:** If a property is listed, the fee is typically paid by the seller and the cost is subtracted from their funds at closing. But in some cases, the buyer may pay a buyer's agent commission out of pocket at closing.
- **Inspection fees:** If you hire property inspectors, which I recommend and talked more about in the chapter on due diligence, you'll often pay their fee at closing

Most residential, owner-occupied mortgage lenders are required to disclose an estimate of your financing and other closing costs before making a loan. But even if they don't, you can ask your lender, your closing agent, insurance agent, and other team members to send you a list of their costs. Use my list to help you know what to ask for.

Repair Costs

Some of the best deals need repairs. At a minimum they may require cleanup and light cosmetic work like painting and landscaping. And with major fixer-uppers, the property could require a "gut" rehab, where you rip out everything and start over.

Some renovation loan programs will cover a portion of your repair costs. For example, the lender may loan you 80 percent of the repair costs and require you to pay 20 percent from your cash. They would also likely cap their funding at the after-repair appraised value of the property. Ask the lender on your team for the specific requirements of their renovation program.

With hard-money and private-money lenders, the amount of the repairs they will fund depends on the after-repair value of the property. For example, most lenders I've worked with will only loan up to 65 to 70 percent of the after-repair value. If my purchase price and all repair costs totaled 70 percent or less, they would loan me 100 percent of the money I needed. But if my repair costs exceeded 70 percent, I had to use my cash to pay the difference.

Holding Costs

If you buy a rental property that is vacant, you will have to pay costs until you get it filled with a renter. These costs include the following:

- **Mortgage payment:** usually principal and interest
- **Property taxes:** even though you pay this once a year, I like to set aside money in a savings or a lender-required escrow account so that I have the money available
- **Property insurance:** same as taxes; annual cost that I like to save for monthly
- **HOA fees:** homeowner or condo association fees to save for monthly as well
- **Utilities:** electric, water, and gas bills while the property is vacant

- **Landscaping maintenance:** pay to keep landscaping looking good or to remove snow in winter for colder areas

All these costs together could be thousands of dollars per month, depending on your situation. If your rental property is in perfect condition, you could still be paying these costs for one or two months until you find a renter to move in and start paying. And if you have a remodeling project, your property could be vacant for many months.

When you are estimating your cash needs for holding costs, be conservative. Even if you think you can rent a unit in one month, give yourself two. And if you think the repairs will take two months, set aside enough cash to pay for six months, just in case. You'll be happy to have the extra cash if things don't go smoothly.

Cash Reserves

The final category of cash you'll need for a rental purchase is cash reserves. For some reason, I've found that investors ignore this category more than the others. But setting aside cash reserves has saved me many times during my twenty years of investing.

I can't tell you exactly how much cash to set aside. This is one of those personal choices that depends on what makes you sleep well at night. But in my own rental business, I started by setting aside $5,000 per property in a savings account. This money was a cushion to help me when a tenant moved out or stopped paying or when I had a major, unexpected repair expense.

As my rental business grew larger, I switched to setting aside enough cash to pay for three to six months of our fixed property expenses. These are the expenses that must be paid no matter what, like mortgage payments, taxes, insurance, and maintenance. Just like an emergency fund in personal finance, this rental reserve fund gives me peace of mind that I have a "runway" to keep our business afloat during tough times. The more conservative you want to be, the more months of cash you should set aside.

Summary of Cash Needs

To give you a summary of how much cash you might need on a typical deal, let me share an example. Let's say you buy a property for $200,000 with a 20 percent down payment. You get a typical conforming mortgage, and the property needs only a minimal number of cosmetic repairs (painting, cleaning, landscaping, minor repairs, etc.). After closing, it takes you two months before receiving your first rent payment. Here's how much cash you might spend:

- $40,000 = down payment (20 percent)
- $5,000 = closing costs
- $10,000 = repair costs
- $3,000 = holding costs
- $5,000 = reserves
- **$63,000 = total cash needed**

Of course, your actual numbers could change depending on the financing you use and the details of your property. But this gives you an idea of how to calculate the total cash needs for your own deal.

CREATIVE WAYS TO FIND THE CASH FOR YOUR DEALS

If you've made it this far in the book, I assume you are a disciplined and motivated person. Therefore, I also know you'll be spending less than you earn to save more money. Over time, that boring but important process of saving your own cash will be the engine that helps you achieve financial independence.

But especially in your growth as an investor, you've got to get creative just to get started or to continue your momentum. That's where some of the strategies that I'll now explain can help. They are ways to find cash for your deals so that you can keep building wealth on your way to increased financial independence.

PASSIVE MONEY PARTNER

If you don't have enough cash to do a deal, you can partner with someone who does. I used a money partner on my very first deal, and then I tweaked and repeated the process several times over the next few years as a young investor. It was a strategy that helped me gain momentum and safely build my rental portfolio. I'll explain how I did it so that you can get some ideas for how to do it too.

Finding Money Partners

You may not believe it yet, but there are people out there with money who would love to fund your deals. They may have money in low-interest bank accounts, or they may not feel comfortable having all their money in the stock market. They would like to invest some of that money into real estate, but they may not have the time or energy to make it happen.

You can find these potential partners by talking with family, friends, work colleagues, and other real estate investors about what you do. The ideal money partner is someone you trust, who you would enjoy doing business with over a long period. They'll likely be someone who already likes real estate and has a solid understanding of finance and investing. And of course, they should also have enough cash and credit to do a deal. Do not use a money partner who has limited financial resources or who is a beginner investor.

You can start by just telling everyone what you do as a real estate investor. You buy quality properties that produce income and grow in value. You make money by collecting rent, paying down your mortgage, and holding the property until it grows in value. And most important, you sometimes use a passive money partner to do the deals with you.

If they show interest, you can tell them more details about how a deal could work. As your money partner, they'll provide the cash and potentially get a loan. As the entrepreneur, you'll find a good deal, buy it, manage it, and handle the active work so that the investor can be completely passive. Then you'll split the profits, preferably fifty-fifty.

How to Structure Deals with a Money Partner

There are dozens of ways to structure a deal with a money partner. But in my own experience, I try to keep things as simple as possible. Instead of a long-term partnership, I use a joint venture arrangement (JV). This means we do one deal together, and we divide the responsibilities and profits for that one deal. If it works out, we can do more deals together. But it keeps the business relationship much simpler and more focused.

When it comes to splitting the profits, many investors are used to complicated arrangements that require a PhD in finance to understand. And not only are they complicated, but the entrepreneur who puts the deal together often gets the better deal by earning fees and commissions before the money partner even earns their profits. I wanted to keep my money partners happy and coming back to me for more deals. So, I avoided those complicated, entrepreneur-favored deals.

I found the simplest arrangement on long-term rentals was a fifty-fifty joint venture (JV) that I learned from John Schaub. In this JV, the money partner puts up all the cash needed for the deal. Then, the money partner and entrepreneur split the positive or negative cash flow fifty-fifty while it's rented. And when they sell the property, they return the money partner's original investment and split the sales profits fifty-fifty. The entrepreneur doesn't charge a management fee, and the money partner doesn't charge interest. And they agree not to sell for five years or until some predetermined profit goal is reached, whichever comes first.

Holding Title to Joint Venture Deals

The money partner has the most at risk, so my goal was always to protect their money first. The simplest way was to let them, or their LLC, buy the property. This was also practical because they often got a loan to buy the property, and the lender required that the property be in their name. After the property is bought, you have a couple of options to protect your interest as the entrepreneur.

The first way is for the money partner to deed you an undivided 50 percent interest in the property. This type of ownership is known as tenants in common. This is not a partnership, and it doesn't require filing a partnership tax return. You legally own an undivided interest in half the physical property, which means you own half the lot, the building, etc. You could technically sell your 50 percent interest, although you'd find it tough to find a buyer. You and your money partner should sign a simple joint venture contract to ensure you're on the same page with your goals and plans for the property. Also run this arrangement by your real estate attorney to get their feedback and suggestions.

A second way to protect your interests is through a master lease option. The money partner still owns the property, but they master lease the property to you. You make sure the rent payment is enough to cover the mortgage, other expenses, and roughly splitting the cash flow. You then split any future repair costs fifty-fifty.

To participate in the future price, you get an option contract to buy 50 percent of the property once you pay 50 percent of the original down payment. Both the master lease and option could last long enough in the future, like five or ten years, so that the property has time to make money.

Of course, another alternative is to form some sort of entity, like an LLC, to hold title to the property. Just keep in mind that properly forming and running an entity isn't as easy as it seems. Annual paperwork, meetings, and tax returns are just part of the formalities you must follow. And getting financing and insurance is often more difficult with an entity. For this reason, most of my single-deal joint ventures avoided forming an LLC and just used some variation of the arrangements mentioned before.

Example Deal

To make this concept more real, let me share an example with numbers. Let's say you find a newer single-family house that's in a great location. It's worth $250,000 and you can buy it at a lower price of $200,000. The rent is $1,800 per month, and the taxes and insurance are $4,200 per year or $350 per month.

You put the property under contract, subject to due diligence and financing approval. During that contingency period, you share the deal with your passive money partner. She likes the deal and agrees to put up all the cash and credit for the deal. As the deal-finding entrepreneur, you invest none of your cash up front.

You then assign the contract to her, and she closes on the property purchase. She puts $60,000 or 30 percent down and gets a $140,000, thirty-year, fixed-interest loan at 6 percent interest and a payment of $840 per month. With a rent of $1,800 per month, that leaves $960 per month to pay for expenses and cash flow.

After the property is purchased at closing, you pay half of your money partner's closing costs and agree to pay half of the holding costs until it's rented. And she signs a master lease agreement and an option agreement with you. Your initial master lease payment is $1,495 per month, which gives the money partner enough to cover the $840 mortgage payment, $350 of monthly taxes and insurance, and $305 of cash flow. You get $305 per month of cash flow, which is the difference between $1,800 and $1,495. You and the money partner then agree to split any future repairs and vacancy costs fifty-fifty and adjust the master lease annually, as needed.

Because you picked an excellent location, you end up increasing rents several times over the next ten years. This boosts the overall cash flow to both joint venture partners. And the price appreciates enough that you're able to sell it to your tenant at the end of year ten for a net price (after closing costs) of $400,000.

By that time, the loan has also been paid down to $117,000, so the net proceeds from the sale are $283,000 ($400,000 – $117,000). Your money partner gets her $60,000 back, and you split the remaining $223,000. That's $111,500 profit to each of you.

You earned monthly cash flow and a big profit using *none* of your own money. And your money partner earned a monthly cash flow and a big profit using little or none of her time. When I did deals like this, my money partners were very happy and wanted to do more deals as soon as I had them. And as the entrepreneur, I was happy to do wealth-building deals that could never have happened because I didn't have the money.

In addition to money partner joint ventures, there are other creative ways to find the cash for your deals. I'll share a few more to get you thinking.

SECOND MORTGAGES FROM A PRIVATE INVESTOR

Once you've established yourself, you could simply borrow some or all the cash you need from your private investors instead of doing a joint venture. Instead of splitting profits, you would just pay your investor interest. And since you'll likely have a first mortgage with another lender, this private money loan would be a second position mortgage.

Using our prior example, here's what it could look like. You would buy the property worth $250,000 for $200,0000 and get a $140,000 loan from another lender. If the first lender allowed it, you could borrow $60,000 from the private money lender in second position. After closing, you'll owe a total of $200,000 in debt. And let's say you pay the private lender 6 percent interest or $300 per month.

When we first started, we paid our lenders 10 percent interest. We could afford to because we were quickly flipping the properties for a profit. But as we used this approach to buy rentals, we lowered our interest rate to 6 percent and paid them a steady monthly cash flow. We found these were attractive loans for some of our investor friends who had self-directed retirement accounts.

One downside of this approach is that you're highly leveraged. As I warned in an earlier chapter, you want to be careful with debt. When you borrow 100 percent, it's easy to become upside down (aka owe more than a property is worth) if property values drop. It's also very difficult to make a positive cash flow.

Another downside is that many residential mortgages don't allow second mortgages to help you fund your deal. They usually have strict requirements that the down payment funds must come from you personally. And you always want to follow the requirements of your mortgage lenders.

But for the right deals where you have sufficient cash flow, enough equity, and a cooperative first mortgage (like seller financing or a portfolio lender), a private lender second mortgage can be a tool to get deals done. My business partner and I used this technique to fund many of our deals early in our career. We especially used it when we bought properties well below their full value. Our goal was that our private lender's loan would be at or below 70 percent loan to value.

We also had a goal to pay these debts off. We used our positive cash flow and profits from other deals to pay off every one of these second mortgages. And now that we've grown as investors, we can use our own cash to fund our deals.

SECOND MORTGAGES FROM SELLER FINANCING

If you're short on cash, you can also consider asking the seller to take back a second mortgage. Like private mortgages, many residential mortgages from banks don't allow second mortgages from a seller. But this tool can make sense if you're using a portfolio lender or private lender in first position who allows it. You can also use this tool when buying a property subject-to a mortgage.

For example, let's say you find a seller who is behind on their $150,000 mortgage and facing the possibility of foreclosure. Their house has a full value of $250,000, and you negotiate a price of $200,000. You agree to buy subject-to their $150,000 mortgage, and you offer the seller a $50,000 seller-financing mortgage in second position. The seller financing will have no payments and no interest for ten years, unless you sell or refinance the property sooner.

The seller has avoided further credit problems and losing their equity to foreclosure. And you've been able to buy a property with little cash out of your pocket. The cash flow for the property will probably be positive as well because you're not paying interest on the $50,000.

When you get financing with zero percent interest, just keep in mind that the IRS has a rule called "imputed interest." Even if the financing doesn't pay interest, both you and the seller will need to report and pay taxes on what the interest *would have been* had you paid interest. Your tax professional can help you look up the IRS applicable federal rates to report this correctly.

HELOC OR 401K LOANS

Just like borrowing your down payment from a private lender or seller, you could also borrow the funds you need from a HELOC (home equity line of credit) on your home. And in many 401k plans, you can borrow up to $50,000 and repay your retirement plan with a reasonable interest rate. Just as with private lender second mortgages, you want to be very careful with this approach. You're essentially using 100 percent financing, so it's easy to get upside down with cash flow and equity.

But every entrepreneur I've known has taken risks early in their career. When you don't have a lot of funds to work with, you have to make a leap in order to move forward. So if you're careful, using a HELOC or 401k loan for part or all your cash needs may be a risk you're willing to take.

Just ensure you have enough cash flow to pay the loan interest. Also be sure you fully disclose your plan and the source of the funds on any applications for a first mortgage. Some lenders will allow this, and others won't. Also have a plan to pay off the HELOC or 401k loan balance as quickly as possible. This will avoid too much risk and make the loans available for another deal, if needed.

BRRRR METHOD

You might have heard of the BRRRR method to invest with little or none of your own cash funds. BRRRR stands for Buy, Rehab, Rent,

Refinance, Repeat. There is an entire BiggerPockets book , *Buy, Rehab, Rent, Refinance, Repeat*, by David Greene on the topic if you want to go deep on it.

The secret of BRRRR deals is to buy properties well below their full value. This kind of deal is normally available because it needs a lot of work, so you remodel the property to prepare it to rent. Then you get it rented to a quality tenant. And finally, you refinance the property at its increased value.

Here is an example of some numbers on an ideal BRRRR deal. A house is worth $250,000 after being fixed up. Using a hard-money or private-money loan, you buy it for $130,000 and perform repairs costing $50,000. With closing costs and holding costs added, your total investment in the property is about $190,000. You then rent to a tenant for $1,800 per month.

After a seasoning period of between three and six months, you apply for a refinance. The new appraisal comes in at $250,000, just as you had planned. The refinance lender agrees to loan you 75 percent of the full value, or $187,500. This pays off most of your purchase loan and costs and recycles most of your personal funds to use on another deal.

I have only used the BRRRR strategy a couple of times during my investing career. I used most of the other strategies I've shared in this chapter a lot more. This was mostly because I've always been a self-employed entrepreneur. Especially early in my career when I made less money, this made getting approved for refinance loans difficult. If I were starting today with easier-qualifying DSCR (debt service coverage ratio) loans available, I may have used the BRRRR method more.

But I also had a healthy respect for the difficulty and risk of the BRRRR strategy. It has a lot of moving parts, and there are factors outside your control—such as whether you can get a loan from the refinance lender. What happens if the credit market freezes between the time you buy the property and when you try to refinance? If you're doing too many of these deals, you could find yourself in trouble trying to handle the short-term balloon payments on your hard-money and private-money loans.

I've also seen investors who successfully use the BRRRR strategy get hypnotized into the perpetual debt religion. Because you *can* pull out your cash on every deal, you *do* keep pulling cash out of every deal. After all, it's how you maximize your returns! But this means you'll always have a lot of debt and risk, and it will be difficult to ever get off that growth treadmill.

Whether it's the BRRRR strategy or any other tool in this chapter, I've benefited by learning when to use the power tools and when to put them away. Starting your career with little or no cash is common. But if you're still using the same no-money-down power tools five or ten years later, you may want to pause and consider why you don't have more cash and where it's all going.

THE CONFIDENCE TO USE FINANCIAL LEVERAGE

The past three chapters have been all about financing your deals. The confidence to use financial leverage is partly about knowing which tools to use, like mortgages, private loans, money partners, and other creative financing strategies. But it's also about knowing how to use the tools safely. Remember cautionary stories like Dave Ramsey's, and follow my smart debt rules and your own gut feeling to stay out of trouble. When used well, financial leverage can be the key to your success in real estate investing.

But there's one more aspect of real estate investing that gives you the confidence to borrow and *pay back* millions of dollars. This final and essential piece of the real estate puzzle is owning and renting properties. Without being successful at this, nothing else will work.

That's why in the next part of this book, I'll share stories and lessons I've learned after owning hundreds of rental properties. This isn't always the sexiest part of the business, but it also doesn't have to take all your time and energy. I currently spend about an average of two hours per week managing my rental business.

I'll begin in the next chapter by showing you how I approach being a landlord and working with tenants. Then I'll share how to build systems for your property maintenance, bookkeeping, administrative tasks, and more.

PART V
GUIDE TO RENTAL PROPERTY OWNERSHIP

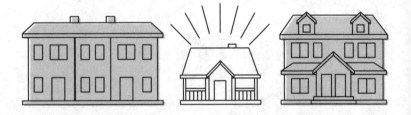

CHAPTER 21
PROPERTY MANAGEMENT TIPS AND BEST PRACTICES

As I write this, I am living in Granada, Spain, with my family for twelve months. I am over 4,200 miles (or 6,700 kilometers) from our rental properties in South Carolina, yet the income from these properties pays all our bills in Spain. And most weeks I spend no more than two hours managing my rental property business. The rest of my time can be spent on whatever I want, like practicing my Spanish skills and writing this book!

The fear of property management hassles keeps many people from owning rental properties. They're sold on the idea that rentals are bad because they're not as passive as investments like stocks. After all, who wants to be stuck in one place managing properties and getting calls at midnight about a leaky toilet? Some existing landlords don't mind this false perception because it reduces competition. But as someone who believes we need more small and mighty landlords, I like to tell a different story.

Most of the rental properties that my business partner and I own are managed by third-party management companies. But currently I also self-manage eight properties from a distance. Over the years, we've built systems, leveraged technology, found excellent team members, and attracted self-sufficient tenants. This has made our rental properties much more passive. The time I do still spend is usually on bookkeeping (yes, I still do that), responding to occasional property manager or contractor messages, or chatting with my business partner.

But it wasn't always that way. We invested a lot of time up front to find, buy, and stabilize these properties. The rentals each began as little time-intensive businesses, but they've become relatively passive investments. It's now possible for us as rental owners to travel the world, have other interests, and sleep through the night without getting calls about leaky toilets.

We've made a lot of mistakes and learned painful lessons in the process of getting to where we are as rental owners. In this chapter, I want to help you avoid some of those same mistakes by sharing property management tips, techniques, and best practices that we've learned. Although I'm very familiar with short-term rentals and have owned a couple, most of my direct management experience is with long-term rentals. That's where I'll focus in this chapter. And one of the first topics I want to cover is whether you should self-manage or hire third-party managers for your rentals.

SELF-MANAGEMENT VS. THIRD-PARTY MANAGEMENT

There is no right or wrong answer to whether you should self-manage your rentals or hire a third-party management company. It will depend on your personal temperament and interests. And it will also depend on the type of properties you own and whether you are local or long-distance.

For example, most long-distance investors use third-party property managers for the benefits I'll explain next. But local investors have more liberty to decide between self-management and third-party management. Whatever situation you're in, I'll share some tips below to help you decide.

Learn to Sweep the Floors First

Before we get into the positives and negatives, I first want to say that I agree with the advice that it's best to begin by sweeping the shop floors before you own the store. In other words, start by doing the nitty-gritty details of your rental management whenever possible. This will teach you how to be a landlord so that you'll know what to expect. Then if you choose to outsource management to someone else, you'll do a better job of holding them accountable.

And I also want to say that it's possible to continue managing your properties yourself for the rest of your life. John Schaub, who I've talked about several times in this book, continues to happily self-manage his twenty-five to thirty single-family rental houses almost five decades after he began investing. And as I said, I still self-manage eight properties, which happen to also be single-family houses. But I've chosen to outsource our more management-intensive student rental apartments to others.

Here are what I see as the positives and negatives of self-managing rental properties:

Positives of Self-Management
- Learn the business from the ground up
- Keep more cash flow in your pocket
- Handpick your tenants
- Build relationships with tenants
- Care more about the details of your property
- Save more on maintenance costs (or maybe not, because sometimes managers negotiate lower rates with contractors)
- Potential for substantial tax advantages (search for: real estate professional status and short-term rental tax loophole)
- A source of fulfillment and feeling productive after leaving a full-time job

Negatives of Self-Management
- Takes your personal time (although it can be *very* part-time)
- It may be necessary to be there in person (especially during tenant turnovers)
- Problems may occupy your mental thoughts and energy

- More difficult to own larger number of properties
- Less extensive network of contractors (maybe)
- Must stay up to date on latest laws affecting rentals
- Must handle tenant problems and evictions yourself

The self-managers I know don't mind a little bit of extra time and effort for a lot more control. They like to personally get involved with their tenants and in the details of their properties. And they find ways to be efficient with their time using technology, systems, and low-management properties.

For example, my easiest properties to self-manage are single-family houses in B or C areas. We have self-sufficient tenants who stay for years, which means less work for me. I also use low-cost or free property management software to screen tenants, collect rent, and organize maintenance. And in the next chapter, I'll share all the systems in my rental property business.

Now let's look at the positives and negatives of hiring a third-party management company:

Positives of Third-Party Management
- Allows owner to be more hands-off and mentally "off duty"
- First line of communication for tenant problems and complaints
- Go-to expert for rental market knowledge when buying new properties
- Internal team of people professionally trained to do the job (if you pick a good property manager)
- Cost benefits of scale; manage dozens or hundreds of properties
- Network of reliable maintenance contractors on call
- Systematized tenant screening process
- Potential source of new deals
- Give you the flexibility to invest from a distance

Negatives of Third-Party Management
- Less urgency filling vacancies because they're not paying the operating expenses
- May pay less attention to your property with so many others to manage

- Tenant-screening criteria could be different from yours
- Management fees (typically 8 percent to 11 percent of the monthly rent)
- Turnover of internal team members can affect service to your tenants and to you
- Potential misalignment of interests due to fee structure (for example, when the property manager receives an increased fee during turnover or if they actively try to turn tenants into homeowners and represent them as a buyer's agent)

Like any profession, not all property managers are equally good. I've been fortunate to find several excellent property managers who have done their job as well as or better than I could myself. When you find the right property manager, their services are well worth the cost. This is especially true for people who invest long-distance, because having a reliable, trustworthy property manager is likely your most important team member.

How to Decide—Self-Management vs. Third-Party Management

If you're on the fence and still in the early phases of your rental business, I'd recommend that you start doing it yourself. If you put in the effort, you'll get paid to learn and build a skill you can use for the rest of your life. The technology and systems to manage properties today have never been easier, and you can always outsource the management later.

For everyone else, the decision often comes down to where you'll get the highest return on investment for your time. For example, if you are a doctor who earns hundreds of thousands of dollars per year doing surgeries, self-management is not what you want to do. When you have other high-income opportunities, outsource property management and focus on making and saving more money to invest.

Or if you're a long-distance investor, I usually recommend that you hire a property manager both to save time and as a resource. Build their cost into every deal that you analyze so that their fees aren't an issue. Their network of contractors, knowledge of the local market, and ability to handle problems locally will make owning long-distance rentals much more enjoyable. In some markets, it is also legally required that the manager of the property is local.

And as you grow your rental property business, also think about the highest leverage real estate activities for your time. In my business, the highest paid task is always negotiating to buy properties. If I buy one extra property, it could make me hundreds of thousands of dollars for a few weeks of up-front work. That's a pretty good hourly rate that pays more than management. With a limited amount of time, this influences my choice of what to outsource.

Ultimately, remember that this decision isn't permanent. I started by self-managing and "graduated" into paying for property management once the income was sufficient to both cover my costs and justify my time. At the same time, I can always decide to go back to self-management even after hiring a third-party property manager.

Whether you decide to manage a property yourself or not, you still need to know the best practices of property management. That's what we'll cover in the rest of the chapter. And we'll start by looking at what makes the ideal tenant.

THE IDEAL TENANT

In this book so far, I've focused a lot on the numbers and the technical aspects of rental properties. But at its core, real estate is a people business. The better we serve our customers—our ideal tenants—the better we'll do as a rental property investor.

In my experience, renting to ideal tenants makes property management easy. But renting to the wrong tenants can make property management miserable. Here's how I define an ideal tenant:

- Pays on time
- Takes care of the property
- Is self-sufficient and responsible
- Stays for a long time

We'll soon look at how to screen for ideal tenants who match these criteria. But we need to start by putting the responsibility on *ourselves* as property owners. If we want to attract the best tenants, we need to own the best properties.

THE BEST PROPERTIES ATTRACT THE IDEAL TENANTS

I've talked to a lot of rental owners who complain about bad tenants. But when I see their properties, I'm not surprised. The properties are usually in a bad location, and they haven't bothered to fix up or maintain the property. Do they expect to get something different than they give?

Your ideal tenants have a choice of where to live. And they will choose to live in the best location, in a property that meets their needs, at a price they can afford. If you make sure you own properties that meet their criteria, you'll never have problems finding those ideal tenants. That's why I spent two entire chapters of this book teaching you the fundamentals of a good location and the right type of property.

My business partner and I own rentals in a college town. Our ideal tenant is a responsible student who stays for three or four years, pays their rent on time, studies a lot, and doesn't trash their rental unit or throw big parties. Most tenants who fit this description are graduate students or responsible second- or third-year students. Many of them prefer to live alone or with only one roommate so they don't have to deal with roommate drama. They also like to be close to campus and on a bus line so they can get back and forth to campus easily and inexpensively.

I remember inspecting one of my properties and instantly knowing we had one of our ideal tenants. It was a two-bedroom apartment on one side of a duplex. The tenant, who was an engineering major, lived there alone, and the place was immaculately clean. In the second bedroom was the equipment for his side-hustle business of carving wood to make artisan axe handles (apparently that's a thing). This business helped pay his way through school.

Every market is different. Your ideal tenant may be in the Section 8 program, a hospital worker, a police officer, or a retiree living on social security income. You can use the lessons from earlier in this book on finding an ideal investment location to discover the unique types of ideal tenants in your town. But then the principle remains the same in every market. If you own and maintain the best properties, you'll get ideal tenants.

Now let's look at how to find those ideal tenants so they can rent your property.

HOW TO FIND TENANTS FOR YOUR RENTAL

Finding tenants for your rental is like the process of finding good deals. It's a marketing funnel. And that means you need to generate leads from prospective tenants. Here's a list of my favorite ways to market for tenants, in order of importance:

1. Real estate listing websites (Zillow.com, Apartments.com, etc.)
2. Sign at property
3. Website for our rental properties
4. Word of mouth (referrals from tenants, friends, other managers)
5. Social media (Facebook Marketplace)
6. Craigslist (less effective in some areas than others)

I use a property manager for most of my properties, so they do a lot of this marketing themselves. In addition to these options, they promote our student rentals at the university's in-person housing exhibitions. Plus, one manager has a physical location near the university and gets a lot of walk-in traffic.

With the properties I self-manage, we use online landlord software to market our property, receive tenant applications, perform a credit and background check, sign and store paperwork, and collect rent. I'll talk more about this technology later. But in terms of marketing to find tenants, this software makes the process very easy. You upload your pictures, videos, and description once, and the software sends it to multiple marketing websites at one time.

As I said earlier, the best properties attract the best tenants. That means finding tenants for those properties is usually easy. If you have the right property, excellent photos, a walk-through video, and a detailed online listing, you will typically generate interest from many potential tenants.

For example, I have one single-family house in a good location that I self-manage. I usually get dozens of interested tenants in the first few days after posting an online listing. Within a week, I typically have it rented to excellent tenants.

When I don't get enough interest in a property, there is either something wrong with my property, my listing (like bad photos), or my price. Over the years, we've gotten rid of our properties that were hard to rent.

But during the Great Recession of 2008–2009, for example, I still had some of those properties. And we had to drop rental rates slightly on some properties (especially the worst ones). But even then, we were able to quickly find the market price and fill the rentals consistently.

TENANT SCREENING 101

The next step after marketing your rental is to screen for those ideal tenants. After buying the right property, this is probably the most important skill you'll learn as a rental owner. The biggest mistakes I've made with tenants could have been avoided with a better screening process.

For example, I let tenants who did not have the full security deposit move in to one of our lower-rent properties early in our career. They were always late on their rent, and eventually we had to file an eviction and force them to move. This was painful for them and painful for me, but I ultimately took the responsibility because I didn't screen them properly in the first place.

The Benefits of Written Tenant Qualification Criteria

The key step of the tenant-screening process is establishing written tenant qualifying criteria. When I hire a management company, I share my criteria and ask them to use them for all our properties. Occasionally they'll suggest some changes, which can be a good discussion. But in the end, we get on the same page. It makes my manager's job easier because they know what we want, and it makes me feel better that they're picking the best tenants for our properties.

Having written criteria also takes the emotion out of the tenant application and approval process. Especially if you self-manage, people will tell you sad stories and ask you to bend your rules and rent to them. But you must look deeper into every situation, past the heart-tugging story, and find the facts of whether this person will make a good tenant or not. That's what the qualifying criteria help you do.

Not only are written qualifying standards a good business practice, but they also help you treat people fairly and stay in compliance with the U.S. Fair Housing Act[54]. This law prohibits discrimination based on race, religion, national origin, gender, age, familial status, or physical or mental disability (which includes recovering alcoholics and people with a past drug addiction). Many local and state governments also prohibit discrimination based on marital status or sexual orientation. By ensuring your written standards comply with the law and then fairly and consistently applying your standards, you will avoid illegally discriminating.

How to Choose Written Tenant Qualification Criteria

You may be wondering what you can legally include in your tenant qualification criteria. The answer is criteria that help you make a good *business decision*. Here are some that I like to use:

- **Minimum Credit Score:** A credit score is a number between 300 and 850 that measures someone's creditworthiness based on their public credit history. It's easy today to pull a potential tenant's score and credit history using online software so that you can see if it meets your criteria. Our minimum score ranges from 600 to 650, with the lower score being for our lower-priced rentals.

- **Minimum Income-to-Rent Ratio:** You can set a minimum ratio of verifiable income to rent. We currently use 3x for our lower-priced rentals and 3.5x for our higher-priced rentals.

- **Debt-to-Income Ratio:** Instead of or in addition to an income-to-rent ratio, you can set a minimum debt-to-income ratio. Even someone with a high income can have too many debts to pay, so this metric gives a good indication of how a person can afford your rent payment.

- **Landlord References:** You can require that someone have positive landlord references. You want to learn how they paid, how they treated the property, and whether this landlord would rent to them again. But be careful with the *current* landlord reference. They may sugarcoat the truth about a bad tenant to get them out of their property. So, be sure to ask for multiple landlord names and not just the current one.

---

54 "42 U.S. Code Chapter 45—FAIR HOUSING," Cornell Law School—Legal Information Institute, last accessed on 12/23/2022, https://www.law.cornell.edu/uscode/text/42/chapter-45.

- **Eviction History:** You can require that a tenant has no prior evictions. This can be a good way to avoid problem tenants, and the information is part of the public records.
- **Steady Employment or Income:** You can ask for proof of steady employment or income (in the case of self-employed individuals) for a period, such as two years. This can give you an indication of their financial steadiness and reliability.
- **Pets:** You can decide whether to accept tenants with pets in your property, and if you do accept them, you can charge an extra pet deposit, fee, and/or rent. You cannot, however, deny or charge extra to tenants with assistance or emotional support animals.
- **Length of Stay:** With long-term rentals, I like tenants who plan to stay for longer periods of time. While nothing in the future is guaranteed, if someone tells me they plan to leave after one year, I'll prefer another qualified tenant who plans to stay for multiple years.
- **Cash for Deposit and First Month's Rent:** You can require that a tenant have enough cash to cover your security deposit and first month's rent. Some states have a law that limits how large a security deposit you can charge.

I want to emphasize that these criteria will help you find an ideal tenant, but that doesn't mean a *perfect* tenant. While they must meet minimum requirements, some of my best tenants didn't have perfect credit or the most income. You are looking for honest, hardworking people who'll take care of your property and stay as long as possible. If you set your criteria too high, you may find future homeowners who stay a short time, but you won't find your best tenants.

How to Communicate Your Criteria to Prospective Tenants

Once you establish your own criteria, write them down in a document. I keep mine in a Google Doc that's easy to share. Then I communicate them early and often to prospective tenants.

First, I include a few of the important criteria in my online listing and on my rental property website. Next, when I email or message a tenant who is interested in the property, I'll share the criteria with them. Or when I talk to them on the phone to discuss their interest in the property,

I mention the criteria and ask if they meet them. I also mention the criteria on my voicemail recording, which is a unique Google Voice number just for my rentals.

When you communicate your criteria up front, tenants often pre-screen themselves. This saves them and you time and trouble pursuing a property that they won't qualify for. And it makes the tenant phone calls, showings, and application process much easier and smoother.

Tenant Calls

Most tenants show interest in a property by messaging you through the online listing company, emailing you, or calling you. As I said, these early communications are a good opportunity to prescreen the prospective tenants by telling them about your tenant qualifications. I find it easiest to talk about some of the big, objective criteria like credit score, income, and cash for a security deposit and first-month's rent. Those are very clear criteria that you either have or you don't.

Then I ask about their story. Why are they moving? What are they looking for in a place? How many people will live there? Do they have a pet? And when do they need a rental?

One of the biggest red flags is a tenant who is too urgent. If they want to move this Friday, I would like to know why. Are they being evicted? Are they leaving their current landlord without paying? The best tenants have given their landlord a thirty- or sixty-day notice, so they're not moving in right away.

And it's also a smaller but important red flag if they can't communicate well or follow simple instructions. I like it when a tenant asks qualifying questions of me. That shows they care about finding a good property and a good landlord. And there are many small tests along the way, like being on time for an in-person showing, that will tell you how responsible a person they are.

Property Showings

Property showings have changed over the years. The popularity of online booking sites like Airbnb and the distancing requirements of the COVID-19 pandemic made people more comfortable with renting properties with pictures and videos. But people often still prefer to see the unit in person, so you can set up times to show the unit.

I recommend limiting these showings to two or three times during the week. This makes it easier on your existing tenant and on you. It also creates urgency and an auction-like atmosphere when prospective tenants see other people interested in the property. And as I said, this gives you a chance for one more prescreening of the tenant. For example, if they don't show up on time and don't bother to call to warn me, that's a disqualification. And then talking to a tenant in person becomes like a job interview where you get to know them better and figure out if they are a good fit for your "team."

While these initial communications and showings are helpful, you ultimately want to have a more formal screening process. After a tenant views the property virtually or in person, they'll usually let you know if they want to rent it. That's when you begin the final, more formal screening process of a tenant application.

Tenant Applications

The many online landlord apps out there today are fantastic for making the tenant application process easy. Once a prospective tenant is interested, you can direct them to your online application to complete it on their phone or computer. When they're finished, you'll be notified and can access all the information in your online software. As someone who began my career with paper applications that had to be scanned, faxed, or physically handed back, this is a simple but beautiful innovation!

My application includes questions that help me evaluate the tenant based on our qualification criteria. It also has their contact information, current address, previous addresses, employment information, whether they smoke, and whether they have been evicted or refused to pay rent. We also ask for the names and ages of the people who will be living with them and the type and weight of any pet. We require all adults who will be staying in the property to complete an application and be approved.

With most online apps, the tenant can pay for their required credit and background check at the same time as their application. This prevents you from having to process payments yourself. When they've paid for the report, you can view their credit report and criminal background check along with the completed application.

Typically, we'll tell prospects that we're leaving the application period open for a certain length of time, like the first week of the listing. Then we'll begin reviewing and processing the applications. Like the rest of this process, you need to be consistent and fair with application reviews to comply with fair housing laws and to treat your applicants well.

Accepting and Rejecting Applications

As you review the applications, there are three possibilities:

1. Decline an applicant
2. Accept an applicant with conditions (such as requiring an additional security deposit)
3. Accept an applicant

Declining an applicant because they didn't meet one or more of your criteria is the simplest choice. You let them know with a simple application denial email. This written denial is required under the Fair Credit Reporting Act[55] anytime you reject an application based in whole or part on criteria from their credit report.

Declining an applicant with conditions is also possible. You could accept someone but require a 50 percent higher security deposit because they didn't meet one of your criteria. If you had a difficult-to-rent property with few applicants, this might help you get the property filled. But in practice, I like to stick with the original tenant qualification criteria. I'd rather compromise on price than compromise on the qualification criteria. I'll just keep lowering my rent or offer other incentives until I find a qualified tenant.

Accepting an applicant is simple if you have one tenant who meets your criteria. But having multiple applications that meet the minimum qualifications can be a good but tricky problem to have. Not only may it be difficult to decide whom to rent to, but you also risk applicants feeling slighted or even discriminated against if you're not transparent about your decision-making process.

Dealing With Multiple Qualified Applicants

Some landlords use a first-come-first-served decision-making policy for applications. This is certainly the simplest and easiest to explain, and

---

55 "16 CFR Subchapter F - FAIR CREDIT REPORTING ACT," Cornell Law School—Legal Information Institute, last accessed on 12/23/2022, https://www.law.cornell.edu/cfr/text/16/chapter-I/subchapter-F.

some local governments have even passed laws that require landlords to use this approach. But following this policy may not give you the best tenant in the end. My preferred approach is to choose an applicant who is most qualified based on *all* our criteria.

For example, we once chose a qualified applicant who had less income and a lower credit score than another. The applicant with the higher income and credit told us that they only needed our rental for a year, while the other applicant planned to stay for the long term. That made the latter more qualified with our criteria because our ideal tenant stays a long time. Two years later, the tenant we chose is still in the house and will likely renew their lease for another year.

If you choose to use a "most qualified tenant" policy, just make sure to disclose it to applicants. Mention it in your ads, in your application, and in your communications during the acceptance/denial process. When you tell people up front that there are multiple applicants and you'll take the most qualified (not the first) one, there will be fewer surprises and hard feelings in the end.

LEASE SIGNING AND MOVE-IN

Congratulations! Your hard work has paid off and you've accepted a tenant's application. But the work to get your rental filled and cash flow positive isn't finished yet. You still need to collect your new tenant's security deposit and the first month's rent and sign a lease contract.

Get Real Money Before Handing Over Keys

In an ideal world, you will have marketed and found the new tenant a month or two before your previous tenant moved out. This minimizes vacancy time between tenants. But whatever the timing, you'll want to get real money from the new tenant before taking the property off the market.

This means getting a cashier's check or having an online payment clear their bank account (this can take many days). Collect the security deposit at a minimum, but preferably get the first month's rent at the same time. Don't accept personal checks, which can bounce easily. And don't take the property off the market or let someone move in before their money shows as "cleared" in your bank account. If someone moves in and bounces their check, it could take weeks or months to remove them from the property.

A detailed review of a lease or rental agreement is beyond the scope of what I can cover in this book. But it's an important document that's more than simply a legal contract that allows you to evict someone if they don't pay you. It's also an opportunity to communicate your expectations and set the tone for the entire landlord-tenant relationship that will follow.

The Rent Talk

Mike Butler, a longtime rental owner and author of *Landlording on Autopilot*, recommends what he calls a "rent talk." This is a conversation that lasts an hour or more where you review the lease and discuss the important points of how this relationship needs to work. Mike tells his tenants that their role is more like an employee who has a job to do. Their job is to pay their rent on time, take care of the property (including lawn maintenance if it's a house), and stay for a long time. Of course, the landlord also has a job to provide a safe, decent house that functions well so that the tenant can enjoy living there.

On the properties I self-manage, I've found this rent talk to be a critical step of the process. In a normal scenario, the tenants and I sign the lease and get on the same page about operational details. This includes how to pay the rent, what happens in an emergency (call the police, call the plumber, etc.), and what happens at the end of their lease.

But from time to time, the long, deliberate rent talk will cause a non-ideal tenant to show their cards. They may not like our rules, or they may begin making unreasonable requests. It's better for this to happen during the rent talk than three months after they move in. They're better off finding another property, and you're better off finding another tenant.

But if all goes well during the rent talk, you'll have a signed lease and the tenant's money in the bank. Once the current tenant moves out, you'll fix any damage and have the property cleaned and prepared for the new tenant. And they'll get the keys and move in.

The Move-In Inspection

The final step of a tenant's move-in is to fill out a rental inspection form. As a more hands-off landlord, I don't do this inspection with the tenant.

Instead, I give them the form and ask them to fill it out and get it back to me within two days of moving in.

This form is very important for your tenant because it's what you'll use to evaluate the property when they move out. Any damage you find that wasn't on this inspection form will be charged to their security deposit. The form will also make you aware of any maintenance items you missed during the turnover, and you can resolve them up front.

HANDLING TENANT PROBLEMS

If you apply everything you learned in this chapter, you'll rarely have problems with tenants. We've had an amazing experience with most of our tenants over the past twenty years. But if you make property or screening mistakes like I did early in my career, you could find yourself with tenant problems. And if you're in the business long enough, a rare bad apple will sneak through your screening process no matter what you do. That's when you need to be prepared for problems and know how to handle them.

Late Rent Payments

The most common problem is late payment of rent. With our rentals, we have a rent due date and a grace period of five days before late fees begin. If someone hasn't paid by the fifth, our rental software sends them automated messages that let them know the rent is late and late fees have begun. We also reach out to the tenant by text or email to ask if everything is okay.

Life events happen, say, when a tenant has an emergency medical situation, a car engine fails, or some other unexpected expenses come up. Ideally, they would have an emergency fund to handle those, but that's not always the case. And ideally, they would contact us before the fifth of the month to let us know what's going on.

If our tenant communicates with us and has a reasonable plan to bring their payment current, we work with them. And in most cases, they resolve the problem, and we all move on with our lives. But sometimes a tenant stops communicating with us altogether. Or they promise to make payments on a payment plan, but they don't follow through. That takes the problem to a different level.

When to File an Eviction

An eviction is a legal process to take back a property from a tenant. The most common cause of an eviction is nonpayment of rent, but it's also possible to evict someone for breaking other terms of the lease, like having an unauthorized pet. Because eviction procedures vary from state to state, you should make it a priority to understand your local laws. You should also have a standard procedure that you follow to help take some of the subjectivity out of the decision-making process.

In our case with nonpayment of rent, if we haven't received a payment and the tenant is not returning our communication, our policy is to file an eviction no later than the fifteenth of the month. Going to court is *never* ideal, and we'd always rather work things out directly. But at the same time, we can't accept empty promises or wait for problems to solve themselves. Things will only get worse.

We'll also file an eviction if a tenant repeatedly fails to follow through on a payment plan. Before that happens, however, we'll try to have a conversation with the tenant and acknowledge that it's not working out. We'll even offer to return a portion of their security deposit if they can move out relatively quickly. Sometimes the problem is unaffordable rent, and a lower-priced property will work better for them.

If you must file an eviction, you'll need to decide whether to do it yourself (if your state law allows it) or hire an attorney or your property manager to handle it. In either case, make sure you follow every rule and procedure in detail. One mistake, incorrect paperwork, or missed deadline could cost you weeks or months of missed rent.

YOUR EDUCATION AS A RENTAL OWNER

As rare as it is, having to evict a tenant can be emotionally and financially difficult. I didn't enjoy having to go through the experience, and I know it was especially hard on the tenants. But this and other difficult experiences are part of the school of hard knocks. They teach you valuable lessons, and they make you better as an investor and a person. I would like to think I've gotten better, and tenant problems today are rarer than they were ten years earlier.

I hope this chapter and this book will be a shortcut of sorts that helps you avoid some of my worst mistakes. But I also want to encourage you to continue your real-world education. Don't let the fear of making mistakes cause you to avoid the benefits and the growth that lie in front of you as a rental property owner.

As you let the tips and lessons from this chapter sink in, let's continue with one more valuable topic for rental owners. In the next chapter I'll share how to look at your rental properties and your business as a group of systems that you can automate, outsource, and eventually step outside of to become a more passive owner.

CHAPTER 22
HOW TO SYSTEMATIZE AND AUTOMATE YOUR RENTAL BUSINESS

In December of 2003, one and a half years after I graduated from college, I officially entered the real estate business. My business partner and I had piles of paper and three-ring binders spread out on his living room floor. It was the first annual meeting of our brand-new real estate company, and it felt like an important milestone.

Looking back on that moment, I realize how laughably new and naïve we were. We had one property under our belt, but we still didn't know much about real estate. Like many new investors, we had big dreams to build a real estate empire. But we didn't yet have the skills, knowledge, or resources to close the enormous gap between our dreams and our reality.

We did, however, have one thing going for us. Before we even started this business, someone recommended that I read a book called *The E-Myth Revisited* by Michael E. Gerber. I devoured the book in a couple of days, and I felt confident that what I had learned could help our brand-new business succeed in the long run.

WORK ON YOUR BUSINESS, NOT IN YOUR BUSINESS

The e-myth stands for the entrepreneurial myth, which is a misunderstanding that traps most small entrepreneurs. These entrepreneurs start with dreams of owning a business that will give them passive cash flow and free up their time. But instead, they end up with a business that owns them because it can only survive financially by the owner doing everything themselves. They create a job for themselves even though a job was what they were trying to escape from in the first place.

For example, many small rental property owners do everything themselves. They buy the properties, apply for financing, paint the walls, fix the toilets, collect the rent, do the bookkeeping, and more. And for a time, there's nothing wrong with that. When you're new, there's a lot *right* with doing all these things so that you can learn.

But if you ever want a relatively passive real estate business, you must change your approach. You can't be only the technician working *in your business*. You must also be the business owner working *on your business*. Successful small and mighty investors play both roles.

I came to our first annual company meeting armed with this idea. My business partner and I were still rookies with a lot to learn, but we were ready to work on our business even while we did all the work inside of it. Instead of simply creating a job, we were going to create a real business with systems and automation that could eventually run without us.

YOU ARE NOT YOUR BUSINESS

In the year 1913, Henry Ford revolutionized the automobile industry by building Model T cars with an assembly line. This innovation reduced the time it took to build a car from more than twelve hours to one hour and thirty-three minutes.[56] This created a chain reaction of value, including being able to sell the Model T for only $260 in 1925 when it had sold for $825 in 1908.[57] The increased efficiency and lower prices made the car more accessible to ordinary people and led to more than

---

56 "1913: Ford's Assembly Line Starts Rolling," History.com, last accessed on 4/14/2023, https://www.history.com/this-day-in-history/fords-assembly-line-starts-rolling.

57 "The Moving Assembly Line and the Five-Dollar Workday," Ford.com, last accessed on 4/14/2023, https://corporate.ford.com/articles/history/moving-assembly-line.html.

fifteen million sales of the Model T over its lifetime.[58]

In part, Ford's innovation was about systems. He broke the process of car building into eighty-four discrete steps that were easier to understand and to replicate. It was also about people. Because Ford paid his assembly line employees more than double their previous wages and reduced their work hours to a forty-hour week, he attracted some of the best workers to his plants.[59] And finally it was about new technology he used to run the assembly line.

For our purposes, the key principle to take from Ford's story is that he saw his business as an entity outside of himself. He innovated and tinkered with each part of his business—people, systems, and technology—like a mechanic would on a car engine. He was able to create massive value and make more money because he was able to see how all the parts worked together. And we can do the same thing with our rental property business.

The paperwork and three-ring binders on the floor at our first business meeting were our attempt to start doing this. The three-ring binder was the first version of our business operations manual, which is like an instruction manual for how to run your business. Our operations manual has evolved many times and will continue to evolve as we learn more, but it became the guiding structure of our business for the next twenty years. In fact, the ideas you're reading in this book came in large part from the best practices, systems, and technology we accumulated in our operations manual.

Now let's learn about the pieces of that operations manual, beginning with the people part of your business.

PEOPLE

The "people" in your business may initially just be one person—yourself. But eventually it will also include other team members that you hire as independent contractors or employees. And there are different, necessary roles for each team member to play. The roles that we created for

---

58 "The Model T," Ford.com, last accessed on 4/14/2023, https://corporate.ford.com/articles/history/the-model-t.html.

59 "The Moving Assembly Line and the Five-Dollar Workday," Ford.com, last accessed on 4/14/2023, https://corporate.ford.com/articles/history/moving-assembly-line.html.

our rental property business include:

- **CEO/Asset Manager:** makes strategic decisions, oversees entire operation
- **Acquisitions Manager:** does marketing and negotiations to buy properties
- **Financing Manager:** acquires financing
- **Remodel Manager:** oversees remodels and maintenance
- **Leasing Manager:** rents properties, handles tenant customer service
- **Sales Manager:** sells properties, for instance, flipping houses
- **Collections Manager:** collects rent, handles delinquencies
- **Bookkeeper:** pays bills, organizes financial information
- **Administrator:** handles paperwork and administrative tasks

Even if you are a one-person business, think of yourself as playing all these different roles. Switching between the roles in your mind will help you understand how the business functions. Like individual players on a basketball team, these roles work together to run your business. Without each of them, the business won't function at its best.

Outsourcing: Delegating vs. Abdicating

As brand-new entrepreneurs, my business partner and I filled most of these roles ourselves. In fact, I vividly remember that first meeting when my business partner and I went down the list and assigned the roles to each other. It was like we had just hired ourselves for multiple jobs all at once!

But over time, we began outsourcing some of the roles to reliable team members. Today, we still play the role of co-CEOs and bookkeepers, but almost everything else is done by someone else. But the process wasn't smooth or easy.

For example, early on we contracted with contractors, CPAs, bookkeepers, attorneys, and others whom we later had to let go. We liked most of the people we hired, so this was a difficult experience. Looking back, the mistake we made with these early hires was abdicating our jobs instead of delegating.

Abdication occurs when you don't know what you're doing, and you hope the other person you hired is trustworthy and has good systems.

You've basically given up all responsibility for the job to that person. Delegation, on the other hand, happens when you first have systems and an understanding of the business results you want. You then train other people to deliver those results for you.

This doesn't mean you have to understand or do every detail of a job as well as an expert does. If you hire an attorney to perform a real estate closing or to create a contract for you, you don't have to first go to law school. But you do have to understand their role enough to clearly communicate the job you want them to do. Delegating means taking responsibility for everything in your business. Abdicating means sticking your head in the sand.

If you want to learn how to successfully delegate, you first need to create systems for your rental business. That's what we'll look at next.

SYSTEMS

In *The E-Myth Revisited,* author Michael Gerber says, "Systems permit ordinary people to achieve extraordinary results predictably.... Systems run the business and people run the systems." In our case, systems are charts, checklists, paperwork, and processes organized in a virtual or physical operations manual.

Systems ensure our rental business works well. Without them, our team running the rental business would experience uncertainty and chaos. And our tenants would not have a consistently good experience with us.

For example, the tenant screening criteria that I explained in the last chapter is a system. Without that system, we might rent to unqualified tenants, get in trouble with fair housing laws, or have a stressful experience renting our properties. But with a tenant qualifying system, we put our best practices in writing. It gives us a baseline process to follow that we can continuously improve over time

The Systems of a Rental Property Business

A rental property business has its own unique structure and systems. And they can be divided into categories based on the function of the business. I organize my own business categories by creating subfolders within an online file system like Google Drive.

Here are the different rental property business categories I use:

1. Acquisitions
2. Financing
3. Leasing
4. Rent Collections
5. Tenant Turnover
6. Maintenance and Remodel
7. Bookkeeping and Administration

Within each subfolder is a series of instructions, checklists, paperwork, and other details related to implementing that system. For example, every time I acquire a property, I use my acquisitions checklist so that I don't forget any steps. And every time I make a mistake or learn something new, I edit and improve the checklist for next time. This is how you continuously innovate and improve your business.

I get very nerdy with this systems stuff. In fact, I made a large, detailed chart called a mind map with all the systems of my rental property business. You can get a copy of the mind map at www.biggerpockets.com/smallandmightybonus.

One of the benefits of studying other rental investors, as you're doing reading this book, is that you don't have to start from scratch. Instead of reinventing the wheel, you can "steal and deploy" systems that already work for someone else. To help you understand and implement the systems I use, I'll summarize and explain each category in more detail.

1. Acquisitions

These are the systems that help you buy good deals. We've covered this topic extensively. When successful, this system allows me to consistently buy deals that build wealth and produce cash flow. Although the specific implementation of marketing strategies has changed over time, the core process still works very well after twenty years.

Here are the subcategories of instructions, checklists, and paperwork within our acquisitions system. They roughly follow the chronological process of the deal funnel:

- **Marketing/Lead Generation**
  - *Buy Box Description:* explains our buy box for a good deal
  - *Marketing Plan:* outlines my marketing budget, lead generation

goal, and the specific marketing systems we plan to implement to achieve that goal

- *Marketing Systems:* contain instructions, checklists, documents, and resources related to each marketing campaign, like Driving for Dollars, Multiple Listing Service (MLS), networking, signs, and direct mail

- **Lead Capture, Analysis, and Negotiation**
  - *Lead Tracking System:* a spreadsheet or software system to track and follow up on leads. More on this in the technology section of this chapter.
  - *Deal Worksheet:* document used to collect information on the seller, property, and property value during phone and in-person negotiations
  - *Back-of-Envelope Formulas Cheat Sheet:* summary of the formulas used to analyze a deal using back-of-the-envelope approach
  - *Analysis Spreadsheets:* computer spreadsheets to analyze a deal in more depth, including formulas like internal rate of return

- **Offers and Follow-Up**
  - *Memorandum of Offer:* simple template to make offers on properties
  - *Follow-Up System:* digital or physical system to follow up on promising leads and offers over time

- **Purchase Contract, Due Diligence, and Closing**
  - *Purchase Contracts and Addendums:* paperwork needed to put a property under contract to purchase
  - *Due Diligence Checklist:* the reminders and details to follow during the research process you perform before entering into a business transaction
  - *Closing Checklist:* the details, due diligence steps, and events needed to successfully close on a property acquisition

2. Financing

These are the systems that help you implement getting money for your deals. We covered the best practices of real estate financing in earlier chapters. The lender credibility package is a strategy I have used to make a good impression on any traditional or private lenders I'm requesting money from.

The private loan documents help me prepare for a financing closing. When borrowing traditional financing, the lender typically has their own paperwork, processes, and systems that you follow. But with private lenders, you must often guide the process more. Some of your private lenders won't have as much experience with the details of transactions. Therefore, you need more checklists for that.

Here are the subcategories of instructions, checklists, and paperwork within our financing system:

- **Lender Credibility Package**
  - *Executive Summary:* condenses purpose and outline of package
  - *Business Plan:* summarizes your real estate business plan and goals
  - *Credibility:* reference letters, testimonials, before-after pictures, case studies of real deals to provide proof of your credibility
  - *Financials:* financial statement, credit report, property schedule, etc.
- **Private Loan Documents**
  - *Private Loan Closing Checklist:* steps to complete before closing a private loan for purchase or a refinance
  - *Promissory Note:* the debt contract between the lender and borrower
  - *Mortgage/Deed of Trust:* the contract that secures the note with real property once recorded in the public records
  - *Amortization Schedule:* spreadsheet of monthly payments and amortization of the principal of a loan

3. Leasing

These are the systems needed to rent out a property to a great tenant. We covered the best practices for this category in the last chapter. Implementing this system well can either make or break your rental property business.

Because leasing is also one of the most time-consuming parts of property management, it may be one of the first systems you outsource. If you hire a property manager, they usually include leasing in their service. But even if you self-manage, you can hire a leasing agent for a fee to find, show, and qualify tenants. I've found this very helpful when I'm traveling or otherwise don't want to be involved in the leasing process.

Here are the subcategories of instructions, checklists, and paperwork within our own leasing system. They flow in roughly the same chronological order you will use when leasing your property.

- **Lead Generation**
  - ▪ *Marketing Systems:* includes the listing websites, signs, and other systems that generate leads from prospective tenants
- **Showings**
  - ▪ *Open House Instructions:* best practices and instructions for showing property to prospective tenants at set times during the week
- **Tenant Screening**
  - ▪ *Tenant Qualification Criteria:* written criteria for qualifying your tenants
  - ▪ *Application:* online form to complete application questions
  - ▪ *Tenant Denial Letter:* for denying an application when using credit info
- **Lease Signing**
  - ▪ *Lease Signing Checklist:* to use when preparing and signing lease package with an accepted tenant application
  - ▪ *Lease Package:* includes lease contract, addenda, and other disclosures
- **Tenant Move-In**
  - ▪ *Tenant Move-In Checklist:* all the tasks for moving in a tenant
  - ▪ *Move-In Inspection:* form to be completed and returned by tenant within two days of move-in
  - ▪ *Welcome Gift, Letter, Info Packet:* leave for tenant at house at move-in

4. Rent Collections

These are the systems for collecting ordinary rent payments and for handling late rent payments. Rent collection is an ongoing process that is the lifeblood of your entire rental business. It's critical to get this set up right.

The priority of a rent collections system is to make it easy and fast for tenants to pay rent. In most cases today, that means using online payment systems. But a small number of our older tenants still prefer mailing checks or even depositing cash directly at our bank. We currently give our tenants these options, but as legacy tenants move on, we'll eventually be 100 percent online.

Another priority of a rent collections system is handling delinquent payments in a fast, effective way. As we discussed in the prior chapter, you need a procedure for this so that you don't get overwhelmed by the emotions of the situation. This doesn't mean you can't be compassionate and helpful when your tenants have problems. But you need to have rules and deadlines that you stick to. Otherwise, you'll find yourself with tenants who owe you several months of rent that will never be paid back.

Here are the subcategories of instructions, checklists, and paperwork within our own rent collection system.

- **Online Rent Collection Software:** software that allows tenants to pay online, see their balance, download paperwork, and receive or send communications; also gives us a list of tenants, their rent amounts, and whether they've paid on time
- **Mail Address:** a physical mailing address for those who don't pay online
- **Delinquent Payment Checklist:** procedure and dates to charge late fees, for contacting tenant, and for filing evictions
- **Delinquent Payment Notice:** letter to send to tenant for official late notice (if required)

5. Tenant Turnover

The goals of this process are to minimize lost rent from vacancies between tenants while also maintaining or improving the physical condition of the property. Vacancy can become one of your biggest rental property expenses if you're not diligent. To reduce our vacancy cost, we require a tenant to tell us if they plan to renew or move within sixty to ninety days from the end of their lease. Or in the case of student rentals, we ask six months or more before the end date. This gives us time to prelease the property before the move-out.

During the actual turnover process, which may last from one to four weeks, we transfer the utilities to our name so that we can clean and do repairs between tenants. The painter, handyman, and cleaner are all notified of work dates, and they're each sent a separate checklist for their job. Once the unit is empty, we perform a walk-through inspection. We look for any tenant-caused damage and add any necessary work to the checklists for our subcontractors. And when the repair and cleaning work is finished, we take photos and videos to save in case they're needed in the future.

The cost of repairing any tenant-caused damage is deducted from the tenant's security deposit. In our case in South Carolina, we're required to return the balance of their deposit with an accounting of any deductions within thirty days. This process can create disagreements with the tenant if you don't carefully document each step, including the tenant's inspection checklist when they moved in.

Here are the subcategories of instructions, checklists, and paperwork within our own rent collection system.

- **Tenant Turnover Checklist:** the steps for a tenant to complete
- **Turnover Painting Checklist:** sent to painter before turnover
- **Turnover Handyman Checklist:** sent to handyman before turnover
- **Turnover Cleaning Checklist:** sent to cleaner before turnover
- **Security Deposit Procedure:** instructions for processing security deposits
- **Photos/Videos of Unit:** save photos and video in case needed in the future

6. Maintenance and Remodel

In the rental property business, you'll have major remodel projects and ordinary maintenance. Major remodel projects normally come up front when you buy the property. But they could also come down the road if you identify improvements that could make you money, like finishing a basement, remodeling a kitchen, or improving landscaping.

The system for major remodels includes creating a scope of work, getting price estimates, and receiving W-9 tax forms and work contracts with your contractors. We touched on the scope of work and estimating process in the due diligence chapter. I also keep a list of capital expenses for each property where I record large repairs we've already done and other improvements we plan to make down the road.

Ordinary rental property maintenance is a different process. Staying on top of maintenance gives your tenants a quality place to live and prevents larger costs down the road. You'll find some maintenance items during turnover inspections. Other times, you want to have a good process for receiving and processing maintenance requests from tenants.

In most cases, the tenant maintenance request system looks something like this:

1. **Receive maintenance request:** preferably in writing and with pictures so that it's easy to track and forward to others. Give your tenant a dedicated maintenance number (like a free Google Voice line) or an email address to send requests to.
2. **Create work order:** many online management applications, which I'll talk about more in the technology section, automatically create work orders when a tenant makes a request. A work order is an online task that includes the details of the maintenance request and the contact information to get into the property.
3. **Assign to a contractor:** assign the work order to the appropriate contractor who can handle the task. Don't forget to confirm the date and time they will visit the property.
4. **Follow up on work:** work rarely gets done on time or as expected. You have to follow up. Online systems let you make notes and changes to work orders as this process evolves.

In the case of emergency maintenance, you also want to have a procedure and explanation of what the tenant is to do. This can be as simple as giving them a list of contractors and their phone number so that they can call the appropriate one in an emergency. You also want to show your tenant how to turn off the water to the house in case of a major leak. For other emergencies, like fire or break-ins, remind them to call 911.

In addition to regular maintenance, we like to have a system for preventative maintenance. For some preventative maintenance, such as roof inspections, cleaning leaves off roofs and gutters, and cleaning HVAC systems, we create reminders in Google Calendar. We find other items during regular inspections of our rental properties.

Many rental owners avoid preventative maintenance because it costs extra money. But it's actually an investment. By spending money on preventative maintenance, you avoid emergency problems, maintain high property standards, and often save money over the long run.

Here are the subcategories of instructions, checklists, and paperwork within our own maintenance and remodel system.

- **Preferred Contractor List (by category):** keep updated so that you, your tenants, or your property manager know who to call.

- **W-9 Forms from IRS:** require all contractors to fill one out before getting paid. You'll need this info to submit the required 1099 forms each year.
- **Independent Contractor Agreement:** for larger remodel projects, sign some sort of agreement with contractor about the scope of work, cost, deadlines, and procedure to change the work done.
- **Estimating Spreadsheet:** I used the one that comes as a bonus in *The Book on Estimating Rehab Costs* by J Scott. It's the best I've found, and the habit of updating a list of your repair costs within different categories is very helpful.
- **Maintenance Call Procedure:** the process outlined above to receive and handle a maintenance call from a tenant.
- **Scheduled Calendar Events:** schedule specific preventative maintenance items and regular inspections by yourself or your property manager.
- **Capital Expense Log:** track any major repairs (aka capital expenses) done for each property. You'll appreciate having these records in the future so that you can make better decisions.

7. Bookkeeping and Administration

Everything that happens in our rental business, from rent collections to maintenance, gets recorded in a bookkeeping system. This means setting down the date, amount, who paid (or got paid), and any other relevant details. In addition, we try to save some sort of evidence for all our income or expenses, like an invoice for an expense or property management report for rental income.

In the case of a property my wife and I self-manage, we use a simple spreadsheet for recording these bookkeeping entries. In the case of my larger rental business, we use bookkeeping software called QuickBooks. And in both cases, we scan and save all paperwork using Evernote, a cloud-based file system.

Bookkeeping and administrative work can seem tedious. It's not as exciting as marketing or buying a new deal. And it's not as urgent as collecting rent from your tenant so that you can pay your bills. But creating and maintaining an excellent bookkeeping and administrative system can make you a rental property superhero.

The Benefits of an Excellent Bookkeeping and Administration System

I'm a big fan of the futuristic sci-fi movie *The Matrix*. Having good bookkeeping systems is like being Neo, the hero of the movie played by Keanu Reeves. You see your entire business in a series of slow-moving numbers. Instead of being chaotic, you are calm and organized. And you react to events and changes within your business with clarity and power.

The specific benefits of having an excellent bookkeeping and administration system include:

- Paying all your bills and financial obligations on time as agreed
- Tracking key performance indicators (KPIs) like cash flow, profits, and net worth
- Comparing your growth (or lack of growth) from year to year
- Managing your cash so that you don't run out
- Knowing whether certain business strategies actually worked well or not
- Analyzing which rental properties perform better than others (so you can sell some and keep others)
- Preparing for yearly tax returns without extra stress
- Saving money on tax preparation because your CPA or other professional doesn't bill you for time spent getting your information organized correctly
- Avoiding extra time and stress digging up information in case of an IRS audit
- Avoiding potential IRS tax penalties or back taxes because you can't defend deductions you claimed
- Raising capital with lenders and partners using real data from past performance

When you have bad or no bookkeeping systems, each of the benefits above will just be their opposite. You'll have less financial awareness, more stress, and more risk of business problems in the future. In my experience, it's worth the time to get good at this.

Bookkeeping Tasks Over Time

You can divide the bookkeeping system of our rental business into the following weekly, monthly, quarterly, and annual tasks:

Weekly

- Check physical mail, email, and online system for bills, rent, or other deposits
- Pay bills and record them in the bookkeeping system
- Deposit money (if needed) and record deposits in bookkeeping system
- Scan all relevant paperwork, label, and save to online records

Monthly

- Perform bank reconciliations—reviewing transactions in bank statement to transactions in your bookkeeping system to make sure they match
- Receive owner draw deposit from property manager
- Enter income and expense details from property manager report into bookkeeping system; be sure to separate details by property to make financial reports possible

Quarterly

- Pay estimated quarterly taxes (for self-employed)
- File quarterly tax reports (if required)
- Review bookkeeping for errors and missing or mislabeled transactions

Annual

- Review bookkeeping for errors and missing or mislabeled transactions (again)
- Tax planning and strategy session with CPA
- File income tax return or send info to accountant for tax return preparation
- Prepare and send required 1099, 1098, W-2, and unemployment tax forms (if applicable)
- File business or rental license applications with local government and pay fees
- Review and update insurance policies, as needed
- Review property financials for property pruning or strategic refinances
- Have annual LLC meeting of members and file annual reports (if required)

To give you the real story, I'll admit that we don't always stay perfectly up to date on our bookkeeping. While I've been living in Spain this year, for example, we were several months behind on our bank reconciliations. We're having to play catch-up at the end of year.

But we always have a good idea of what's going on with our core finances, like rent collections, major expenses, cash flow, and cash in the bank. And eventually we do catch up and produce tidy, organized books that we can use for business decisions and income tax preparation. You'll find an approach that works for you as well, but I highly recommend you implement a strong bookkeeping and administration system for yourself. It's one of the most underrated yet powerful parts of a successful small and mighty real estate investing business.

It's possible to run a successful rental property business with only people and systems. But a third and final component—technology—allows you to run your entire rental property business much more efficiently, smoothly, and passively. That's what we'll look at next.

TECHNOLOGY

In my earlier story about Henry Ford, I mentioned that his innovations were partly about technology. His assembly line used some of the latest machines that stamped out parts and chain-driven conveyor belts to carry cars along the assembly line. Along with his people and systems innovations, this technology produced an automobile revolution.

As a small and mighty real estate investor, you may not be building millions of cars, but you can also use technology to revolutionize your business. You can use it to add more value to your customers and the people who work with you. And you can use it to free up more of your time so that you can spend it doing what matters most to you.

The Best Technology for the Rental Property Business

Technology changes so fast that I'm not going to list the names of the actual software and tech I use here in the book. But you can visit the companion website for the book (www.biggerpockets.com/smalland mightybonus) to get a list. I'll do my best to keep it updated with some of my favorite software and tech for small and mighty real estate investors.

But here in the book, I will list the different types of software and technology that small and mighty investors that I know use. This will give you a starting point to implement the technologies for yourself. I'll divide the list into the same categories we used in the section on systems.

1. Acquisitions

- *Spreadsheets:* for deal analysis
- *Lead generation websites:* for search engine optimization and paid advertising (Google/Facebook)
- *Deal-finding app:* for automation of lead generation activities like Driving for Dollars, direct mail lists, sending direct mail, pulling comparable sales, skip tracing owner contact information, sending text messages, and more
- *Project management app:* for collecting, organizing, and following up on leads
- *Answering service:* to receive seller lead phone calls and gather initial info
- *Smart phone:* to make acquisitions calls with sellers from anywhere

2. Financing

- *Online banking:* to schedule and automatically pay all regular expenses like mortgage payments, taxes, insurance, etc.
- *Cloud file storage:* to save all financing documents for easy access when needed

3. Leasing

- *Property website:* for property photos, descriptions, and virtual tours
- *Marketing syndication:* to promote rental listing to multiple sites automatically
- *Google Voice number:* for a free, dedicated leasing phone number and voicemail
- *Showing assistant:* for tenants to automatically schedule appointments and receive automated text and email reminders; you get organized showing process
- *Virtual showings:* to show rental units remotely through prerecorded or live tours

- *Tenant lead management*: to manage the communications, applications, and information for all tenant leads in one place online
- *Online applications:* for prospective tenants to fill out an application online and upload all supporting documentation, like pay stubs or bank statements
- *Tenant screening:* to perform credit and background checks, user-friendly dashboard; automate acceptance and denial communication to stay in compliance
- *Digital signatures:* to easily sign leases online with no physical paperwork

4. Rent Collections
- *Online rent payments:* for tenants to make their payments online manually or automatically each month, which saves time and creates more transparency
- *Tenant online portal:* to allow tenants to access their paperwork and payment account information anytime
- *Automated payment reminders*: to automatically send email or text payment reminders on set dates and/or when payments are late
- *Payment reports:* for easy-to-understand reports for tenants and property owners

5. Tenant Turnover
- *Photo/video storage:* to save property photos and videos before and after tenant turnover for evidence of security deposit deductions, if needed
- *Contractor scheduling software:* to set up appointments, follow-ups, and access without constant back-and-forth phone calls or emails
- *Smart locks:* to easily change locks between tenants and give temporary access to contractors with programmable lock codes

6. Maintenance and Remodel
- *Online maintenance requests:* for tenants or managers to create work orders that can be assigned to contractors and tracked until completed
- *Inspections*: for your property manager or a third-party vendor to schedule and manage property visits and inspection reports with online software

- *Digital signatures:* to sign contracts with contractors online without physical papers
- *Photo/video storage:* to save property photos and videos during remodels for remote project management and clear communication with contractors
- *Smart home:* to manage HVAC thermostat, lighting, and utilities remotely. Especially useful for short-term and mid-term rental owners

7. Bookkeeping and Administration
- *Online bill payment:* to schedule all payments online and avoid physical checks
- *Online bookkeeping:* to record transactions and pull reports online and remotely from any location
- *Online records:* to scan and store invoices, statements, and other financial records online for easy access, sharing, and backup
- *Smartphone service*: to make business calls and manage business from anywhere in the world using flexible date and phone plans

By the time you read this, there will probably be even more useful tech applications for real estate investors. The main point here is to just get you thinking about what's possible. Pay attention to the technology that is working for other investors as the industry continues to evolve.

As we end this section, I also want to give you a warning. It's easy to become so enamored with technology that you waste a lot of time and money with it if you're not careful. Technology should always make business sense. This means using technology to automate or assist with key systems that can make or save you a lot of time or money. Using technology on low-value processes just because it's possible doesn't make business sense.

For me, acquisitions systems always make a lot of money. Therefore, using technology in that area was usually profitable. Rent collections and paperwork are also important and require much time, so using technology makes us money. The point is to just be thoughtful about how and when you implement your own technology tools. Evaluate each one to ensure it gives you a return on investment that moves your business forward.

GET TO WORK ON YOUR BUSINESS

Twenty years after that first company meeting in my business partner's living room, our small real estate business has come a long way. We now have trustworthy people on our team, proven systems to guide our work, and technology to automate many of the processes. Our business isn't perfect and will always need to keep improving. But it's in a good enough place to give us the financial benefits and personal fulfillment we always wanted with a very part-time involvement from us as the owners.

If you aspire to have a similar rental property business, now you know how to create the systems and automation to make it happen. Results don't come all at once, so don't beat yourself up if it takes time. But as soon as you can, do get to work *on your business* even while you're working *in your business*. Your future self will thank you.

And while you're doing that work, don't forget about the big picture of your rental property business. We've spent a lot of time in the previous chapters on the nitty-gritty tactics of buying, financing, owning, and automating rental properties. In the final part of the book, I'll show you how to put all those tactics together into a successful long-term strategy. In other words, I'm going to teach you how to win the real estate game.

PART VI

HOW TO WIN THE REAL ESTATE GAME

CHAPTER 23
PLAYING A DIFFERENT FINANCIAL GAME

Do you remember Liz and Tom, Couple No. 1 in the story at the very beginning of the book? They own ten single-family houses in St. Louis, Missouri, that are free and clear of all debt, which gives them a very resilient, low-risk portfolio. After all expenses, their properties produce cash flow of $120,000 per year, which meets their fat financial independence (FI) number and allows them to be financially independent. And because the properties are well-located and carefully chosen to attract long-term tenants, Liz and Tom's job of self-management is low hassle and flexible.

I compared Liz and Tom's story to Couple No. 3, Lauren and Mike, who have more properties and money but don't have as much flexibility or freedom. At the time of this story, Couple No. 1 is in the Ender phase. But Couple No. 3 has chosen to move back into the Wealth Builder phase, which has more risk and hassle.

The point of this story isn't to make Couple No. 3 wrong. I'm sure they thought about their reasons for continuing to grow. I simply want to illustrate the different choices they made.

Couple No. 3 chose to keep playing the wealth-building game, while Couple No. 1 chose to switch to a different game called being an Ender. I think of this as the choice of financial freedom. The details of each person's choice will look slightly different. But it's one that everyone who builds more wealth eventually faces. In this chapter, I want to help you figure out when and how to start playing a different financial game yourself.

STOP PLAYING THE GAME

Dr. William Bernstein is a retired neurologist, prolific author of books like *The Four Pillars of Investing*, and investment adviser. Bernstein is famous for encouraging people to make the choice we're talking about in this chapter with this quote:

"If you've won the game, stop playing."[60]

In my former life, I was a team captain for the Clemson University football team as a middle linebacker. When we were winning in the final minutes of the game, our coaches would change their strategy. If we had the ball on offense, they would become extremely conservative to avoid mistakes that could lose the game. The quarterback would simply take a knee as soon as the ball was snapped, and the clock would run out so that we won the game.

In your personal finances, the equivalent situation is when you've built enough wealth to achieve financial independence. This is when Bernstein says you should stop playing. His advice is to go ahead and take a financial knee by reducing your risk and switching to a safer approach to investing.

With traditional investing, taking a financial knee means owning fewer risky assets like stocks. Instead, you switch to owning more bonds, annuities, CDs, and cash. In real estate investing, it means switching to an Ender real estate portfolio. For many real estate investors, this means paying off debt, decreasing the number of properties you own, and improving your systems and team.

---

60 "William Bernstein: If You've Won the Game, Stop Playing," The Long View, Morningstar.com, last accessed on January 5, 2023, https://podcasts.apple.com/gb/podcast/william-bernstein-if-youve-won-the-game-stop-playing/id1462214964?i=1000437002756.

This choice is extremely obvious if you're at a traditional retirement age or you just no longer want to work for money. The cost of losing money is much worse than the benefits of getting more growth. If you were to lose a large amount of your wealth and were forced to start over, it would be devastating.

But what if you like your work and don't want to retire? Or what if you want more financial growth to cushion you from an uncertain future? Or what about those who have built wealth young and aren't at a traditional retirement age? To return to the football analogy, should a team leading by fifty points at halftime just take a knee for the entire second half? That's not a good strategy.

I've personally been in all these situations, and the decision to "stop playing" wasn't as easy or clear-cut. I wanted to secure my financial freedom, but I also wanted to keep playing. I started studying other successful investors to see if there was a way to reduce my risk, build an Ender portfolio, yet keep playing the real estate game. I found one of my favorite examples with a longtime investor from California.

A NEW GAME—A LOW-RISK INCOME FLOOR PLUS UPSIDE INVESTING

One investor I know (who requested to stay anonymous) spent years building wealth with rental properties in California. He also had a house flipping business that paid his bills and funded his long-term investments. This investor still loves house flipping. He has no plans to stop, even though he's achieved financial independence and has been working for almost four decades.

But along the way, he made a financial freedom choice. To use a poker metaphor, he chose to take some of his chips off the table. Instead of continuing to play the game of maximizing leverage to grow, he used his cash to pay off the debt on a group of his best rental properties. He basically carved out an Ender portfolio that was low risk, high cash flow, and low hassle. To use a term from earlier in the book, he created a safe *income floor* to protect himself from falling backward financially.

As an aside, one of this investor's mentors told him this choice was crazy. In the mentor's mind, real estate was all about leverage. Paying off fixed-payment, low-interest debt so early in life wasn't in the mentor's playbook of winning real estate moves. But the investor listened to his gut. He knew that his new game required a different set of winning plays.

Once they were debt-free, the investor's properties produced enough cash flow to pay for his lifestyle. In fact, he gave each of the rental properties a job description to pay for a particular personal expense for the rest of his life. For example, one property's $1,250 per month of cash flow might pay for health insurance. Another $1,500 per month might pay for food and groceries. Other properties might pay for transportation, vacations, etc. The rents have roughly kept up with inflation, so today, they pay for the same number of goods and services that they did years ago.

With his low-risk income floor providing a solid base, the investor was free to grow and take risks with all his other time and money. If he later changed his mind and didn't want to spend time flipping houses, he could stop at any time. If any of his new investments flopped, he'd still have the Ender portfolio to fall back on. But instead of either of those negative scenarios happening, he has been very successful and happy. And his wealth has continued to grow.

THE STORY OF MY ENDER PHASE AND INSTALLING INCOME FLOORS

I loved how this investor figured out a way to take chips off the table while also continuing to grow. It made a lot of sense to me and to my business partner. But instead of doing it all at one time, we decided to start installing pieces of our own income floor a little at a time.

In Chapter 6, I shared the story of how my business partner and I didn't have one long, smooth cycle from Starter to Builder to Ender. Instead, we had a series of mini-cycles where we switched from Starter to Builder to Ender, and then started over again. At the end of each mini-cycle, we worked to increase income, reduce risk, and decrease hassle.

In case it's helpful to you, I'd like to share more details about how we transitioned into these Ender phases. Each time we ended a mini-cycle, we created a little bit more of our income floor and a low-risk Ender portfolio. And this process began during the Great Recession of 2008–2009.

The End of Our First Mini-Cycle

During our first investing years of 2003 to 2007, my business partner and I grew at a fast pace and ended up with about sixty rental units (thirty per partner). But for the next few years, we decided to stop growing and switched to a mini-Ender phase. With the goal of decreasing our risk and increasing our cash flow, we sold some properties and refinanced or paid off debt on others. We also worked extremely hard to simplify, systematize, and outsource our rental operations.

This was the time when we began working with a bookkeeper to help us with bookkeeping, administrative, and property management tasks. It was also the time my wife and I stopped working for four months to travel around Spain, Peru, Chile, and Argentina. I learned to love mini-retirements during that year!

But my business partner and I didn't have enough cash flow or resources to permanently become an Ender. Plus, we were still having fun and wanted to grow our wealth more. So, for the next few years between 2010 and 2016, we saved money from jobs and flipping houses to invest into more deals. Then we also took on more debt leverage. Our knowledge and skills had improved since the last mini-cycle, and the market was much better for buyers during that time. This allowed us to buy much better deals with more equity, cash flow, and growth potential.

The End of Our Second Mini-Cycle

By 2016 we had another financial freedom choice to make. Both our rental business and a separate business owned by my business partner had done very well financially. We had the good fortune of having excess cash in the bank, and the risky mortgage debt in our portfolio had either been paid off or refinanced by that time. Our portfolio was in good shape, and we could breathe a sigh of relief after surviving the Great Recession seven years earlier.

We thought about using the excess cash to pay off the debt on a big chunk of our properties. We estimated that after this debt was paid off, our total cash flow would comfortably cover our *normal* FI numbers. This was a very tempting decision.

But we also thought about conservatively investing the cash in something new. One more great deal might put us over the top and past our fat FI goals. We weren't interested in taking on a lot of new risk, but if the right opportunity came along, we were open to it.

We decided to give ourselves a few months to hunt for those great deals. We figured the market would help make the decision for us. And as it turns out, the market decided for us to buy another deal!

The Start of Our Third Mini-Cycle

The deal we found was a very good multi-unit apartment that came to us as a referral from a local friend and real estate broker. The asking price was just over $1 million. But the twenty-eight-unit property (eight buildings) needed some repair work, and the current per unit rents of $375 per month were far below the market rents of $600 per month. We thought that with $300,000 of repairs and upgrades, it could be worth $1.8 to $2 million and produce strong cash flow.

Just as important, the properties themselves were in the heart of our favorite location. They also fit our buy box with two-bedroom units, brick siding, crawl spaces for easy maintenance access, and low-maintenance hardwood floors inside. These were properties we could see owning for a very long time.

We bought the property using a $500,000 commercial loan plus our own cash for the balance of the purchase and repairs. Although we didn't use that cash to pay off debt, we did use it to make a conservative purchase. With an after-repair value of over $2 million, the loan to value ratio was a very low 25 percent.

We hired the broker who brought us the deal as our property manager. He also happened to be a contractor, so he could handle the remodeling of the units and the tenant turnovers. In the past, my business partner and I had managed these types of value-add deals ourselves, so this was something new. But our manager performed even better than we could, and we were able to step back from many of the details of the project.

Having a third party manage the property and the remodel also allowed my family and me to live in Ecuador for seventeen months. My kids were 3 and 5 years old at the time, and we wanted them to learn to speak Spanish at this age in local schools. Taking mini-retirements at the end of a mini-cycle was becoming a tradition!

This apartment purchase represented the end of our second mini-cycle and the beginning of another cycle of growth. We now had more than thirty properties with about 110 rental units. Once stabilized, the properties produced more than enough cash flow to meet our normal FI number. And it was relatively passive because we had two different property managers to handle the day-to-day affairs.

Our Present Ender Portfolio

As I write this book, my family and I are living in Spain for a year. The mini-retirement tradition continues! And it's been almost six years since the twenty-eight-unit apartment purchase and the start of our latest mini-cycle. At this point, we're clearly in the Ender phase as real estate investors.

For the past few years, we've used extra cash flow to pay off more of our rental property debt. I'll share how we use a version of the rental debt snowball in a later chapter. And although we're not completely debt-free, the balance of our debt owed to third-party lenders is only 13 percent of the value of all our properties. And we will likely pay off most of the remaining debt in the coming years.

We've also sold a couple more properties that weren't ideal for us. Although our local market fundamentals are still strong, we have geographic risk with all our properties in one location. So we're considering investing as passive partners in a couple of deals outside of our market to diversify.

Using Financial Freedom to Do What Matters

I feel good about our current Ender portfolio. Choosing more freedom over more growth has created a sense of calm and peace that I've come to love. That freedom has also created more space and free time for other projects that matter to me.

First and foremost, I get to be an involved parent of young kids. When they get off the bus from school, do homework, or have an after-school activity, I get to be there. I'm certainly not a perfect parent, but I am a present one!

I've also become very involved in my local community. In particular, I've become passionate about land planning and alternative transportation. This led me and a few other local entrepreneurs to start a nonprofit in 2015. Through the nonprofit, we're working to build a network of walking and biking paths in our community called the Green Crescent Trail.

Our nonprofit has helped create a long-term plan for the trail network, raise several million dollars for construction, and engage the support of our local community and leaders. As I write this, the first few miles of trail are being built. The nonprofit and the trail network resulted from the effort of many people. But being financially independent allowed me to lead the effort and consistently contribute a large amount of time, energy, and money with no expectation of getting paid in return.

And finally, financial freedom has given me more time to teach others how to invest in real estate. This book and my Coach Carson podcast, YouTube channel, and courses are the result. I spend more professional time on these projects than anything else because I love doing them. If that changes someday, I'll do something different. But for now, I have no plans to slow down.

Having more financial freedom has also taught me to appreciate "the how" or the method of becoming an Ender in the first place. It's not something I see taught in other real estate education. But it's a topic I want to explore with you in the final part of this chapter. It has to do with thinking like an asset manager.

THINKING LIKE AN ASSET MANAGER

In the last chapter, I shared Michael Gerber's advice from *The E-Myth Revisited* to work on your business, not just in your business. Many of the lessons in this book have been about topics *inside* your rental property business. They included mortgage financing, marketing for deals, negotiating with sellers, performing due diligence, and managing a property. These tactical-level details are incredibly important for your success as a real estate investor.

But to become an Ender who has financial freedom, you must also work more strategically *on* your rental property business. Strategic decisions are made on the level of your entire rental portfolio. These are such decisions as whether to sell or keep a property or whether to refinance or pay off a debt. To successfully make these decisions in my own portfolio, it's been helpful to think like an asset manager.

Large real estate companies hire asset managers. Their primary role is to maximize the return and minimize the risk of the entire property portfolio. They do this by hiring the right people, like property managers, contractors, and real estate agents. And they also do this by making the strategic buying, selling, and financing decisions I just talked about.

As a small and mighty real estate investor, you are your own asset manager. You can get advice from others, but ultimately you must make the important decisions yourself. And the better your decisions, the faster you'll move toward the Ender phase and financial freedom.

In the final two chapters, I will help you understand two important strategic decisions of asset managers. The first is about when and how to sell your properties. And the second is about when and how to pay off your rental property debt.

CHAPTER 24
WHEN AND HOW TO SELL RENTAL PROPERTIES

As my own asset manager, I'm a fan of holding properties as rentals for the long run. The properties that have made me the most money are the ones that I didn't sell. But people, properties, and markets change, and selling a property can be the right thing to do in certain situations.

In this chapter, I'll help you figure out when to sell and when to keep properties. And once you decide to sell, we'll look at the best methods to sell your properties as an investor. If you're careful and strategic about selling, you can use it as a tool to improve your finances and move you closer to your financial freedom goals.

STRATEGIC SELLING

Selling can be a useful tool to help you on your journey through the real estate phases of Starter, Builder, and Ender. For example, if you have very little cash to invest as a Starter but you have a lot of equity in your home, you could use a home equity line of credit (HELOC). But you could also sell and use the profits to reinvest in another property.

Below I'll share a list of strategic reasons you might decide to sell during your real estate journey.

1. Live-In Flip

As I shared in Chapter 4 with strategies for the Starter phase, selling your residence for a profit (aka a live-in flip) uses one of the best tax incentives in the U.S. tax code.[61] The key is that you must buy a residence and then live there for at least two years. Then you can sell your home and make a tax-free profit of up to $250,000 as an individual or $500,000 as a couple.

Let me share a quick example of how fantastic this tax incentive can be. Let's say you buy a home for $200,000 and invest $50,000 into repairs for a total cost of $250,000. Then two years later, you sell it for $350,000 after all your sales costs. The $100,000 profit would be *tax-free*.

And unlike a 1031 exchange, another strategy I'll talk about later, the tax-free profit of a live-in flip doesn't have to buy a replacement property. You can just put the money in the bank! This gives you a lot more flexibility.

In Chapter 7, I told a story about Mindy and Carl Jensen who used this one strategy multiple times to accelerate their wealth building. By their early forties, they were financially independent and had a multi-million-dollar net worth. Yes, they had to move a few times to achieve that. But if you could earn hundreds of thousands of dollars that could eventually grow into millions of dollars, would it be worth it? Even if you only do it once or twice early in your career, it can be an amazing financial move.

There are a couple of other nuances about the live-in flip that I want to mention. The IRS rule says that you only have to live in the residence "two years out of the last five years." This means you could move, rent for a couple of years, and still have time to earn the tax-free profits. That gives you some flexibility if it makes more sense to wait before selling.

The rule also gets more complicated if you choose to move into a property that was first a rental investment. You can't move into a rental and just wipe out the entire taxes you owe. There are still some benefits to doing this, but they're prorated based on how long you live there. If you're interested in that strategy, do some research and ask your CPA for more details.

---

61 Tax laws change, so be sure to ask your CPA. This statement was accurate at the time of writing in January 2023.

2. Fix-and-Flip

This book has primarily been about rental properties, but a lot of rental investors I know also fix up houses and flip them on the side. You don't get the same tax incentive as flipping your primary residence, but it can be a great strategy to generate chunks of cash for your long-term investments. You can then use those funds to invest in more rentals that produce residual monthly income.

Flipping houses is more of an active business than rental property investing. But if you have the time and if you're already looking for rental properties, you'll naturally find some properties may make more sense as a flip than a rental. Even flipping one or two extra houses per year can make a lot of money on the side.

My business partner and I sold many houses this way during our first ten years in real estate. In our best years we had a multi-six-figure flipping business. We used the cash flow to pay our bills, save cash reserves, and invest in rentals. We rarely flip houses now, but it was an essential part of our early growth strategy.

3. Value-Add Rental Properties

A value-add rental property is one that has opportunities to increase the property value by fixing it up or increasing its net operating income in other ways. Most BRRRR method deals fit into this value-add category. And my twenty-eight-unit apartment deal in the last chapter was an example because the rents were far under the market value. By fixing up the property and repositioning it, we were able to generate higher rents, higher net operating income, and a higher value.

In our case, we decided to keep the property as a rental. It fit very well into our buy box criteria for a long-term rental. But with value-add deals, you could choose to sell the property and cash in on the profits. You will have a long-term capital gains tax bill because of the sale. But it could make sense to pay the tax and use the profits to pad your cash reserves or to pay off debt. Or you could also decide to use a 1031 tax-free exchange, which I'll talk about next.

4. Trading Up with Tax-Free Exchanges

Whether you're selling a value-add rental or selling a rental for another reason, you can defer paying taxes by trading one property for another property of "like kind." But this is not an easy transaction because there are many rules, moving parts, and timelines to follow. The rules are found in section 1031 of the Internal Revenue Code of the U.S. tax laws.[62] Here are a few of the important ones to know about:

- **Like Kind:** Replacement property must be like kind. For example, you can trade apartment buildings for land, but you can't trade an apartment building for stocks or bonds.
- **Deadline to Identify:** You have forty-five days from when you sell to identify a replacement property.
- **Deadline to Close:** You have 180 days from when you sell to close on the replacement property.
- **Escrow of Funds:** You can't hold the funds of the sale before another property is purchased. An intermediary must hold the funds on your behalf.

I've found the hardest rule to follow is to identify a replacement property within forty-five days from your sale. Many investors make poor decisions by purchasing a bad or mediocre real estate deal because they are rushed to meet this deadline. Therefore, it's smartest to find good replacement properties well before you even sell. I'll give you additional tips on how to do this later in the chapter.

If you can pull off a sale using a 1031 tax-free exchange, it can be a fantastic way to grow and compound your wealth. For example, I had a student named Paul who saved $32,000 in taxes selling a duplex with a 1031 exchange. He then reinvested that money into another property. At a 10 percent compounded return for twenty years, that tax savings alone will grow into over $215,000 of wealth!

PROPERTY PRUNING

In addition to selling for strategic reasons, my business partner and I have sold properties that were no longer ideal for us. I've come to think of the process as "property pruning." Like pruning fruit trees, we've cut back on the bad growth of our real estate portfolio so that it would be healthier overall.

---

62 "26 U.S. Code Chapter §1031 - Exchange of Real Property Held for Productive Use or Investment," Cornell Law School - Legal Information Institute, last accessed on 1/8/2023, https://www.law.cornell.edu/uscode/text/26/1031.

I first heard this idea in a seminar with John Schaub. He described an annual process where he makes a list of his rental properties and puts them into two categories: keepers and sellers. Then when he finds the right time, like during a sellers' market, he sells the properties on the sell list until he has no more to sell. At that point, he has a healthy portfolio of ideal properties.

We copied John's process and made a spreadsheet of all our properties that we review regularly. The best properties that attract our ideal tenants, have the least maintenance, and go up in value I highlighted with green. The worst properties I highlighted in red to remind us to sell them. And I highlighted others in yellow that had good qualities but had other problems to be solved, like a refinance to pay off a balloon note or to increase our cash flow.

We've been pruning our rental portfolio for over a decade now. Sometimes we use a 1031 tax-free exchange to trade the property for a better rental. Other times we turn the property into a note by seller financing it to our tenant. And still other times we sell a property for cash and use the funds for reserves or to pay down debt.

GOOD REASONS TO SELL DURING PROPERTY PRUNING

The important part of pruning is deciding the criteria important to you and then regularly reviewing your portfolio. The list below will give you ideas of good reasons to add properties to your sell list. But feel free to create your own criteria. Then continue to revisit the process at least every year because properties, neighborhoods, and your own criteria change over time.

1. Neighborhood Is Bad or Getting Worse

I once owned a property in a neighborhood where crime was a regular problem. My tenants got robbed multiple times, and our air-conditioning unit was stolen. I knew I had made a mistake on the location, and I also knew I could find other deals in better locations. It took a couple of years, but we sold the house for a small loss.

2. Neighbor Nuisances That You Can't Solve

Back in Chapter 15, I shared a list of red flag nuisances to avoid, such as bad smells from a nearby commercial property or a dangerous dog in the yard next door. I discovered most of these problems firsthand after experiencing them at my own properties! In a few cases, it affected our ability to rent to and keep our ideal tenants. If we couldn't easily solve these problems, we sold and moved on.

3. Weird Properties

I've owned some properties with weird layouts. For example, in one you had to walk through one bedroom to get to another. I've also owned other properties with weird configurations of buildings, like a converted garage rental in the backyard of another rental. My business partner and I bought these properties early in our career at prices that produced a strong cash flow. But over time, we learned it was difficult to keep good tenants for long periods because of their weirdness. We sold them and moved on to more standard properties.

4. High-Maintenance Properties

Excessive maintenance costs can quickly turn a property into a cash-flow alligator that eats all your money. I've owned several high-maintenance properties that I originally thought were great deals. It either wasn't possible or wasn't profitable to spend money to prevent the problems, so we sold them.

In some cases, these were older properties that weren't completely remodeled. The physical systems, like sewers, electrical wiring, plumbing, driveways, and siding were wearing out. Or the original builder or subsequent owners used low-quality materials that wore out easily and cost a lot of money.

In other cases, the lot, not the building, was high maintenance. We've had dozens of trees near a house that dropped branches or fell on the house during storms. And we've had water run-off issues that required dehumidifiers and constant vigilance to avoid moisture and mold problems. Even when these problems can be solved, the solutions cost money and rarely make for good rentals.

5. Landlord Regulations Getting Worse

Both state and local governments can impose rent controls, eviction moratoriums, or other rental regulations that make your rental strategy unprofitable or difficult. I would be careful to leave the market too quickly just because of regulations if all the other criteria are good. But if regulations continue to get worse and negatively affect your financials, selling the property could be a smart move.

6. Tired of or Uninterested in Being a Landlord

If you own good properties and build good systems, it's possible to own properties for the rest of your life. I have several investor friends in their eighties who still happily own rentals. But you may find yourself tired of owning rentals or just uninterested. If that's the case, strategically selling some or all your properties could make sense.

I especially like selling with owner financing in this situation in order to maintain an income stream without having to manage a rental. For example, a former landlord I bought a property from is still receiving passive interest income from me today. He no longer has the hassle, but he gets to benefit from the monthly income and the security of real estate.

BAD REASONS TO SELL A RENTAL PROPERTY

You've now seen a list of good reasons to sell when you're pruning property. But you may also be tempted to sell for bad reasons. Here's a list of situations where I'd encourage you to hold on to your property until you find a better reason to sell.

1. You Had One Bad Tenant

A bad tenant can be emotionally difficult. I'll admit that in weak moments I've wanted to sell a property after dealing with a tenant who didn't pay or who caused other problems. But in my own case, a good night of sleep and a few conversations with people in my inner circle reminded me to think about the bigger picture.

One bad tenant doesn't mean you should sell a property. Just solve the tenant problem and move on with your business. If, however, you find a particular property continuously attracts the wrong tenants (like two or three in a row), you may have a different problem. First, you may need to make sure you've done your part and fixed the property up to attract the best tenants. But if you've done that or if the economics don't make sense to fix it up, you may need to prune the property and sell.

2. Someone Wants to Buy Your Property

With your best rental properties, there will *always* be someone wanting to buy it. I get letters and text messages almost every day from other investors wanting to buy my rental properties. And with my best single-family house rentals, most of my tenants would like to buy one. But that's not a good reason to sell it. You should keep properties that attract the best tenants, go up in value, and cost you the least to operate. Hold them until something changes that makes them not as good of a rental.

I will occasionally make exceptions to this rule if I can get exceptionally high resale prices. For a price to be "exceptionally" high, I need to be able to easily reinvest the resale money (after tax) into similar rentals and make much more income as a result. For example, we have one property where the land is more valuable for redevelopment than it's worth as a rental. Because we can sell for three or four times its income value, we're considering doing it. We'll then reinvest that money into something else that produces even more cash flow.

3. It's a Seller's Market

If you need to sell a property, a seller's market is the best time to sell. A seller's market occurs when demand for housing exceeds the supply. You can usually get top dollar with fewer contingencies or concessions by selling at that time.

During 2008 and 2009, we held on to some of our bad rental properties until the worst of the recession and buyer's market was over. Then we sold them as the market turned into a seller's market. The properties were not profitable while holding them, but we came out ahead in the end.

Just because you're in a seller's market doesn't mean you need to sell all your rentals. Only sell if you have a good reason to sell. Your best properties will make much more money by keeping them as rentals for the long term.

4. Bad News in the Overall Economy

You probably know this, but news headlines are designed to scare you because it makes media companies money. But most news should not affect your decision to sell or keep a rental. In many cases, news is about the national real estate market, which is not always relevant to your local market.

In other cases, the economic news may indeed be bad, but it still doesn't mean you should sell. For example, I held many of my best rentals through the deep recession of 2008–2009. I'm now very happy we didn't panic and sell these rentals just because the overall economy dropped. They all remained rented, with only a slight dip in rent prices for a year or two. And now they're worth much more than before the recession.

5. You're Not Getting Enough Tax Deductions

I love the tax benefits of real estate. But I find that many investors don't really understand how they work. And beyond that, they let taxes control their decisions more than the core financial benefits of real estate, such as cash flow, amortization of loans, and price appreciation.

For example, let's say you've owned a property for so long that you no longer have any depreciation. That simply means you'll shelter less rental income from tax. But if this is an excellent property with good long-term prospects, don't sell it. Smart investors own excellent stock investments that produce dividend income with *zero* depreciation shelter. You can also own excellent real estate investments in the same way.

6. Too Much Equity in a Property

Over time as you build more equity in a property, your return on investment will naturally go down. Your investor friends or a financial adviser may tell you that a property with a lot of equity is hurting your return, so you should sell or refinance it. That may be true when you're trying to maximize growth in the Builder phase. But remember that an Ender plays a different game with different priorities. Having a lot of equity can increase income, lower risk, and lower hassle. Selling or refinancing an excellent rental property simply because your return isn't as high doesn't make sense from the perspective of an Ender.

WHAT IF YOU LOSE MONEY SELLING A PROPERTY?

During the process of strategically selling or pruning back properties, you may lose money. I've certainly been there. If that's the case for you, don't let your shame from doing a bad deal cloud your judgment.

We all make mistakes. If you make a mistake that costs you money, just accept it and move on. Think of it as a real-world seminar, and your loss was the cost of buying the "education." You'll learn more from these painful lessons than from any other source because you won't forget them!

I have sold bad deals where I even had to bring cash to the closing. It was painful after investing years of my time, sweat, and money into the property. But aggressively selling a bad deal is better than holding on to it. It's a mistake to try and make your money back the same way you lost it. Instead, find a better opportunity and earn the money back somewhere else.

HOW TO SELL AN INVESTMENT PROPERTY

Now I want to talk about how to sell your rental properties. Whether you are selling strategically or pruning back your portfolio, you want to end up with the most money possible after the sale. And ideally you want to also sell in the easiest way possible. Below I'll share some ideas from the different ways I've sold rentals during my investing career.

List and Sell for Cash

The most standard way of selling rental properties is to list with a real estate agent. The benefit is that you can access a large pool of buyers through the MLS. And many of those buyers have cash or third-party loans to cash you out at the time of the purchase.

But there are a couple of downsides to listing with an agent. First, the seller normally pays a commission to the agents, which is often between five and six percent of the sales price. You can find flat-fee listing services where you pay a few hundred dollars for a listing and do most of the negotiating yourself. But when I've done that, I still offer to pay three percent to the buyer's agents so that I can have a large pool of buyers.

A second downside comes with the other costs of the sale. You normally need a vacant property to get the maximum price on the market. Your buyers who pay the highest prices are owner occupants who want to move in immediately. So your tenant must leave, and you'll get no rent during the waiting period. And you'll usually have to spend a lot of money on repairs to put the property in top cosmetic condition.

Even with all of that, we have still often chosen to sell rentals with a real estate agent. Usually, we wait until a tenant leaves before selling. And I have an excellent agent who adds a lot of value in the process. She is willing to manage part of the remodel and even pick the paint colors and light fixtures for us. And in the end, she also stages the property with furniture, pictures, and other small touches that help us get top dollar.

Creative Strategies to Use 1031 Tax-Free Exchanges

I've already explained what a section 1031 tax-free exchange is in a previous section. I love the idea of these exchanges, but executing one that really benefits you as an investor isn't easy. And the primary problem is finding the replacement property in the short period allowed in the IRS rules (45 days to identify, 180 days to close).

To solve this challenge, I've found that the best strategy is to find your replacement property *before* you sell. In one case, we negotiated a purchase contract for a builder to build us a rental house. Then it took several months for the house to get started and built. In the meantime, we got our rental ready and put it on the market to sell. Our house sold about thirty days before the new house was finished. Our 1031 intermediary held the funds from the sale until we were ready to close.

In another case, we used options and lease options to tie up properties that were later purchased with a 1031 exchange. When you are negotiating directly with sellers to buy properties, you can often ask for options or lease options. You may need to pay a significant deposit to have some skin in the game so that the seller says yes. But even a one-year option period can give you enough time to sell your other property and save a lot of money in taxes. In the end, your 1031 intermediary will use the funds from the sale to buy the property that you secured the option on.

As you can probably tell, 1031 tax-free exchanges aren't simple or easy. The potential tax savings must be large (perhaps $20,000 or more) for a 1031 exchange to be worth it for me. For that reason, we've sold a lot of properties early in our career without tax-free exchanges. When you do choose to use this strategy, be sure to pay for competent professionals to help you execute the transaction. Their fees are not cheap, which is also why you need to make enough money to justify it. But without all the correct paperwork and procedures, you could end up making a mistake and costing yourself substantial money in tax penalties.

Lease Options for High Profit Margin Sales

John Schaub, whom I've talked about a lot in this book, sells all his properties using a lease option. I have used this strategy as well. The basic idea is to sell a house directly to an eager tenant-buyer instead of listing the property through a real estate agent. Instead of just a security deposit, the tenant also pays a 3 percent to 5 percent option fee for the right to purchase. You find these tenant-buyers by marketing the property yourself, just like you would when finding a normal tenant. But in addition to the normal tenant qualification process, you want a mortgage lender to evaluate their situation to ensure they can qualify for a loan soon.

The core benefit of selling with a lease option is that you save money and earn a higher profit margin. A lease option allows a tenant to have one or two years to work on saving a down payment or improve their loan qualifications, like credit or debt-to-income ratios. By offering them this big benefit, you can usually sell the property for the full appraised value. As long as the property doesn't have any structural or safety issues, you can also offer it in as-is condition, without major remodeling costs. And instead of waiting three to six months with no rent before selling, you can usually rent the property in thirty days and begin receiving rent until the day the tenant-buyer closes.

All these benefits can result in a 10 percent higher profit margin than a normal sale, which is significant with the high prices of real estate. One downside of lease options could be in a market with rapid appreciation. You could lose out on a lot of appreciation during that year while you wait. In that environment you might want to shorten the option period to six months. You can also negotiate a higher price to anticipate the appreciation.

Seller Finance to Keep the Income but Not the Property Management

We have chosen to sell many properties with seller financing. Usually, we sell to our tenants who have already proven that they can take care of the property and pay on time. Once they save up a down payment of 10 percent, we have a closing where they become the owner and we become their "bank."

Like lease options, seller financing is a way to get a top price without the commissions and costs of selling traditionally. It's also a way to continue receiving monthly income without having to be a landlord. Ever since our first mini-Ender phase in 2008–2009, we have always had some seller-financing notes mixed in with our rentals. It has given us a solid base of cash flow with very little work.

Seller financing does have its downsides. First, when you sell to owner occupants there are now strict federal and state regulations that make financing riskier and more difficult for small investors. Fortunately, there are exemptions when you only seller finance between one and three properties per year, which is usually the case for us. Search online for "Dodd-Frank" and "SAFE Act" regulations to learn more about these rules.

A second downside is that buyers don't always pay on time. We have had to foreclose on some buyers, which can be extremely costly and take a long time. For this reason, seller financing isn't a beginner strategy. You need to have a large cushion of cash reserves to fund any collection or foreclosure issues should they arise.

A third downside is that seller financing has a mixed bag of tax benefits. You do get to defer your capital gains tax until the year you receive the principal. And because you only receive a portion of your principal each year, this allows you to spread out your taxable gain over a longer period and avoid bumping yourself into a higher tax bracket in one year. But unlike a 1031 tax-free exchange, you still must pay depreciation recapture tax in the year of your sale. This could be significant on a property you've owned for a long time.

CONCLUSION—THE CHESS GAME OF REAL ESTATE

I am not an expert at chess, but being an asset manager of your own rentals reminds me a lot of playing the game. To be successful, you must think several moves into the future about how to accomplish your goals. And your properties are your chess pieces that you get to move.

Some of the pieces are extremely valuable, like the king and queen. These are your long-term hold properties that you keep protected on the back row for as long as possible. Other properties are like pawns, which must be strategically sold or "lost" to win the overall game.

The longer you play the game of being an asset manager, the more comfortable you will be deciding when and how to sell properties. You'll also get more comfortable with other strategic moves, like when to pay off the debt on your properties. That's the topic of the next and final chapter of the book.

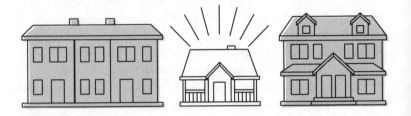

CHAPTER 25
WHEN AND HOW TO GET DEBT-FREE RENTAL PROPERTIES

U sing debt in real estate investing is a fantastic tool. That's why I spent three chapters explaining how to safely use it. But there also comes a time to put the tool of debt back in the toolbox. That means paying the debt off.

In this final chapter, I'll explain why I like to pay off the debt on some or all of my rental properties. Especially in the Ender phase, it's been an excellent decision for our rental property business. If you agree with my reasoning after reading this, the final part of the chapter will then show you the best ways I've found to pay off debt as quickly as possible.

WHY YOU SHOULD PAY OFF DEBT ON YOUR RENTAL PROPERTIES

Paying off real estate debt is a strategy for the Ender phase of your journey. It's one way to meet the Ender goals of reducing risk, increasing income, and reducing the hassle of your business. My business partner and I chose to pay off a large portion of our debt and plan to eventually be debt-free. Here are some of the specific reasons we thought it was a good idea.

1. Loan Risks

The main risk of a loan is that you can't pay it back. If that happens, a lender can foreclose and take back your property. And if you have a personal guarantee, which most loans do, the lender can also come after your personal assets if they lose money.

If you follow my Safe Debt Rules in Chapter 18, the probability is low that you won't be able to pay back your loan. But even then, the probability isn't zero. Unexpected, extreme events can happen in the world or your life. The less debt you have, the more resilience you will have when those unexpected problems happen.

2. Deflation Risk

Real estate deflation happens when property values or rent prices drop. During the Great Depression of the 1930s, U.S. housing prices dropped by more than 67 percent and stayed down for a decade.[63] During the same time, rent prices dropped by 33 percent.[64] Japanese residential real estate dropped in value by 70 percent between 1991 and 2001,[65] and prices still haven't recovered as I write this over thirty years later.[66]

63 Tom Nicholas and Anna Scherbina, "Real Estate Prices During the Roaring Twenties and the Great Depression," *Real Estate Economics*, Vol. 41, No. 2 (Summer 2013), pp. 278–309, https://www.hbs.edu/ris/Publication%20Files/Anna_tom_59f6af5f-72f2-4a72-9ffa-c604d236cc98.pdf.

64 Chris Salviati, "The Ghost of Renters Past: A Portrait of Renters in the U.S. since 1930," Apartmentlist.com, last accessed on January 8, 2023, https://www.apartmentlist.com/research/time-machine-portrait-renters-u-s-since-1930#fn-1.

65 John H. Makin, "Japan's Lost Decade: Lessons for the United States in 2008," American Enterprise Institute for Public Policy Research, March 2008, last accessed January 8, 2023, https://www.aei.org/wp-content/uploads/2011/10/20080225_22772EOMarch_g.pdf.

66 Bank for International Settlements, Residential Property Prices for Japan [QJPN628BIS], retrieved from FRED, Federal Reserve Bank of St. Louis, last accessed January 7, 2023, https://fred.stlouisfed.org/series/QJPN628BIS.

More recently during the U.S. financial crisis of 2008–2009, national housing prices fell by 27 percent.[67] But it was worse in some markets like Las Vegas, which fell over 60 percent and didn't fully recover until the housing boom of 2021.[68] Fortunately for landlords, rent prices didn't fall and actually increased in most markets during this period.[69]

Compared to a variety of other risks, deflation isn't the top thing I worry about. It seems unlikely to me. But as an asset manager of an Ender portfolio, I have to prepare for whatever possibilities might come. Even if it's unlikely, the consequences of deflation on a leveraged rental portfolio are catastrophic. Let me show you by assuming your average rental properties had the following statistics:

- Value of $200,000
- Debt of $160,000
- Debt payment (principal/interest) of $900 per month
- Rent of $1,500 per month

If the value dropped by 50 percent, you'd owe $160,000 on a property with a value of $100,000. If the original value didn't come back for ten years, would you be okay? If you didn't have a balloon payment that forced you to refinance, you could hold on and survive. By the way, most commercial mortgages do have a balloon payment, which shows you why they are risky.

But what if the rent values dropped by 30 percent? You would collect $1,050 of rent with a mortgage payment of $900 per month. With another $400 per month of taxes, insurance, management, and maintenance costs you'd have negative cash flow of $250 per month or negative $3,000 per year.

67 S&P Dow Jones Indices LLC, S&P/Case-Shiller U.S. National Home Price Index [CSUSHPINSA], retrieved from FRED, Federal Reserve Bank of St. Louis, last accessed January 7, 2023, https://fred.stlouisfed.org/series/QJPN628BIShttps://fred.stlouisfed.org/series/CSUSHPINSA.

68 U.S. Federal Housing Finance Agency, All-Transactions House Price Index for Las Vegas-Henderson-Paradise, NV (MSA) [ATNHPIUS29820Q], retrieved from FRED, Federal Reserve Bank of St. Louis, last accessed January 8, 2023, https://fred.stlouisfed.org/series/ATNHPIUS29820Q.

69 U.S. Bureau of Labor Statistics, Consumer Price Index for All Urban Consumers: Rent of Primary Residence in U.S. City Average [CUUR0000SEHA], retrieved from FRED, Federal Reserve Bank of St. Louis, last accessed January 7, 2023, https://fred.stlouisfed.org/series/CUUR0000SEHA.

If you owned ten properties like this, you'd have $30,000 of negative cash flow per year. With twenty properties, you'd have $60,000 of negative cash flow per year. Could you cover $30,000 to $60,000 of negative cash flow for a year? What about for ten years?

The point is that a leveraged real estate portfolio would get crushed during deflation. If you want to protect yourself from this scenario, no matter how unlikely it is, you should pay off some or all the debt on your properties. I'll quote Warren Buffett one more time, "If you risk something that is important to you for something that is unimportant to you, it just doesn't make sense. I don't care if the odds you succeed are 99 to 1 or 1,000 to 1."[70]

3. Increased Income

When you completely pay off a debt, it instantly increases your cash flow. Especially when you pay off an older mortgage, the cash flow increase can be significant. Here's an example.

- $100,000 debt
- Nine years remaining of twenty-year loan at 5 percent interest
- $1,155 per month payment of principal and interest

By paying off that $100,000 loan, you free up $13,860 per year of cash flow. That's a cash-on-cash return of almost 14 percent. Let's say the property already had $350 per month or $4,200 per year of positive cash flow. With the debt gone, it now has about $1,500 per month or $18,000 per year of total cash flow. If you needed $36,000 per year to achieve Lean FI, you'd just have to pay off the debt on two properties to get there!

Yes, you do miss out on the growth of principal pay down when the mortgage is paid off. And you could invest that $100,000 somewhere else for growth and income. But where else can you get a 14 percent *cash return* while also reducing your risk and hassle significantly? I haven't found any other investments like that yet.

---

[70] Marcel Schwantes, "Warren Buffett Says These Simple Habits That Most of Us Ignore Separate Successful People From Everybody Else," Inc.com, June 21, 2018, https://www.inc.com/marcel-schwantes/6-common-sense-things-warren-buffett-says-you-must-do-to-be-happy-successful.html.

4. Simplicity and Less Hassle

When you allocate money to pay off debt, that means you're not investing it in new properties. You're maintaining the same portfolio size, or you're decreasing its size if you also sell some properties. This combination simplifies your real estate portfolio and your life.

And simplicity is a good thing. It means you'll have fewer tenants to manage, fewer things to break, and less details to pay attention to. You can focus on excellence and improvement, and not just growth. You can enjoy the details and the craft of your rental business instead of experiencing it as a fast-moving blur.

OBJECTIONS TO PAYING OFF RENTAL PROPERTY DEBT

Reasonable people can disagree on important topics. You may never plan to pay off any rental property debt, and that's okay. But just in case you're on the fence, here are a few objections I typically hear from people, along with my responses.

But Shouldn't You Keep a Mortgage for the Tax Benefits?

When you pay off a mortgage, you no longer pay interest. Because this is one of your biggest expenses, you'll now make *more* money. And as a result, you pay *more* taxes.

If you started a business, would you say it's a good idea to make *less* profits so that you could save on taxes? That's the same as saying you should keep a mortgage for the "tax benefits." It's a silly argument that gets tossed around too often in real estate investing.

Now you could argue that the money you spent to pay off the mortgage would make *more* money somewhere else. But let's look at that as well.

But There's an Opportunity Cost! Isn't Paying Off Debt a Bad Return on Investment?

Even if you agree that keeping a mortgage expense doesn't give you tax benefits, you might argue that there is an opportunity cost of paying off your mortgage. Instead of paying off a $100,000 debt, for example, you *could* invest that cash into something else. For example, you could make a $25,000 down payment on four new leveraged rental properties.

It's true that you could make more money by growing bigger and using leverage. Especially if you bought good deals, you could make more cash flow and more growth with these new properties. But these two situations aren't the same in terms of risk and hassle. To an Ender, comparing them is like comparing apples-to-oranges.

To help make these apples-to-oranges comparisons, asset managers look at something called *risk adjusted return*. When you compare the opportunity cost of doing something else, the alternative investment needs to have a similar risk profile. If the alternative has more risk, you should earn a risk premium. In our example, investing with leverage in four new rental properties *should* make more money, because it clearly has more risk.

From a risk and hassle standpoint, paying off debt is more like investing in a U.S. Treasury bond, which is considered ultra-low risk by investors. As I write this in January 2023, ten-year U.S. Treasury bond interest yields are about 3.5 percent. If you're paying off a debt that costs more than 3.5 percent, you're earning a higher risk-adjusted return. At different interest rates, however, like a 2 percent, thirty-year mortgage, maybe you would make a different decision.

But Doesn't Paying Off Debt Hurt You with Inflation

Inflation is a real risk as you build and maintain your wealth. If your monthly groceries cost $1,000 today, with 3 percent annual inflation, the same amount of groceries will cost $1,344 in ten years or $1,806 in twenty years. Inflation reduces your future buying power.

To maintain your buying power, your investments need to at least keep up with inflation. This is also called a good hedge against inflation. Fortunately, real estate has a strong long-term track record of being a good inflation hedge.[71] This means that the resale values and rents of real estate will likely be larger in the future than today. This is especially true if you follow the advice in this book on buying in the right location.

When you pay off your rental property debt, you still own the rental property. If your rental property is worth $200,000 and rents for $1,500 per month, paying off $100,000 of debt won't change the asset. If it's in the right location, its value and rent could still increase by 3 percent per

---

71 "Is Real Estate an Inflation Hedge?" AvisonYoung.com, last accessed on January 9, 2023, https://www.avisonyoung.com/is-real-estate-an-inflation-hedge.

year over the long run. If inflation was also 3 percent, your rental income would still buy the same amount of groceries in the future.

Even with real estate being a good inflation hedge, I agree with this concern to an extent. It's not enough to hope that real estate barely keeps up with inflation. My solution is to build more of a wealth cushion in case inflation is higher or in case my spending increases. That's why I use an income floor *and* a growth portfolio, like I talked about in Chapter 23.

A growth portfolio is the extra wealth that exceeds what you need to meet your lean or normal FI number. The core real estate income floor, which includes debt-free properties, gives you stability, peace of mind, and some inflation protection. The growth portfolio gives you the extra growth and cushion you need just in case.

WHEN YOU SHOULD NOT PAY OFF DEBT ON YOUR RENTAL PROPERTIES

I've made my case for paying off some or all of your rental property debt. Hopefully, you also think it's a good idea. But while paying off rental property debt is *eventually* a good idea, there are times when it doesn't make sense to do it. Here are a few of the times when you may want to wait before paying off your rental property debt.

- **Inadequate reserves:** If you don't have personal and business reserves or an emergency fund, fix that before paying off debt.
- **Still have dangerous personal debt:** If you owe high interest credit card or personal loan debt, pay those off before your rental property debt.
- **Funding rental property growth:** During the Starter and Builder phases, cash for growth is tight. After I funded reserves, I used almost all my cash to fund growth when I was a Starter and Builder. Cash during those stages is like fuel for your growth vehicle. Remember, however, that I also used mini-cycles where you might pay off some debt earlier before choosing to grow again.
- **Funding retirement accounts:** Retirement accounts have excellent tax benefits, and I've tried to maximize my contributions to them throughout my career. With limited cash, you may have to make tough choices between investing in your real estate growth and

fully funding your retirement account. But before I paid off rental property debt, I fully funded my retirement account.

- **Plenty of liquidity:** I've met some investors who got into rental property investing after having a large liquid portfolio of other investments like stocks and bonds. If real estate is a smaller percentage of my overall portfolio and I could easily sell shares to pay off my debt, I may be in less of a hurry to pay off rental property debt.

HOW TO PAY OFF YOUR RENTAL PROPERTY DEBT

Now that I've finished explaining why you should consider paying off rental property debt, let's look at how you could do it. My own journey to pay off debt has been gradual and continues today. It didn't happen all at once. And one of the tools I've used to help me track this journey has been the loan-to-value ratio.

Track Your Loan-to-Value Ratio

In my role as asset manager, I like to track the loan-to-value ratio (LTV) of individual properties and of my entire rental portfolio. The LTV is the ratio of your mortgage balance to the market value of your property or of a group of properties. On the portfolio level, it's a rough indication of your overall level of risk with debt. I've also found it to be a helpful tool to track your overall progress of paying down rental debt.

If you have no debt, your LTV ratio is zero percent. If you bought a property for its full value and put 20 percent down, your LTV ratio is 80 percent. When a bank or other institution makes you a loan, the LTV is often one of their most important qualification factors. This is because the higher the LTV, the higher their risk as a lender.

I've also noticed that the most financially healthy and resilient large public corporations and REITs (real estate investment trusts) have low LTV ratios, if they have debt at all. These mature companies balance growth maximization with lowering risk for their investors. I want to do the same with our portfolio.

Early in our career, our portfolio-level LTV ratio was around 70 to 75 percent. Now it's less than 15 percent. We are comfortable staying at this level for a while, but eventually we plan to get to a zero percent LTV.

In the next sections, I'll share a few of the ways we've paid off debt and decreased our LTV ratio.

1. Strategic Refinance

Even before you save up cash to pay off debt, you can use a technique called a cash-out refinance to improve the cash flow and risk of your portfolio. With this type of refinance, you pull out cash from your equity in a property. But instead of spending that money to buy another property or a vacation, I suggest that you use the money to pay off another debt. This is another strategy I learned from John Schaub, and I think of it as strategic refinance.

A strategic refinance won't necessarily decrease your portfolio's LTV ratio, but it can decrease the LTV ratio of one property, increase your income, and decrease the risk of your entire portfolio. Let me explain with a simple example that assumes you own two properties with the following details:

STRATEGIC REFINANCE — BEFORE

	Property No. 1	Property No. 2
Value	$200,000	$200,000
Debt Balance (6% interest)	$80,000	$80,000
LTV	40%	40%
Mortgage Payment	$675 per month	$675 per month

Let's say you decide to strategically refinance property No. 1 with a new 80 percent LTV loan of $160,000 at 5 percent interest, with a fixed payment of $859 per month for thirty years. You'll have to pay off the existing $80,000 loan, but you also get $80,000 cash for your equity. You then use that $80,000 to pay off the debt on property No. 2. Assume you pay the closing costs out of pocket.

Here's what your two-property portfolio looks like after the strategic refinance.

STRATEGIC REFINANCE — AFTER

	Property No. 1	Property No. 2
Value	$200,000	$200,000
Debt Balance	$160,000	$0
LTV	80%	0%
Mortgage Payment	$859 per month	$0 per month

The LTV ratio of your entire portfolio is the same at 40 percent. But your total debt payment has dropped from $1,350 to $859 for an increase in cash flow of $491 per month. And I would argue that you've also reduced your risk with your lenders.

Property No. 2 has no debt, so your risk is clearly reduced. Property No. 1 has an 80 percent LTV, which on the surface seems like you have more risk. But think about what would happen in a worst-case scenario where you couldn't make your mortgage payments for some reason. Which lender will be quicker to foreclose on you—the one with a 40 percent LTV or the one with an 80 percent LTV?

In my observations during the depths of the credit crisis of 2008 to 2010, the lenders with 40 percent LTV were quicker to foreclose. I had an investor friend in a similar situation, and a balloon note on his commercial loan came due. His lender refused to refinance and told him to come up with the cash or they would foreclose.

When asked, the lender wouldn't extend his loan or work with him at all. They knew that if they foreclosed, they'd get all their money back quickly, which was their goal. My friend had to sell the property for an extremely low price to avoid foreclosure.

At an 80 percent LTV ratio, however, that lender might have had a different attitude. By foreclosing in a down real estate market, they would have probably lost money. Working with my friend to extend the loan or to come up with a different plan would have been in their best interest.

My business partner and I did a lot of strategic refinancing during our early Ender phases. The refinances didn't always look exactly like this example, but the principle and the benefits were the same. It increased our cash flow and decreased our risk without adding any more properties. That extra cash flow allowed us to invest in some of the other debt-payoff strategies I'll tell you about now.

2. Buy New Properties for Cash

If mortgage interest rates in the open market are much higher than the rates of your existing rental properties, you could save up and pay cash for a *new* rental instead of paying off existing debt. For example, if new mortgage interest rates are 7 percent, you would rather avoid a new loan and keep your existing 4 percent interest, thirty-year mortgages in place. This especially makes sense if you're in the Builder phase and still want to add a few more properties in a safe way.

By using this strategy, you'll begin to lower the risk and the overall LTV of your portfolio. Your new debt-free property will also produce cash flow that you can use to buy more properties or to pay off debt in the future. Like a strategic refinance, it's a sort of hybrid strategy that you can use in the early stages of getting more debt-free properties.

3. The Rental Debt Snowball

The primary strategy we've used to pay off debt is the Rental Debt Snowball. It's a simple method to pay off the debt on your rental properties in just a few years instead of waiting for twenty to thirty years. The strategy is like the personal finance debt snowball taught by people such as Dave Ramsey. But instead of paying off personal and credit card debt, you're paying off debt on rental properties.

My version of the concept is simple and works like this:

1. **List your debts:** Create a list of your rental property debts and rank them based on these four criteria (or whatever is important to you):
   - Smallest principal amount (pay off first) to largest (pay off last)
   - Highest payment-to-debt ratio (pay off first) to lowest (pay off last)
   - Highest interest rate (pay off first) to lowest (pay off last)
   - Most dangerous debts (pay off first) to least dangerous (pay off last)
2. **Saving:** Save as much cash flow as possible, both from your rental property cash flow and from your personal income.

3. **Concentrated Paydown:** Use all the cash savings to make extra payments on the first rental property debt on your list until it's paid off.
4. **Saving:** Add the new cash flow from the paid-off debt to your existing saving strategy and begin saving money again.
5. **Concentrated Paydown:** Use this larger "snowball" of cash savings to make extra payments on the *second* rental property debt on your list until it's paid off.
6. **Repeat:** Keep using the strategy until all debts are paid off or until you want to take a break.

The magical momentum of this strategy comes from focused effort. If you spread your cash flow out over multiple debts, it's like using a weak flashlight instead of a laser beam. It will take longer to pay off all the debts. This is also why you don't want fifteen- or twenty-year amortizing loans. They automatically increase your principal payments and spread the debt paydown over multiple properties.

Instead, you'd rather have thirty-year amortizations or even interest-only loans. The lower payments allow you to save more cash flow and focus it like a laser beam on one debt at a time. This focus creates momentum and a growing snowball of cash flow each time you pay off another debt. Here's an image of what that looks like.

THE RENTAL DEBT SNOWBALL PLAN

We were not too rigid with the four criteria I shared to rank the list of debts. Feel free to rearrange them in a way that you prefer. We just used it to help get our thinking straight. It usually became obvious the next debt that needed to go, and we just focused on it until it was paid off. Then we decided on the next one and started again. It became a fun game!

We also adjusted the method of making payments on the debts. The traditional snowball method is to make extra payments every month with your cash savings. Mathematically, this is the smartest approach because you save the most interest. But my business partner and I preferred to save cash until we had enough money to completely pay off the debt.

While this wasn't mathematically as smart, it gave us more flexibility. Sometimes our plans would change during that time, and we'd choose to pay off a different debt. Or other times, we'd have a new, incredible deal opportunity that we could use the cash to purchase. Being flexible with our debt snowball was a strategic choice that worked out better for us in the end.

4. Buy More Properties Than You Need, Sell Off the Extras

In addition to the Rental Debt Snowball, we sold some of our rental properties to generate cash for debt paydown. This began as an accident because we bought too many properties during our first Builder phase from 2003 to 2006. We decided to sell off the extra properties to reduce our risk and simplify our rental business. But the accident became a strategy that we used to pay off debt over the long run.

The strategy basically works by buying extra rentals beyond what you need for your FI number goal. Instead of long-term holds, these extra rentals will be short-term holds. You'll then wait and sell them at the ideal time in the next one to five years. The after-tax cash proceeds from the sales will then be used to pay off debt on your long-term holds.

In my first book, *Retire Early with Real Estate,* I called this the Buy 3, Sell 2, Keep 1 strategy because you normally need to sell two properties to have enough after-tax cash to completely pay off the debt on the third. I explained this strategy in much more detail in that book, but I've included an infographic below that summarizes how it can work.

Buy-3-Sell-2-Keep-1 Plan

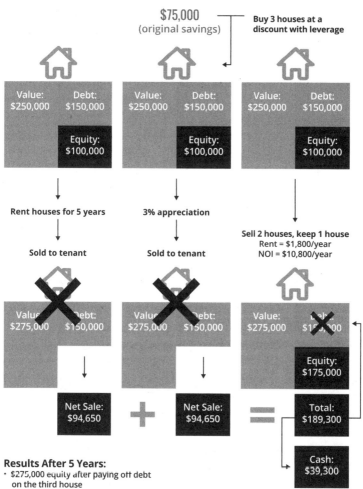

$75,000
(original savings)

Buy 3 houses at a discount with leverage

Value: $250,000 | Debt: $150,000
Equity: $100,000

Value: $250,000 | Debt: $150,000
Equity: $100,000

Value: $250,000 | Debt: $150,000
Equity: $100,000

Rent houses for 5 years

3% appreciation

Sell 2 houses, keep 1 house
Rent = $1,800/year
NOI = $10,800/year

Sold to tenant

Sold to tenant

Value: $275,000 | Debt: $150,000

Value: $275,000 | Debt: $150,000

Value: $275,000 | Debt: $150,000
Equity: $175,000

Net Sale: $94,650

+

Net Sale: $94,650

=

Total: $189,300

Cash: $39,300

Results After 5 Years:
- $275,000 equity after paying off debt on the third house
- $39,300 Cash
- $10,800/Year Income

Whichever approach you choose, the main idea is simply to generate extra cash flow by selling rental properties. You could also accomplish the same thing by flipping properties short-term, but you'll typically pay more in taxes, holding costs, and transaction costs than holding them as rentals. Instead, I like to hold them patiently and then sell to my tenant using a lease option, which I explained more in the previous chapter.

OPTIMIZATION IS NEVER OVER

We've now come full circle. Throughout this book, I've shared stories of people who are winning the real estate game. And now you know how to do it. Particularly with the final part of your real estate journey, remember to be patient with yourself and enjoy the climb. The hardest part is the persistence that it takes to stick with your plan and finish.

I also want to say that even with a stable, low-debt Ender portfolio, there never comes a point when you're completely off the hook. There are other important topics to learn that I couldn't cover here, like tax optimization, asset protection, and estate planning. And you'll still need to continue optimizing your overall financial portfolio even as an Ender. The world is always changing, and unless you grow and change with it, it can leave you behind.

Winning the financial game as a small and mighty real estate investor really means having more freedom, control, and autonomy with your life. But along with that freedom always comes added personal responsibility. There is no one else to make decisions for you. The buck stops with you and no one else! That's both terrifying and exciting. But more than anything, it means that the greatest *continued* investment you can make is in your own mind, skills, and relationships.

By reading this book, you've demonstrated that you're willing to make that investment. I hope you'll also find that this journey of growth and learning as a small and mighty investor can be amazing by itself. The greatest pleasure of my professional life, even more than material wealth, has been the personal growth I've experienced as an entrepreneur and investor. Every day I'm still learning something new, and I plan to continue that until my last breath. I wish the same for you.

CONCLUSION

A wealthy American real estate investor took a much-needed vacation to a sleepy town on the coast of Mexico. After a stressful morning call to solve a few problems back home, he finally got away to walk on the beach. As he strolled past a small pier, he noticed a single fisherman docking his boat. Inside were several large yellowfin tuna.

The American complimented the fisherman and asked, "How long did it take you to catch the fish?"

"Only a little while," was the fisherman's reply.

Noticing an opportunity, the investor then asked why he hadn't stayed out longer to catch more fish.

"I have enough fish to feed my family and to share with friends," answered the fisherman as he began unloading the fish into a cooler.

"But … what do you do with the rest of your day?"

Smiling, the fisherman said, "After cleaning the fish, I'll walk the kids to school, work on my hobbies, and take a siesta with my wife. Each evening, I stroll into the village, where I sip a beer and play guitar with my amigos. I have a full life."

Surprised at the wasted business opportunities, the American investor cleared his throat. "Señor, I think my years of business experience could help you here. If you spent more time fishing, you could sell the surplus to generate more cash. With that extra cash, you could scale your business and buy more boats and hire more fishermen. With this fleet of boats, you could then catch even more fish and generate even more cash flow."

"What then?" asked the fisherman.

"With your increased supply of fish, you could cut out the middleman and sell directly to consumers. Then you could open up a cannery and increase your profits even more. You would now control the product, processing, and distribution. You would need to leave this small fishing village, of course, and move to Mexico City, then Los Angeles, and eventually New York City, where you could run your expanding empire with proper management."

"But Señor," asked the fisherman, "how long will this all take?"

"Fifteen to twenty years," replied the investor.

"But what then, Señor?"

The American laughed. "That's the best part! When the time is right, you would announce an IPO and sell your company stock to the public and become very rich. You would make millions."

"Millions? Then what?"

"Then you would retire," said the investor. "You could move to a small coastal village where you would walk your grandkids to school, work on your hobbies, take a siesta with your wife, and stroll into the village each evening, where you could sip beer and play guitar with your amigos."

THE GOOD LIFE

This has been a book about real estate investing. At its core, however, it's really a book about living a good life. It's about doing what matters with that most precious resource of all—your time.

The Mexican fisherman was clear on what mattered to him. And he resisted the urge to get bigger and chase shiny promises of future happiness. He already had the good life, and staying small allowed him to enjoy it more fully.

In your own way, you can make that same choice. It's the choice of the small and mighty real estate investor. It's the choice to use real estate investing and wealth building as a tool to improve your life.

The definitions of a good life and success are always personal. My goal in writing this book was to give you both the philosophy and the practical tools to turn your personal version of a good life into reality. I hope you now have the inspiration, knowledge, and the clear path to do that.

I wish you much success on your personal journey as a small and mighty real estate investor! If this book has been helpful to you at all, I'd love to hear about your feedback, progress, and accomplishments. Send me an email at book@coachcarson.com or search for "Coach Chad Carson" on Twitter or YouTube and leave a comment.

Best of luck, and enjoy the journey!

ACKNOWLEDGMENTS

F irst and foremost, thank you to my wife, Kari, and my daughters, Serena and Ali, for understanding the crazy itch I had to write this book and for being patient with me during the many months I spent putting it together. Your unconditional love and support are my rock and foundation.

Thank you to my parents, Tom and Nancy, for your support, wisdom, and examples of being excellent human beings. I was lucky to win the ovarian lottery!

To my business partner, Tommy, you helped to shape, test, and ultimately succeed with the ideas in this book as much as I did. Thank you for your friendship and wisdom. I couldn't ask for a better person to work with all these years.

As someone who calls himself "Coach," I know mentorship from others is one of the most precious gifts in my life. Thank you to my real estate and life mentor and friend, Dr. Louis Stone. Knowing I can always call for a conversation or to take a walk means the world to me. And specifically for this book, thank you to John Schaub for the inspiration, emails, and lessons over the years that helped me to formulate many of the ideas I've shared here.

To my brother Andrew Carson, I'm so grateful to have you as a friend and sounding board in business, investing, and life. And thank you to my sister-in-law Emily and niece and nephew Bea and Gibbs for your love and support.

Writing this book wouldn't be possible without my own small and mighty business teams behind the scenes. Thank you to Eric Newton and the Tiger Properties management team, Martin Tiller and the Orange Real Estate management team, and April Breton and Wendi Setzer at Real Estate Market Place. Thank you to my Coach Carson team, including Michael Nguyen, Joe Jimenez, Megan Thomson, and Kelli Jagmin. And thank you to my CPA Brandon Smith.

I was inspired to write this book by thousands of real-life small and mighty investors who shared their stories after following me on my Coach Carson newsletter, podcast, YouTube channel, and blog at coach carson.com. Your comments, emails, and messages were *invaluable* to me, and I am extremely thankful, even though I often can't respond and acknowledge every one of you personally!

Fifty-eight people went even further and allowed me to ask them detailed research questions in a small and mighty investor survey in preparation for this book. Unfortunately I wasn't able to feature all of you directly in the book, but I want to thank each of you here because your feedback and stories helped me to shape the book you have in your hands. These amazing people include: Ali and Josh Lupo, Erion Shehaj, Tim Robinson, Lisa Tilstra, Karen and Robert, Rachel Richards, Garrett Diegel, Cory Binsfield, Ryan Brennan, Shane Gaboury, Adam Cranmer, Jackie Walker, Megan Greathouse, Jon Rudy, Nick Ford, Rodd Gortney, Meridith Wardle, Sean McKay, Sam Dogen, Dustin Heiner, Will and Veronica Pritchett, Anthony Petz, Gregg Branham, Betty Cruz, Dorsie Boddiford Kuni, Maria Fristrom, Paula Pant, Phillip Leonard, Nick Bushyager, Sunitha Rao, Rick Hamilton, Pearly Leung, Brooks Rogers, Barbara Sloan, Nasar El-Arabi, Kyle Ball, Antoinette Munroe, Zasha Smith, Brie Schmidt, Myra Oliver, James and Emily Lowery, Jeff Daubenmire, Sarah King, Tiffany Baker, Ethan Board, Joe DelGrosso, Jonathan Bradley, Vlad Stinga, Ashley Hamilton, Eitan and Noga Sella, Ray Zhao, Gorden Lopes, Sarah Wilson, Diego Corzo, Joe Jimenez, Jillian Johnsrud, Amy Wright Webber, and Rolando Archila.

I have amazing friends and colleagues who let me bounce ideas off them or who agreed to read sections of the book for feedback. Thank you to Michael Nguyen, Joe Jimenez, Eitan Sella, Sean McKay, Anthony Petz, Joe Breslin, Bradley LaBrie, Martin Tiller, Travis Dodge, Joe Gibson, Kyle Ball, Joel Larsgaard, Matt Altmix, Elliott Savage, and Tony Crumpton for your feedback and support.

Last but not least, I want to acknowledge and thank the team at BiggerPockets for working with me on this book and for promoting the mission of serving small and mighty investors. Thank you to Katie Miller for your leadership and confidence in me as an author and speaker. Thank you to Savannah Wood for your editing skills extraordinaire and for your support throughout the writing process. And thank you to Kaylee Walterbach, Peri Eryigit, and others on the marketing team for getting this book in the hands of people who can benefit from it. Joshua Dorkin, thank you for the vision and hard work to create such an incredible platform in the first place. Scott Trench and Mindy Jensen, thank you for your leadership, support, and friendship. And Brandon Turner, thank you for getting me into this "book author thing" in the first place and for paving the way with your example.

To doing what matters!

Chad Carson
Granada, Spain, 2023

More from
BiggerPockets Publishing

If you enjoyed this book, we hope you'll take a moment to check out some of the other great material BiggerPockets offers. Whether you crave freedom or stability, a backup plan, or passive income, **BiggerPockets** empowers you to live life on your own terms through real estate investing.

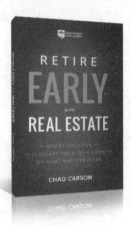

Retire Early with Real Estate
Escape the 9-to-5 work grind, retire early, and do more with your life! This book provides practical methods to quickly and safely build wealth using the time-tested vehicle of real estate rentals. Experienced real estate investor and early retiree Chad Carson shares the investment strategies that he used to create enough passive income to retire at 37 years old. Learn from more than twenty real estate investors and early retirees profiled in this book—retiring early is possible with a step-by-step strategy at hand!

Long-Distance Real Estate Investing
Don't let your location dictate your financial freedom: Live where you want, and invest anywhere it makes sense! The rules, technology, and markets have changed: No longer are you forced to invest only in your backyard. In *Long-Distance Real Estate Investing*, learn an in-depth strategy to build profitable rental portfolios through buying, managing, and flipping out-of-state properties from real estate investor and agent David Greene.

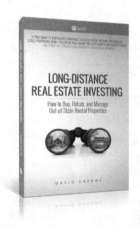

Find the **information**, **inspiration**, and **tools** you need to dive right into the world of real estate investing with confidence.

Sign up today—it's free! Visit **www.BiggerPockets.com**

Find our books at **www.BiggerPockets.com/store**

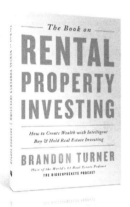

The Book on Rental Property Investing

With nearly 400 pages of in-depth advice for building wealth through rental properties, this evergreen best-seller imparts the practical and exciting strategies that investors across the world are using to build significant cash flow through real estate investing. Investor, best-selling author, and longtime co-host of *The BiggerPockets Podcast* Brandon Turner has one goal in mind: to give you every strategy, tool, tip, and technique you need to become a millionaire rental property investor!

The Book on Managing Rental Properties

From the top-selling author of *The Book on Rental Property Investing*, this companion book will be your comprehensive guide to effectively managing tenants in your rental properties. Being a landlord doesn't have to mean middle-of-the-night phone calls, costly evictions, or daily frustrations with ungrateful tenants. With this book, you'll learn every trick, tool, and system you need to manage your rentals—leading to more freedom, less drama, and higher profits from your real estate business.

Looking for more?
Join the BiggerPockets Community

BiggerPockets brings together education, tools, and a community of more than 2+ million like-minded members—all in one place. Learn about investment strategies, analyze properties, connect with investor-friendly agents, and more.

Go to **biggerpockets.com** to learn more!

 Listen to a **BiggerPockets Podcast**

 Watch **BiggerPockets on YouTube**

 Join the **Community Forum**

 Learn more on **the Blog**

 Read more **BiggerPockets Books**

 Learn about our **Real Estate Investing Bootcamps**

 Connect with an **Investor-Friendly Real Estate Agent**

 Go Pro! Start, scale, and manage your portfolio with your **Pro Membership**

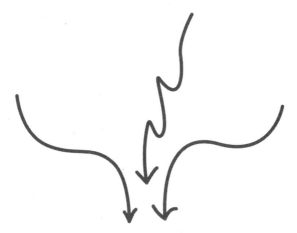

Follow us on social media!

Sign up for a Pro account
and take **20 PERCENT OFF**
with code **BOOKS20**.

 BiggerPockets®